Take It from the  Mouth

Copyright © 1999 by The University Press of Kentucky

Scholarly publisher for the Commonwealth,
serving Bellarmine College, Berea College, Centre
College of Kentucky, Eastern Kentucky University,
The Filson Club Historical Society, Georgetown College,
Kentucky Historical Society, Kentucky State University,
Morehead State University, Murray State University,
Northern Kentucky University, Transylvania University,
University of Kentucky, University of Louisville,
and Western Kentucky University.
All rights reserved

Editorial and Sales Offices: The University Press of Kentucky
663 South Limestone Street, Lexington, Kentucky 40508-4008

03 02 01 00 99   5 4 3 2 1

Library of Congress Cataloging-in-Publication Data

Pitrone, Jean Maddern, 1920–
    Take it from the big mouth : the life of Martha Raye / Jean Maddern
    Pitrone.
        p.   cm.
    ISBN 0-8131-2110-8 (cloth : alk. paper)
    1. Raye, Martha.   2. Entertainers—United States—Biography.   I. Title.
PN2287.R248P58   1999
791'.092—dc21
    [B]   98-49383

This book is printed on acid-free recycled paper
meeting the requirements of the American National Standard
for Permanence of Paper for Printed Library Materials.

Manufactured in the United States of America

*A special thank you to Steve Allen,
whose generosity provided a more penetrating insight
into the complex personality of his friend,
Martha Raye.*

*And my gratitude to all my family
for their encouragement and help,
especially to Julie, Joyce, Joe, and Chuck.*

Contents

Illustrations follow page 120

1

The Sudden-Death Circuit

The plaintive wail of bagpipes drifts across the Fort Bragg, North Carolina, military cemetery where a plain wooden coffin, draped with an American flag, rests on supports above an open grave. The date is October 22, 1994. The few family members of the deceased—famed actress, comedienne, singer, and dancer Martha Raye—are divided now as they have been for a few years. Her fifty-year-old daughter sits with her uncle's widow on folding chairs at the side of the grave. The forty-five-year-old husband of the seventy-eight-year-old Raye sits, with his daughter from a former marriage, at the foot of the grave.

As bagpipes drone "Amazing Grace," uniformed Special Forces veterans stand in a half-circle near the burgundy canopy sheltering the waiting grave of Honorary Lieutenant Colonel Raye. "Colonel Maggie," as she was known to her "boys" in Vietnam, has the singular honor of being the first civilian ever laid to rest at Fort Bragg.

Raye had served valiantly, bringing entertainment, good cheer, and tender nursing care to soldiers in precariously situated jungle outposts of Vietnam. In 1994, shortly before her death and in recognition of her outstanding service, not only in Vietnam but also in Korea and during World War II, President Clinton presented Raye with the prestigious Medal of Freedom. The nation's highest civilian honor had previously been presented to such luminaries as Lech Walesa of Poland and Margaret Thatcher of the United Kingdom.

Raye often said, in purposeful self-deprecation, that she thought

1

of herself as primarily a clown. "Yup, a clown, that's me," she would say, flashing her famous grin. But melancholy lurked behind her raucous laugh. "She was one of the world's four best comediennes," Milton Berle had said, "but she lived a life of personal disaster."

On learning of Raye's death, Bob Hope issued a statement to reporters regarding her popularity with the GIs in Vietnam where, he said, "she was Florence Nightingale, Dear Abby, and the only singer who could be heard over the artillery fire."

It is likely that neither Berle nor Hope knew that Raye's melancholy and disastrous tendencies were rooted in what she considered a disability: her lack of education. Her own awareness of this deficiency had taken its toll on her psyche and even on her relationship with her daughter, her only child.

Martha Raye was, indeed, a multifaceted personality with an assortment of names to match her temperamental disposition. Her birth name was Margy Reed (sometimes changed, on a whim, to O'Reed). She also answered to Maggie, Teresa, Martha, Yvonne, and various last names resulting from seven marriages.

She was Mom to her daughter when the two of them were together. But when the young girl was packed off to boarding school or when Raye was away performing—which was a great deal of the time—the girl felt alienated from her mother and thought of her much less often as Mom, from whom she was unwillingly detached, than as Martha. Martha the singer and comedienne. Martha the star, to whom a glittering career was the focus of her life.

A great number of the stories Raye told about her life were products of her lively imagination and of her eagerness to cover up the facts. Still, the stories she told of her birth in the bleak mining town of Butte, Montana, must have been true because each time she spoke of her parents and the date she was born, August 27, 1916, the details were consistent.

The manager of the Maguire Opera House was not impressed by the vaudeville team of The Girl and the Traveler, who came into his office in August 1916 and pleaded for a job. He stared at the nineteen-year-old girl, who looked ready to give birth any day, and at her older, debonair husband. Just another down-on-their-luck pair, he must have thought, striking out on their own and traveling what seasoned performers called the "sudden-death circuit."

The manager shrugged when the fast-talking Pete Reed boasted of how he and his wife recently had packed in audiences that overflowed into the aisles back in "Frisco." Here in Butte, the manager told them, they ran four shows a day. It was a tough schedule. Still, the Reeds looked as if they really needed a job. The manager relented. "Well, okay. You can start tonight."

By 1900, the population of Butte had zoomed to 30,000, although in other respects the mining town had changed very little from its boom-town beginnings in the 1880s. Butte had become one of the ugliest, wildest towns in the West as Irish immigrants, spurred by reports of silver and copper, came northwest to mine the riches of Butte Hill. These lusty Irish miners were followed by others from the coal and tin mines of Wales and Cornwall, then by a sprinkling of Slavs and Italians.

At the end of their shifts, grimy miners put aside their picks and shovels, trudged away from the pits, and headed for tin-bucket washups and hot meals at their camps or boardinghouses. Afterwards they crowded into Butte's saloons or jammed into the opera house, stamping their boots and applauding whenever their favorite singer of sentimental songs, golden-haired Kathie Putnam, was the attraction. Road company fare varied, though, and the miners also watched tear-jerking productions of *East Lynne* and *Ten Nights in a Barroom.*

On that August evening of 1916 when the Reeds bounced out onto the opera-house stage, they were introduced as an "Irish immigrant team." But Maybelle "Peggy" Reed had been born in Montana to Teresa Sanchagrin and Samuel Hooper, who worked as a smelter in Great Falls. Mining towns also were familiar territory to Pete Reed, since his Irish relatives still worked back home in the mines of County Clare. So neither of the Reeds was unaware of the problems that existed between mining companies and their employees in the early 1900s.

Just two summers previously, the barren town of Butte—its wood buildings gray with smoke from ore smelters and its vegetation shriveled into nothingness—had erupted into a bloody riot and martial law had been imposed. The mining company still refused to recognize a worker's union, and resentment smoldered among the mixed ethnic population.

Wearing a loose fitting dress to conceal her swollen figure, Peggy fastened a bright smile on her face as she thumped on the piano and then joined her husband in the song-dance-comedy routine that they were accustomed to present on splintered wood platforms that often served as mining camp stages. At such performances, colored lamps, hanging on each side of the stage, and footlights helped to glamorize the setting. In winter, a couple of blazing woodstoves tended to deglamorize the set. But there was no need for ugly stoves now. The heat was oppressive. Perspiration beaded Peggy's forehead at every performance, and behind her fixed smile she worried about the baby who soon would be born.

Both Peggy and Pete eagerly anticipated getting paid for their performances in Butte so they could pay for the downtown furnished room they had rented in Mom's Block. They also needed money for food and a doctor's services. When Peggy's faint labor pains began, Pete hurried to the opera house. There he discovered that the manager had skipped town with the box-office receipts.

Pete Reed had no choice but to take his wife to St. James Hospital, where she was admitted as a charity case. Comforted to some degree by the knowledge that her baby would be born in a hospital, Peggy endured hours of hard labor. The baby girl's name was recorded on her August 27 birth certificate as "Margy Reed."

Two days later, Peggy tucked her daughter into a basket backstage, then danced out onto the platform with her husband. They were back on the circuit again, riding the Anaconda and Pacific to Deer Lodge and moving, with baggage and baby, to perform their routine on any makeshift stage in any raw, western town as they gradually worked their way to the Midwest.

Margy would later follow the pattern set out by her parents and sometimes, using O'Reed as a last name, claimed to be of Irish descent. Part Irish, yes, but her maternal grandfather, Samuel Hooper, the smelter, had been born in Michigan to English immigrants.

Before Margy's second birthday, the Reeds found work in a tab show. Pete Reed considered it a stroke of luck to be a part of the miniature musical comedy in its tour of midwestern cities because Peggy was now expecting a second child. The Reeds were still with the tab show in Grand Rapids, Michigan, when Peggy went into labor. A second delivery would be much easier, her vaudeville friends assured her. There would be no need for a hospital this time. Douglas, nicknamed Buddy, was born while Peggy lay on a cot backstage, attended by chorus girls who were no novices to births behind the velvet curtains.

Once more the Reeds were moving from town to town. Each day, they took their children, Margie (as they now spelled her name) and Buddy, from damp basement dressing rooms of third-rate theaters to a boardinghouse or dingy hotel room where there was no relief from heat in summer or from cold in winter.

Backstage, Margie poked into her mother's powder boxes and rouge pots. At age three and a half, she wandered onstage as Pete and Peggy went through their routine. Caught in the brightness of floodlights, the blue-eyed girl looked up expectantly at her parents. In the tradition of vaudevillians, they had taught their small daughter to sing several popular songs. Now Peggy quickly moved to the piano and began to play "Jada," signaling for Margie to sing. Dressed in blue pajamas her mother had made, her hair cut in Buster-Brown style with bangs, the child sang into the floodlights. "Jadaa. Jadaaa. Jada, Jada, Jing Jing Jing."

Margie's earliest memory was of the sound of applause echoing backstage. But now the applause was for her, from out front, the sound of it rising around her while she curtsied as she had been taught.

From that time, Margie was part of the family act. Soon after their arrival in Chicago, another daughter was born. Melodye was a decided complication in the Reeds' lives. Young Buddy already was being trained by his father to take part in the family act, but with the birth of her third child, Peggy was becoming more and more disturbed by the frequency with which her husband drank himself into oblivion whenever he could get hold of a bottle of illegal "moonshine."

They changed the name of the family act to the Reed Hooper

Revue, to see if their fortunes would improve. With Margie prancing about, dressed as a miniature bride in white dress and veil, and Buddy serving as her even smaller groom, Peggy jazzing it up in her usual role of pianist, and Pete performing his song and dance, the Reed Hooper Revue had no better luck than had The Girl and the Traveler.

Now, with both Margie and Buddy involved in the family act, Peggy worried about their schooling as the Reeds moved from one city to another, playing vaudeville houses wherever they could get bookings. When no gigs were available to them, they went back to Chicago, a kind of home base. (Years later, when the famous movie and television star Martha Raye was asked about her education, she usually would say that she was sent either to public or parochial school, depending on convenience, for short periods while her parents worked at odd jobs and on different shifts in Chicago restaurants or saloons. Her claim of attending school periodically was not true, but she took this protective stance to avoid not only embarrassment but what she feared even more—scorn.)

The family's friends were vaudevillians who, like the Reeds, were on the move much of the time and considered themselves lucky to stay in one town any longer than three days for a gig. Gerry Society representatives, who were supposed to check on children who were performing onstage and not enrolled in school, found it very difficult to catch up with families like the Reeds and their friends, the O'Connors. Marveling at the O'Connors' ability to survive with six children on the vaudeville circuit, Peggy carefully counted the days between her menstrual periods and breathed a sigh of relief each month when a new period began.

The two families remained close, sharing backstage baby-sitting chores and exchanging tips on possible bookings. In 1925 when the O'Connors' seventh child was born at the Oriental Theater in Chicago, Peggy suggested the name Donald for the boy who would become a singing and dancing star on Broadway and the silver screen.

In her concern for her daughter's education, Peggy got hold of an elementary-school speller and drilled Margie on word lists, which the little girl was very good at memorizing. But Peggy's concerns for educating her daughter were often superseded by her more pressing need to provide milk and food for the children. Spelling lessons were pushed aside, too, by the more compelling and practical need to rehearse for the family act. It was not surprising, then, that Margie grew up only marginally literate.

Rehearsing for the family act was troublesome for the children as their father changed their lines or came up with new interpretations of their roles in his anxiety to make the act more entertaining. Both Pete and Peggy were likely to run out of patience when Margie or Buddy did not pick up their cues or memorize their lines as quickly as the parents expected. When the yelling and cursing began, the children cowered in fear, remembering nothing of their lines as their father or mother slapped them or clipped them on the ears, as if each blow would teach them to remember next time.

Onstage, though, they were a devoted family as Pete and Peggy proudly introduced Margie to each audience. At her mother's cue, the child would plunge into a hip-swinging, lusty rendition of "I Wish That I Could Shimmy like My Sister Kate."

After being introduced by his father, Buddy, too, launched into a well-rehearsed song and dance. Eventually Peggy and Pete realized that their two children consistently were drawing much more applause than were the parents. As a matter of practicality, they decided that the children's act would highlight their show. Billed as Bud and Margie Reed and drilled relentlessly, the young brother and sister quickly adapted themselves to their starring roles as more and bigger bookings began to come their way.

The Reeds were moving again now—to Pottstown, Philadelphia, Pittsburgh, and on to Dayton, Sioux City, and Des Moines on the Loew's Theater circuit. Pete Reed bought a used car, a Pierce Arrow, as the kids hit the big time. "For a while, I was enrolled in the Professional Children's School in New York City," Raye would say in later years. But this claim, too, was not true.

When the Bud and Margie Reed act accelerated to a $400 weekly salary, the Reeds reveled in their new prosperity and status. They were on top at last, they exulted. But then, before they had an opportunity to catch up with all their bills, they were over the top and slipping.

Now there were weeks when there was no work for Bud and Margie. And when a week's billing was offered, the salary was lower.

Why? Why? the Reeds wondered. The act was as good as it had ever been. The kids were more polished performers. So, why? Peggy and Pete could find no answers, but the time from one week's gig to the next was stretching. Was it true, they wondered, that the decline of vaudeville had begun?

Desperate for work, the Reeds agreed to a tough schedule performing in Thomas's Tent Show, traveling across the country in trucks and making one-night stands along the way. The rumbling of traffic after midnight became the children's lullabies until they awakened, each morning, in a different town. Since show admission was only twenty-five cents, the tent show had to attract large audiences if it were to survive.

At the season's end, the Reeds went back to accepting split-weeks in small cities, moving on to Passaic and Patterson, New Jersey, then on to Lancaster, Pennsylvania, in the same week. Once again, the family was living meagerly, vying with third-rate magicians and animal acts for a favorable spot on the bill. The Reeds considered themselves fortunate to get signed up for a small theater where they were required to give three or four performances a day.

The new family act that Pete had worked out was one of pure fantasy. Young Buddy, in the role of a spoiled, in-your-face rich kid, had most of the good lines and drew most of the laughs as his father took the part of a butler, a foil for Buddy's wisecracks.

Somehow, Pete managed to hold on to the battered Pierce Arrow and to keep it running. Often the car served as a shelter for the night as the five Reeds rode as far as sixty miles to fill a one-night date at an Eagles' Club and were paid as little as fifteen dollars for their efforts. To accommodate his family in the automobile, Pete stacked all the scenery for the act so that it made a platform level with the tops of the car seats. While Pete drew up his knees to sleep on the front seat, Peggy and the three children huddled together to sleep on top of the platform.

When they could afford slightly better accommodations, their shelter was usually a room in a boardinghouse catering to "artists."

As soon as the family settled into the furnished room, they hauled their "stove trunk" inside and unpacked their hot plate and a few pots and pans. In the meantime, Margie stuffed the door cracks with paper to prevent cooking odors from seeping into the hallway. Cooking in the rooms was forbidden, but Peggy Reed was more concerned with feeding her family than with observing rules.

To put food on the table, Pete Reed tried selling Christmas cards door to door. Peggy washed dishes in restaurants. Margie tried, with little success, to sell raffle tickets on various items to other entertainers, many of whom had no more money to spare than did the Reeds.

By the time Margie was twelve years old, she nourished a growing desire to push ahead in the entertainment world and to escape the crumbling boardinghouses and dingy dressing rooms that smelled of mildew and urine. She was a rapidly developing girl whose eyes reflected her changing moods—depression as she chafed at the poverty and the quarreling parents and the loneliness of having no friends of her own age; elation when she dreamed of her name in lights above a theater marquee, and of fame and success and plenty of money for a comfortable home. She knew, though, that her father had pinned his hopes on Buddy. Pete spent countless hours coaching the boy in comedy routines and seeing to it that Buddy practiced each day on the guitar. Margie was second-best in her father's eyes. She was well aware of that.

When the family was once more living in Chicago and scrambling for survival, Margie learned that an Erie Street theater was featuring an amateur night with a prize of three silver dollars. Margie ached to win the money and to prove to herself that she could strike out on her own and make it as a performer.

Sneaking out of the boardinghouse and over to Erie Street, she saw a doorman stationed at the theater entrance. Uniformed attendants with gilt shoulder epaulets were no novelty, of course, to any vaudeville child. Young as she was, Margie soon convinced the doorman that although she had no entrance pass, she was one of the amateurs scheduled to perform.

A dozen young contestants, most of them trembling with stage fright, took their turns on the stage. When it was Margie's turn, she sang "Dinah" lustily and confidently and went home with the silver dollars jingling in her pocket. The family made good use of most of the money. With the remainder, Margie splurged on candy. A secret cache of licorice and "red hots," she discovered, could buy a lot of friends. For the first time, Margie enjoyed a few days of popularity among neighborhood youngsters. Then it was time for the Reeds to move on.

Now the car became their shelter at night even more often as the family trekked from one midwestern city to another. Pete and Peggy fought more violently as their bookings dwindled away, and they directed much of their frustration toward the children, punishing them harshly even for minor offenses. Yet despite the meager wages, they always managed to buy liquor.

In 1929, the family was down on its luck after a short gig in Detroit when Margie, spindly legged but full-breasted at age thirteen, put on a pair of high heels and, hoping that she could pass for seventeen, walked into Detroit's Fisher Theater to ask for a job. "I was born old," she often would say in later years.

Proudly, she reported back to her parents that she had been promised a job, singing with a stage show. When the job at the Fisher ended after one week, the Reeds used their daughter's money to drive down to Cleveland, where Pete heard there might be work. But only disappointment and frigid winter weather awaited them in Cleveland, and recriminations flew back and forth between Pete and Peggy.

While Christmas shoppers thronged Cleveland stores for last-minute holiday purchases, the Reeds tried to keep warm in the sleazy furnished room they had rented with a promise to pay later. There was no money for rent. No money for gas or even for food as Peggy parceled out "the single box of crackers that was all the family had to eat," Raye would reminisce years later.

An embittered, gray-faced Pete Reed walked from one theater to another in search of work while, in the drafty furnished room, Peggy searched the newspaper's help-wanted advertisements and the entertainment section. When Peggy read aloud that bandleader Paul Ash was arriving in Cleveland that very day for a holiday performance, Margie felt a surge of excitement. She knew that Ash used a comedy skit with bit parts, played by locals, for a policeman and a boy who jumped out of a box. If her father and brother could snare these parts while Ash's troupe was in Cleveland, their earnings would carry the family through the Christmas season.

Margie headed for the theater and had no trouble making her way backstage. Going right up to the dressing room door marked with a large star, she knocked. "Come in," a male voice invited. She opened the door. And sure enough, there was Paul Ash, looking at her questioningly.

Margie plunged right into the monologue she had rehearsed on the way down. They were show people, she told him, broke and desperate for any kind of work. She told him about her father and brother and how easily they could take the parts of the officer and the boy. The words poured out until Ash agreed to hire Pete and Buddy, sight unseen. But if the father and brother were as convincing and as spirited as this girl, Ash must have thought, they surely could handle the parts.

Carefully, he wrote down Margie's name and address. As the wide-eyed girl thanked him, he reached into his billfold and pressed a five-dollar bill into her hand. It would be an advance against her father and brother's salaries, he promised.

Bursting with her accomplishment, Margie hurried back to the dismal room where her family waited. Accustomed to mercurial changes in their lives and fortunes, the Reeds quickly responded to the good news. Perhaps they would make it through the winter after all, they reassured one another. And surely by next year, things would take a turn for the better.

The next day, a delivery boy knocked at their door. Peggy opened the door and took the package from the boy. Her hands trembled as she opened it to find a turkey, sent by Paul Ash. Her family would have a Christmas dinner after all.

2

Martha Raye, Girl Singer

The jobs for Paul Ash soon ended for Pete and Buddy, but they had lasted long enough for Ash to take a personal interest in Margie Reed, young as she was, after her brother boasted of her singing abilities to the bandleader. As soon as Ash agreed to have her audition for him, Margie returned to the theater. Ash listened as she sang out, loud and strong. He nodded. The girl was very young but talented; he would keep her in mind and do what he could to help her in the future, he promised.

Paul Ash kept his word and hired Margie to sing with his band in Chicago when the Reed family returned there in midwinter. Following the stock market crash of October 1929, Chicago's jobless stood on street corners and waited in long lines at soup kitchens and employment offices. But Margie's hopes were high. The family act was finished, Maybelle and Pete Reed agreed. The failure pattern, the lack of gigs and money, and the deprivations they had endured had taken their toll on the Reed-Hooper marriage. Pete and his son headed for New York City, where Buddy was determined to become a musician and bandleader instead of a comedian.

Peggy and the two girls stuck together in Chicago. When Margie wasn't singing for Paul Ash, she and Peggy worked as waitresses.

When Ash took his band to New York, Peggy and her daughters went, too. For one week, Margie sang with the band in the pit at the Paramount Theater. Then Ash announced he would take her to audition for Broadway producer Charles Yates.

"I pulled out all the stops," she recalled. "I sounded louder than the Twentieth Century Limited pulling out of Grand Central Station."

Like Ash, Yates was impressed with the volume and quality of the girl's voice. He agreed to try to promote her.

In the rented room she shared with her mother and sister, Margie hand-cranked a portable phonograph and practiced singing along with records. Wanting desperately to sing as successfully as Ethel Merman, the brassy-voiced singer who shared with Mary Martin the enviable title of "queens of Broadway musicals," Margie practiced for hours each day—mimicking Merman and belting out the melodies in a throbbing vibrato.

Margie's first appearance for Yates was at Keith's Eighty-sixth Street Theater on Broadway, which was used for display of new acts by vaudeville impresarios. "But you need a new name, for good luck," Peggy said, opening a telephone directory and looking over the listings while quite disregarding the fact that name changes had never helped the Reeds in their desperate search for success. It was time for her daughter to separate herself from past failures. A first name? How about Martha? Peggy flipped to the R section of the directory. And how about Raye for a last name? "Martha Raye. Sounds good, doesn't it?" Peggy asked. Margie nodded. She depended on Peggy to steer her in the right direction. After all, her mother had gone to school when she was a kid. Peggy could read better than Margie, who had trouble "comprehending" (Peggy's term) the words she managed to recognize in her struggle with reading difficulties.

Before Margie had much opportunity to get acquainted with her new name, it was time to meet Yates at the theater. And there was the name, looking very strange to her on the printed program. *Martha Raye, girl singer.* My name, she reminded herself as she heard the orchestra playing her cue music. Then she was moving out into the spotlight, opening her mouth wide and warbling her first number in robust Merman style, her body pulsing with the thrust of each note. Finishing her song, she smiled and waited for a burst of applause. But the clapping was weak, barely polite. The wide smile froze on her lips. Forcing her numbed mouth to move, she plunged desperately into another song. "Louder," she told herself, determined to get a reaction from the audience. But this time the response was even more feeble.

Martha Raye, bright new personality, had emerged and then died ingloriously in a single night. Dazed, Margie slipped backstage where Yates assured her that she was too far ahead of her time and that the audience just wasn't ready for her great talent. But his soothing words echoed dismally in Margie's mind. She began to wonder if the public ever would recognize Martha Raye any more readily than it had recognized little Margie Reed. Still, she decided to stick with her new moniker. As Yates pointed out, her own name hadn't taken her very far. But to family and friends, who might have found the new name stiff on their tongues, Martha was quickly modified to Maggie—a nickname that would be hers for the rest of her life.

When the Palace Theater—the New York showplace considered by performers as Big Time at its best—stopped presenting vaudeville acts in November 1932, the date would accelerate the decline and demise of vaudeville. The gradual decline had begun with the arrival of "talking" pictures, and by 1932, hundreds of idled vaudevillians were crowding into booking offices, searching for work. The trouble was that most vaudevillians, accustomed to projecting themselves to theater audiences, found they "bombed" when trying to adapt to performing in the close and very personal atmosphere of cafes and nightclubs.

When the newly christened Martha "Maggie" Raye—five feet three inches and short waisted, with blue eyes and dark brown hair, a generous mouth and long shapely legs—began making the rounds of theaters and booking offices after her brief job at the Paramount had ended, she found the offices mobbed with entertainers.

Maggie's hopes spiraled when comedian Ben Blue, who could perform eccentric dance routines, hired her for an act he was taking on tour, opening in Syracuse. For one week, she sang two songs in each show. Then Blue fired her.

"You were just too good, kid," one of the other performers told her. "Blue don't like to be upstaged."

Was it true? Maggie wondered. Was that the real reason? By

The Field Library
914-737-1212

Date charged: 2/6/2015,
13:34
Title: Take it from the
big mouth : the life of
Martha R
Item ID:
31019152248483
Date due: 2/27/2015,23:
59

To renew items call:
914-674-4169

this time, she had learned, though, that people in show business were intensely jealous when it came to protecting their own acts and getting preferred billing. But she was dismayed that Pete and Buddy, still in New York, would hear that she was out of Blue's show and would think she had failed.

Maybe her father was right after all. Maybe Buddy was the one who would make it big in New York. To save her shattered pride, Maggie told her family that she had quit the Ben Blue act. Then she hung around cafes and theaters to buttonhole managers and bandleaders until she finally arranged to audition for Rudy Vallee's band, the Connecticut Yankees.

Vallee's popularity was growing, despite the nasal quality of his voice when he sang his theme song, "Your Time Is My Time." His records, particularly "The Stein Song," had become top sellers. Maggie was thrilled when Vallee praised her performance. He liked her big voice, he said, but would make his decision the next day after auditions ended.

One of the other singers, Maggie noticed, was a pretty blonde with the kind of poise that she envied. The next day, when Maggie gathered up her courage to telephone for the results of the audition, she was told that the blonde—Alice Faye, who soon would become a Hollywood star—had been hired to sing with the Connecticut Yankees.

Maggie's disappointment was forgotten, however, when Benny Davis invited her to join his Star Dust Revue, along with Vilma and Buddy Ebsen, Hal LeRoy, and Little Jackie Heller. But after a short period with the Star Dust Revue, receiving a steady $115 weekly, Maggie could not resist the lure of what she hoped would be her big break—a featured role offered her in Will Morrissey's *The Crooner*.

The Crooner turned out to be a typical depression-era show with little financial backing. When the show folded in Asbury Park, New Jersey, Martha Raye again began haunting booking offices, theaters, and nightclubs. She worked in vaudeville and in cafes, developing the bawdy, raucous style that eventually would bring her recognition. In the meantime, there were many disappointments. One occurred when she was sent to Detroit to fill a date at a private club.

After Maggie tore into "Minnie the Moocher" with lots of body action, she was fired for her raunchy performance as she left the stage.

It was not a good time for an entertainer to be out of a job, even though Prohibition had ended shortly after Franklin D. Roosevelt became president, and nightclubs were legally selling liquor again. Even so, the Great Depression continued to choke the economy. Only the motion picture industry still flourished out in Los Angeles where movie stars commanded high salaries and where income taxes were low. Hollywood and motion pictures, however, were far removed from the boundaries of Maggie's sagging career on the East Coast and in the Midwest. She knew, too, that thousands of girls had moved out to Los Angeles to vie for bit parts in the film world of illusion and delusion.

Returning to New York and to days or weeks of inactivity between gigs, Maggie began going nightly to Fifty-second Street, where Louis Prima and his band were playing at the Famous Door. When Prima picked up his trumpet, Maggie closed her eyes and let the Dixieland jazz rock through her body. Then, whenever the gravelly voiced Prima invited her to sing, she got up on the stage and improvised, her voice soaring up and around the band in punchy syncopation. She sang not only for the joy of it but also for the plate of chow mein that the Famous Door supplied whenever she performed.

Although chow mein was the only remuneration Maggie received, her boisterous singing attracted the attention of a newspaper reporter. A devoted admirer of Prima, he wrote glowingly in his column about Martha Raye and her ability to improvise.

The item caught the attention of Broadway producer Lew Brown, who was looking for a fresh singer for a couple of production numbers in his musical comedy *Calling All Stars.* Maggie's hopes soared again when she learned that Phil Baker, Ella Logan, and Lou Holtz already had been signed for the show, along with Judy Canova and Mitzi Mayfair.

The show opened in New York at the Hollywood Theater in December 1934, then moved on to Boston. At the rehearsal for the Boston opening, Ella Logan, preparing to go into her comedy routine, fell and broke her arm on the mock stairway built on the stage. The director considered cutting the segment from the show. Then some-one suggested asking eighteen-year-old Maggie to try the routine.

Eager to make the staid Bostonian audience respond to her antics, she took her position at the top of the stage stairway on open-ing night. She waited for her cue, heart thudding, and began stag-gering down the spiral staircase in pseudo-drunken abandon. The audience tittered, then burst into laughter as Maggie's heel caught on the stairs and she reeled down the circular steps, tumbling awk-wardly to the bottom. There was more laughter as she sat on the stage, momentarily stunned. But the laughter inspired her. If the audience wanted roughhousing, that was exactly what she was go-ing to give them. Maggie pulled herself to her feet, careened wildly around the stage, and continued to sing in her wide-open-mouthed style until she flipped into the orchestra pit.

When the applause finally tapered off, Maggie realized her right arm had been fractured. But this was a minor inconvenience to Maggie, who soon discovered that the role had brought her recogni-tion as a comedienne-singer.

Although *Calling All Stars* soon collapsed, it had lasted long enough to open new vistas for the young singer. Nightclub booking agents began chasing her now, instead of Maggie haunting them. She appeared in Earl Carroll's *Sketchbook Revue* at Winter Garden Theater in New York, then she sang in Chicago and New York clubs that paid well enough to make it possible for Peggy to open their first bank account. In New York, she appeared at the Casino de Paris with comedian Jimmy Durante (known as "Da Schnozz" or "Schnozzle"), who had become famous as an entertainer on the "gangster circuit"—the New York City nightclubs owned by vari-ous members of the Mob during the Prohibition era. Now, at the Casino de Paris, Durante and Raye were referred to as "the nose and the mouth." The two hit it off so well that they would remain lifelong friends.

In Chicago, Maggie appeared on the stage of the Southtown Theater, a "palatial film and vaudeville house with vaguely Moorish architecture," as entertainer Steve Allen describes it. A youthful Allen attended that Chicago performance. "Her face was pretty enough and her body was certainly impressive," he writes in *More Funny People*. "She had a marvelous sense of comedy and a great singing voice. It is only the fact that Martha eventually became a world-famous comedienne that obscured the fact that in her prime she was one of the best vocalists in the business. From the first she had a jazz singer's sound, with a certain throaty breathiness to it. But unlike most jazz singers—even the best of whom are rarely able to convey emotion—Martha could very effectively perform an emotional ballad."

Allen also points out that jazz vocalist Anita O'Day wrote an autobiography, *High Times and Hard Times,* which paid tribute to Martha Raye's talents as a "presentation singer," meaning that she used her body as well as her voice to present her songs—a technique which O'Day adapted in her own career. When she heard Martha sing, O'Day admitted that "the back of my neck begins to creep." In O'Day's opinion, Martha was "a natural who never pretended to know music," but was "rhythmical, a very good tap dancer, a show-business gal."

When Maggie was offered a $100-a-week booking with the Century Club in Hollywood, she boarded a train with her mother and younger sister, Melodye.

Hollywood was a mecca for beauty pageant winners and leggy chorus dancers who dreamed of becoming another glamorous Marlene Dietrich or Joan Crawford, two of the highest-paid actresses in the 1930s. But visions of stardom began to fade quickly for the clamoring Dietrich-Crawford "wannabees" as they found themselves standing in early-morning lines at casting offices for bit parts and work as extras. Maggie already was a realist. She had learned tough lessons on the pavements of New York and in the cheap boarding-houses of other East Coast and midwestern cities. She did not want to be a part of the lines of Hollywood jobseekers who were paid an average five dollars a day for work, and then were forced to fork over a couple of those precious dollars to those who had selected them as "extras" from the long lines. "Better pay up if you want to work again soon," they were warned. No, Maggie wanted none of that. She had been asked to come to the city of glitter. And that was unbelievably good luck, she and her mother agreed.

She sang for several months at the Century Club and the Casanova. She and Peggy were in agreement, too, that sad songs and ballads were out for Maggie from now on. Peppy, rhythmic pop songs drew the best audience response. These were the kind of songs Maggie wanted to get a chance to sing at the Trocadero, Los Angeles's most glamorous nightspot, crowded with stars, producers, and directors. On Sunday nights, aspiring entertainers, including professionals from other popular nightclubs, waited their turns to perform as guests at the Trocadero. Each hoped, by way of outstanding talent—or, lacking talent, by outrageous exhibitionism—to attract the interest of film moguls in the audience.

Like many others, Maggie had signed up for a turn to appear on the Trocadero stage. When she finally was assigned to a specific Sunday night, she had the worst case of jitters she had ever suffered. Peggy tried to be reassuring, but her hands trembled, too, as she stood backstage with her daughter.

Then Maggie was bounding out into the spotlight, opening her mouth wide and tearing into her song, gaining confidence as she went into her drunk act. And the audience was with her, laughing and applauding at her antics. At the same time, Maggie spotted comedians Joe E. Lewis and Jimmy Durante sitting at tables near the stage. Remembering the fun she had had, singing with Durante at the Casino de Paris and laughing at his rough-voiced complaint that "Everybody wants to get into da act," she began tossing jibes at Lewis and Durante and they wisecracked back, bolstering her comedy performance. When Lewis and Durante jumped to their feet, pretending to be violent, Maggie joined in counter roughhousing until the musicians ducked for cover in mock terror.

Later, as she joked about the success of her Trocadero act, Maggie said, "When I opened my mouth, they thought it was a cave-in. They could hear me in Santa Barbara."

More important than being heard in Santa Barbara was the fact that she had been heard by film director Norman Taurog. The next day, a telephone call came to her hotel room from Taurog's office. "Would Martha come down for tests?"

The tests turned out to be for a part in a movie already in production, starring Bing Crosby. Taurog had been so impressed with Maggie's Trocadero act that he ordered a special part written for her into the 1936 motion picture *Rhythm on the Range*. And within twenty-four hours.

Maggie would recall, years later, that when Peggy had advised her to sign the contract, she left Taurog's office in a daze. She wouldn't have to take the bus home today. She could hail a taxi if she chose. My Lord, she could buy a new car if she wished. With a contract like the one she had just signed, $1,300 a week, she could do almost anything she had ever dreamed of doing. Buy herself a fur cape. One for Peggy, too. Move into a nice home. Have a pet dog. She loved animals, but had never had the chance to keep a pet in the rundown hotels where they had lived.

When Maggie made her first appearance for work on the make-believe dude ranch on the Paramount set, Crosby quickly put her at ease with his laid-back, soft-spoken manner. Former vaudeville comedian Bob Burns was part of the cast, too. Maggie remembered Burns from twelve years previously when he had been in vaudeville and had bought ice cream cones for the seven-year-old girl who was part of the Bud and Margie Reed act. Then there was the security of her old familiar comedy-drunk routine, written into the *Rhythm on the Range* production. Things were falling into place rapidly now for Martha Raye as she also was assigned a poignant ballad, "Mr. Paganini." It was the kind of song into which Maggie could pour all the tender emotions that she hid behind the wide grin and rowdy mannerisms of her clown persona. Most thrilling of all was the opportunity to sing with Bing Crosby and to close the show with an energetic Crosby-Raye duet, "If You Can't Sing It, You'll Have to Swing It." With her career on the upswing, Maggie bought a mountaintop home in Beverly Hills and hired a maid, Lulu, to take care of it. Her father would see now which child was the talented and successful one. Her younger brother, Bud, married at eighteen, was now the father of a baby boy and she knew that Bud was making only twelve dollars a week, leading a band in a small New York nightclub.

When *Rhythm on the Range* premiered at the Paramount Theater in Manhattan on July 31, 1936, Maggie, Peggy, and Lulu traveled to New York for the event. Sitting among Paramount officials and close to Bing Crosby, Maggie often would say, years afterwards, that her skin crawled with excitement as the curtains separated and the movie began. She watched fearfully as her own bigger-than-life image flashed onto the screen. When the Martha-on-screen was only halfway through "Mr. Paganini," the audience broke into applause. Maggie put a handkerchief to her eyes and began to cry. "Bawling so hard," as she described it later, "that I didn't even see myself for the rest of the movie." But she was happy. Deliriously happy. The audience had liked both her singing and her comedy.

The next day, Maggie got hold of newspapers as quickly as she could. With Peggy's help, she read the critiques. Frank Nugent of the *New York Times* described the new Paramount find, Martha Raye, as a "stridently funny comedienne with a Mammoth Cave mouth" and a chest that, "in moments of burlesque aggressiveness, appears to expand fully ten inches." He pointed out that she might have had clever lines of dialogue, but many of them were not heard because the audience began to laugh as soon as she opened her mouth. "Hollywood has found a remarkable pantomimist" who can register various moods "in facial pothooks and flourishes." He described her singing as "a voice with saxophonic overtones and an occasional trace of pure foghorn."

With the help of the talkative and philosophical humorist Bob Burns, Raye stole the picture from "the laryngeal Mr. Crosby." In this musical comedy, "we could have had a mite more of Miss Raye," Nugent stated, indicating an anticipatory desire to see her perform again soon. Although the reviewer also noted the flimsiness of the plot, Maggie was elated, knowing that a *Times* review, often more penetrating and sometimes more caustic than most other reviews, could make or break an actor or a motion picture.

Rhythm on the Range played across the nation to crowds who laughed at the antics of the girl with the rubber mouth and listened raptly as she sang her soulful interpretation of "Mr. Paganini," which later would become a hit recording. As a result, the studio renegotiated her contract in 1937, giving her more money.

Additional offers poured in. Al Jolson, the most popular entertainer on the American stage, hired her to sing on his CBS radio show. Maggie was thrilled at the opportunity to work with Jolson, who had retained his popularity ever since he had reached the pinnacle of success in 1918. She appeared several times on his show.

Paramount then cast her in *The Big Broadcast of 1937* with Jack Benny and Gracie Allen. Public relations people went into high gear and began spreading their hype about the new star who "speaks both Italian and Spanish, and a little French."

But no matter how cultivated or erudite the studio tried to make her appear, Maggie was very much aware of her reading difficulties and of how dependent she was on Peggy as a result. She also became exceedingly desirous of praise and admiration to keep her shaky self-esteem from slipping.

However, Maggie did have a sharp, retentive memory. She knew that the smattering of Italian and Spanish phrases, of which the public relations people boasted, were simply fractured bits of the languages that she had picked up in earlier years from the children of immigrant parents who lived near the seedy hotels where the Reeds rented rooms. She had learned a number of Yiddish exclamations and phrases, too, which she would often use in her comedy routines in later years. Her knowledge of U.S. geography was obtained from the windows of trains and of the Pierce Arrow as the Reeds had trekked across the country. She had learned the nuances of speech from older vaudeville stars who taught the younger ones how to project their voices without the aid of microphones, and she had learned acceptance of people of all kinds by sharing vaudeville stages with midgets and stripteasers and what were known in the trade as "freak acts." Still, at age twenty, she was naive when it came to relationships with men.

A *New York Times* reviewer pointed out that *The Big Broadcast of 1937* was the third in a series, but it still "goes bouncing across the screen with a great deal of geniality and good humor." With so many stars, comedians, and singers in the cast (Jack Benny, George Burns and Gracie Allen, Ray Milland, Shirley Ross, and Bob Burns), "its extravaganzas are no greater than we might expect," the review continued, adding that the motion picture becomes "sheer poetry" when conductor Leopold Stokowski draws the "fullest measure of melody" from his symphonic orchestra as it performs Bach's Fugue in G Minor.

There was special mention of Raye and her "impish clowning" being "almost as funny" as in *Rhythm on the Range* as she "keeps her facial gymnastics and her foghorn swing music on tap." Reminded by Peggy of the competition from all the big stars taking part in the musical, Maggie was pleased with the *Times* recognition.

As the movie played to packed theaters in major cities, Maggie's life took on new dimensions when she was introduced to one of the five Westmore brothers, all makeup men and hair stylists. Young Hamilton "Buddy" Westmore soon became her Svengali, studying her carefully in preparation for the glamorizing process. The figure was good and the legs were great. No need for improvement in that area. Carefully, he arched Maggie's eyebrows above the clear blue eyes, parted her hair on the left, and brushed it smooth on top, then let it fall gently to near-shoulder length, curling into a soft flip. When he had finished applying makeup to highlight the cheekbones and de-emphasize the large mouth, Maggie looked into the mirror and smiled. She was pretty, she decided. Buddy had made her so. And she was ready to take on Hollywood and its press people, with all their hype and puffery.

3

To the Top

When twenty-one-year-old Buddy Westmore promptly fell in love with the glamour girl of his creation, Maggie must have felt like a Cinderella. At the same time, she was being offered several roles in movies. Agents waved radio contracts and personal appearance dates in front of her. Beauty-aid companies sought her endorsement of their products. Orchestra conductor Leopold Stokowski, admiring her vocal improvisations, soon would become such a good friend that she would call him "Stokey." And to give the glass-slipper touch to the wonderful things that were happening to her, Buddy proposed.

Peggy emphatically protested the idea of marriage for her daughter, pointing out that she had known Westmore for only a short time. Right now the important thing was Maggie's career, Peggy insisted, and absolutely nothing must interfere with that. The older woman's vehemence roused Maggie's suspicions that Peggy wanted total control over her life. She had already been persuaded by her mother to hire Peggy's male companion, Peter Bouman, to manage her business affairs, but Maggie had no intention of permitting Bouman and Peggy to supervise her personal affairs. They had no right to decide whether she would marry Westmore, Maggie determined.

Pete Bouman, a former waiter at Hollywood's Cafe La Maze, possessed the kind of take-command personality that had inspired confidence in the mother and daughter at this bewildering and swiftly changing period of their lives. Important decisions regarding contracts and advertising offers had to be made, and both women had been relieved to place such decisions in the hands of the man to whom Peggy was attracted. Peggy had been separated from Pete Reed for several years, and she had obtained an interlocutory divorce decree.

As *The Big Broadcast of 1937* broke a ten-year box-office record, Maggie plunged into a strenuous role of singing and performing acrobatic burlesques in *College Holiday* with Jack Benny, whose weekly radio program earned high ratings as the comedian portrayed a lovable cheapskate who did a squeaky job of playing a violin. George Burns, Gracie Allen, and Bob Burns also filled major roles, although once again a *Times* review cited the film's "negligible plot," adding that there was "nothing crueler than an outline of a musical comedy story." The mention of "Raye's caricature of a strong-armed virgin from the corn fields" was the only thing the reviewer, Frank Nugent, had to say about Maggie's performance as Daisy Schloggenheimer. His comment on the picture overall was that "being trivial, unpretentious and nonsensical on its own admission, the picture demands nothing of the beholder but unlimited patience or an appetite for the ageless rudiments of vaudeville."

Maggie was given her chance to star in another "creampuff" production, *Hideaway Girl* with Shirley Ross and Robert Cummings. The picture came out only three weeks after the release of *College Holiday,* and the *Times* review was not an encouraging one for Maggie to accept if, indeed, she had time to digest the reviewer's remarks among the constant demands of filming. Frank Nugent referred to Raye as "the lusty lark of Paramount's roster of curiosa" and added that "the explosive Miss Raye has but one opportunity left—to swallow a stick of dynamite and light the fuse, distributing her animated self over a Paramount set." Raye, Nugent continued, "is in her customary leather-lunged form, trying abortively to match her matchless 'Mr. Paganini' bathos" by expressing, in song and swing-dance gestures, her preference for "Liszt, Beethoven or Bach" over modern vo-de-o-do. The reviewer summed up the picture as something for audiences to shudder about with "countless juveniles enacting" a corny plot.

The pressures on Maggie persisted when, as soon as the filming for *Hideaway Girl* was completed, Paramount rushed her into *Waikiki Wedding* with Bing Crosby and Bob Burns. The *Times* reviewer found this picture to be "a friendly, inoffensive, reasonably diverting musical." The same adjectives could be applied to Crosby, who commanded a large following of devoted fans, and to his crooning style, admirably fitted to performing "Sweet Leilani" and "Okolehao."

Nugent gave some credit to the plot in this movie as "a workable idea for a musical comedy" but temporized that "the fabric has been stretched so far that it has burst in places." Nugent credited himself with "sticking loyally to his guns" in heralding the performance of "Miss Raye of the elastic mouth, the rubbery legs and the amazing holler."

After the Paramount debut of *Waikiki Wedding* in late March 1937, there was a brief break. On May 30, Maggie and Buddy were together, partying with friends, when, without informing Peggy, they eloped to Las Vegas in Maggie's convertible. Going along with them were Maggie's friend Noreen Carr and Hollywood physician Frank Nolan, who agreed to serve as witnesses for the impromptu wedding.

Shaking out the folds of her blue chiffon evening gown in Las Vegas, Maggie, with an impatient Buddy at her side, waited for the judge at the courthouse, passing the time by grabbing an office rubber stamp and imprinting Buddy and Nolan's white shirt fronts. When the judge appeared, the wedding evolved into a double ceremony as another young couple arrived and requested the same service.

After a champagne breakfast, Maggie wired the news to Peggy, then the four climbed back into the convertible and headed for Beverly Hills. As the newlyweds drove up to Maggie's house, they were surprised to find reporters waiting for them. Maggie was not so surprised to find Peggy in tears, but she was astonished to learn that her mother was preparing to move out of the daughter's house. "They promised me that they wouldn't get married for two years," Peggy sobbed.

Buddy eagerly pointed out to his bride that it was better for a married couple to live alone. But Maggie, basically insecure, was not yet ready to end her dependence on her mother. Mother and daughter had had their spats from time to time, especially when Peggy had too much to drink, but they had always quickly forgotten the quarrels in their need for mutual support. Upset, now, that her mother was leaving, Maggie made up her mind to repair the estrangement.

The quarrel between daughter and mother soon ended, but the relationship between the bride and groom was already strained. Buddy was irritated that Maggie complained of being too tired for sex when she worked late at the studio, which was most of the time. To Buddy, it seemed that she had lost all desire for sex and couldn't care less about his needs. Maggie felt that Buddy had little or no appreciation of the demands placed on her by the studio at this time. Only one month after their wedding, *Mountain Music* was released. Starring with Bob Burns in what the *Times* called a "hillbilly romp," Raye sang a number titled "Good Morning" in typical explosive style. The critic wrote that Rufe Davis's one-man-band rendition of "Mamma Don't 'low no Bull Fiddle Playin' in Heah" was the "musical high spot of the show," but added that Raye's myriad fans would firmly argue that nothing could match Raye's version of "Good Morning."

In this movie, Burns filled the role of a mountaineer suffering from a schizophrenic peculiarity resulting from a jolt to the head. Maggie's home remedy for Burns's problem was supposed to be dousing him with a bucket of cold water from a well. Cameras had rolled as she energetically doused him, accidentally letting go of the handle and watching in horror as the bucket flew through the air and struck Burns at the back of the head. A stagehand had come running with smelling salts. After a few whiffs, Burns, a good trouper, was back on his feet and ready to face the camera again.

Mountain Music, the critic concluded, was a "hodgepodge of horsefaces and horselaughs" introducing bazooka player Bob Burns's eccentric relatives to the public. Scarcely had Maggie finished *Mountain Music* when her studio propelled her into a personal appearance tour that began on July 4 at the Paramount Theater in New York. Buddy decided to accompany his wife (after all, maybe it would give him a chance to be with her more frequently than when she was making movies), but he was unhappy that Peggy and Pete

Bouman decided to go along, too. He was making no attempt now to conceal his resentment of his mother-in-law. He insisted to Maggie that Peggy had no right to interfere in discussions between the newlyweds. Nor did Maggie need to consult her mother on all business and social affairs.

Maggie saw things differently. Her family had been split up. Pete Reed and Buddy were in New York, and her sister, Melodye, who had serious health problems including alcoholism, had moved back to Chicago. Maggie felt she couldn't desert her mother. "Not after the sacrifices Peggy made to help me become a success," she told Buddy in one of the dramatic statements to which she often resorted regardless of whether they were true, partly true, or not at all true.

Despite Buddy's protests, Maggie's arrival in New York was complete with entourage. While Maggie drew crowds of admirers to the Paramount Theater, the feud between Buddy and his mother-in-law and Bouman escalated.

Maggie, earning $5,500 a week for her Paramount appearance, felt that she was caught in the middle. The increasing urgency of Buddy's complaints, added to the stresses of her career, made her feel that she surely would explode. Yet, when she appeared on stage, her wide smile and bouncing hilarity were so genuine that no one could have detected any evidence of turmoil. The thrill of performing superseded her problem-ridden existence.

Offstage, the more her husband criticized Peggy and Pete Bouman, the more protective Maggie became. Still holding on to the remnants of patience that Maggie was determined to retain, she kept reminding Buddy that her mother deserved her loyalty because Peggy had been her critic and her best friend all through the tough times.

The reminders were useless. So much hatred festered on both sides that Buddy bought a gun. It was "for protection," he told his wife. He needed the gun, he told others, because Pete Bouman had burst into the Westmores' hotel suite with a pistol in his hand, threatening violence over Buddy's so-called interference between Peggy and her daughter and between Peggy and Pete.

Rumors spread to the press. When Maggie publicly denied to reporters that Bouman had made such threats, Buddy's animosity intensified. As difficult as it was to cope with Buddy's resentment, Maggie continued with the tour, which drew crowds to the Paramount night after night. From New York, she moved to Chicago, where Peggy told reporters that her daughter's strenuous stage acrobatics had resulted in a broken finger. Detroit was to be the next destination.

As Maggie and Buddy—finally minus Peggy and Bouman—arrived on an early morning train at Michigan Central Station in Detroit, the entertainer's splint-bound finger attracted much less attention than did her clothing. "This is a Hollywood costume," she told reporters. A man's suit, fitted to her 120-pound figure. Blue trousers. Blue jacket. Blue beret covering her dark hair. And a yellow vest and tan sandals. "Men's clothes are more sensible than women's and a darned sight easier to get into," Maggie explained.

Her description of her clothing as a "Hollywood costume" was pretty much on target. Bisexual actress Marlene Dietrich had been wearing male evening clothes since the 1920s while performing in Berlin, where gay culture was much admired. In Hollywood in the 1930s, Marlene was outspoken about her preference for male clothing. In fact, she claimed that she would much prefer to be a man. But although the gay lifestyle was accepted in some major European cities, Hollywood studios assumed a sanctimonious attitude by warning homosexual actors that they would lose their contracts unless they carefully concealed their sexual relationships. Since most film contracts at that time contained a "morals" clause that gave studios some control over the personal lives of their employees, stars were pressured to conform to their studios' edicts.

However, it was perfectly all right, even desirable in the view of the studios, to flaunt lavish Hollywood lifestyles with furs, diamonds, and displays of palatial homes equipped with swimming pools, tennis courts, Rolls-Royces, and chauffeurs during the long and terrible years of the Great Depression.

Glittering Hollywood offered motion pictures that brought relief and reprieve to viewers, who temporarily could push aside the ugly and embarrassing distresses that scarred their lives in the 1930s. And an eager and gullible public greedily devoured the puffery distributed by press agents on the golden lives of glamorous stars.

It was a time of smoke and mirrors, a decade when a young blonde wearing a simple skirt and form-fitting sweater and sitting at a drugstore counter could be "discovered" by a producer or talent scout going about like a fairy godmother with a magic wand. Ping! The wand touches the blonde's shoulder and, according to the story that would attain folklore status, she becomes a Hollywood starlet soon known to millions as America's Sweater Girl. If it could happen to Lana Turner, it could happen to anyone.

The essence of the smoke-and-mirrors vogue of those earlier days encircled the man who lived in the White House and represented the hopes and dreams of so many laboring people, employed and unemployed. President Franklin D. Roosevelt's resonant voice reassured Americans by way of his Fireside Chats on the radio. People saw him in newsreels, smiling and waving his long cigarette holder. Every sight of his handsome, tanned face was additional reassurance as he sat in his open car or behind his desk.

Americans were aware that Roosevelt had had polio and was promoting donations to help children and adults stricken with that crippling disease. But Roosevelt projected strength, nonetheless, because the sight of his helpless, steel-braced legs was hidden with the collaboration of a protective press corps. He was seen standing behind a podium while the braces holding him upright were concealed, as was the tableau of the president being hauled by strong men up to a platform. Reporters also helped to conceal from the public the president's long adulterous love affair. It would be decades later (the early 1980s and the 1990s) before the relentless dig-up-all-the-secrets style of investigative reporting would begin to change American society.

Unlike the sudden rise of America's Sweater Girl from obscurity to celebrity status, Maggie's life, up to this point, had been marked by struggle and a desperate clawing up the ladder to recognition. And now, her first day in Detroit was taken up with rehearsals for the next day's opening at the city's top showplace, the plush Michigan Theater. She wanted desperately to draw crowds to the theater to prove her personal attraction to movie fans, despite lukewarm reviews of her most recent movies.

On August 7, 1937, she was thrilled to see throngs of people waiting in front of the theater and jostling each other, trying to push inside and be the first to see "Hollywood's newest comedy star." Extra policemen were called to keep order.

Inside the handsome theater, Maggie went through her act, transformed into a dynamo of slender, flashing legs and whirling arms. She responded with encore after encore as the audience applauded, whistled, and cheered, especially as she sang "Truckin'" and the soulful song that rapidly was becoming her trademark, "Mr. Paganini." Finishing her act with a high kick that sent one of her slippers sailing into the audience, Maggie clowned her way offstage, her heart pounding at her enthusiastic reception.

In the week she stayed in Detroit, each performance was a sellout, with so many theatergoers still wanting to see her act at the close of the week that Maggie agreed to do six shows on the final day. The exhausting schedule hardly fazed the entertainer, who renewed her energies by having Buddy read to her the glowing reviews from Detroit newspapers.

Hollywood's newest star, the papers reported, had broken all admission records at the Michigan Theater, "out-distancing even 'America's Sweetheart,' Mary Pickford," who had made a personal appearance there a few years earlier.

This frantic pace was the kind of life for which Maggie had been primed since early childhood. With success and the adulation of millions finally within her grasp, she had no intention of backing away from the demands of her career, however tiring they might be.

On her return to Hollywood, she was scheduled to perform in *Artists and Models,* starring Jack Benny and Ida Lupino. According to *Times* critic Frank Nugent, she and trumpeter Louis Armstrong "blasted through a high-brow sequence called 'Public Melody Number One.'"

The affinity between Armstrong and Raye was like that of Maggie's earlier musical rapport with Louis Prima. Armstrong's innate talents for jazz, like those of Raye, were palpable enough to heat up the screen when the film was released, and to create a critical controversy in segregated America among those who saw the two musicians' onscreen performance as defying a ban "of interaction between a black man and a white woman," wrote a reviewer of Laurence Bergreen's 1997 biography of Louis Armstrong.

Jack Benny's performance drew plaudits from the *Times* as "the drollest comic on the screen," and *Artists and Models* rated praise as "a suave, witty and polished show, one of the sprightliest of the season's musical comedies."

Maggie moved right into making *Double or Nothing* with Bing Crosby. Comics Andy Devine and William Frawley (the latter gaining fame on television in later years as the grumpy neighbor of Lucille Ball and Desi Arnaz) added their considerable comic talents to the movie. The *Times* reviewer pointed out that Crosby-Raye fans "turned out en masse" (some 3,000 of them) for the opening of the show at 10 A.M. on the first of September. Terming it a "tuneful show" with several "better-than-average numbers," the reviewer wrote that Crosby sang five numbers in his "customary agreeable voice," but that it was the explosive Raye who provided the "brighter moments." He particularly lauded her singing of "It's On, It's Off," a satirization of striptease performers. If the show had less buoyancy and sparkle, the critic continued, it likely was due to unimaginative direction by Theodore Reed.

Maggie could now see that she had a large and devoted number of fans who turned out to see her movies. Her goal remained the same, whatever the pressures might be, to gain top billing on all her movies.

Her commitment to success on the stage and screen was as strong as, if not stronger than, her young husband's commitment to the promotion of the House of Westmore and its makeup artistry. But Buddy, whose salary was only $100 a week (the House of Westmore had not yet attained its peak prestige) should not demand her subjugation to his own life and career, she decided.

Westmore had a different opinion. His wife did not have control over her income. In fact, Pete Bouman had assigned Maggie a monthly "allowance" for her expenses. Westmore felt that he had molded this effervescent girl with the too-large mouth and gauche mannerisms into a glamorous young woman who should be content to let her career command second place to her image as his wife and bearer of the proud Westmore name. He wanted her at his side and in his home, not running around the country making stage appearances.

Westmore was angry, too, over a September incident when his wife wanted him to take her to a nightclub when he was not in the mood. Annoyed, Maggie phoned another man and went out anyway. But Westmore must have followed her, because he engaged in a fistfight with Pete Bouman in the washroom of that Hollywood club, while Maggie and Peggy looked on, screaming. Still, neither man was hurt in what turned out to be a typical Hollywood skirmish of wild swings that never landed in vulnerable spots—if, indeed, they landed at all.

On September 4, 1937, after three hectic months of marriage, Maggie filed for divorce, charging Westmore with cruelty. He had been extremely jealous of her, she complained. While in Las Vegas in August, he had slapped her in the mouth in public and had even threatened to shoot her and himself, she insisted, adding that Westmore had lived in luxury at her expense without making any attempt to support her.

Westmore had a very different version of who was taking advantage of his wife. Under the influence of her manipulative mother and Bouman, he claimed, Martha's earnings were being "dissipated and mismanaged."

Near the end of the month, an interlocutory decree of divorce was awarded to Maggie, complete with a court order restraining Westmore from molesting her. She was free now. Free to concentrate on the goal that lay tantalizingly close to her grasp: the goal of bursting into the inner circle of those box-office stars whose names consistently took top billing on theater marquees. Clark Gable. Fred Astaire and Ginger Rogers. Joan Crawford. Claudette Colbert. James Cagney. Shirley Temple. And, coming up fast, Judy Garland, one of the Gumm sisters who had worked the same third-rate vaudeville circuits that the Reeds had worked.

The competition was frightening, but years later as Maggie

looked back on the year 1937, she would recall her resolve to put any regrets about her short-lived marriage behind her and to dwell instead on her successes. Good roles in five motion pictures for Paramount in a single year. A weekly Tuesday night radio show over WABC with Al Jolson, plus countless other public engagements. She was on her way to the top. The very top.

4

Marriage and the Movies

Maggie's recollections of her fast-paced experiences in Hollywood during the 1930s would seem, even to her, to consist of unreal episodes including her brief marriage to Westmore. So much happened during that relatively short period of time.

Her father, Pete Reed, came back into her life early in 1938 when he took legal action to demand an accounting and share of his daughter's income. His own contributions to his daughter's early theatrical training had been overlooked, he said. The self-styled "forgotten man" wanted $50,000 compensation.

At the same time, Reed filed a suit to have Peggy's divorce decree set aside. He had not contested the decree earlier, he claimed, because his wife had promised to end her relationship with Pete Bouman.

When the appeal to set aside the divorce decree was denied, Maggie's father sued Bouman for $150,000, charging alienation of affections. To add to Bouman's problems and to the clutter of lawsuits, a young St. Louis stenographer filed a $50,000 breach-of-promise suit, charging that Bouman had jilted her and had begun to associate with Peggy Reed instead.

By the time that news of the court suits made headlines, however, Peggy already was married to Bouman. Unknown to Maggie, the wedding had taken place in Phoenix on March 19, 1938, only a few days after Peggy's divorce became final. When Maggie learned of the marriage, she wondered why her mother had not confided in her. She did not yet know that Peggy's eagerness to marry Maggie's business manager was because of her desire to gain greater control, with Bouman's help, over the daughter who had little understanding of financial matters. (Many years later, Maggie's lawyer would say that Raye "doesn't know the difference between $25, $2,500, and $25,000. She has absolutely no concept.")

Since math continued to be so confusing to Maggie, she was unable to assume responsibility for her own finances. Beneath her confident and genial exterior, she was so insecure that she was relieved to retain the pair she thought she could trust to manage her assets. The Boumans now settled into a house bought for Peggy by her daughter.

Leaving money matters to wiser heads while the legal maneuvering continued, Maggie had focused her full attention on achieving greater success in the movie industry as she was assigned to *The Big Broadcast of 1938*, playing the part of W. C. Fields's daughter. Bob Hope, a song and dance man new to film, and Dorothy Lamour also had roles in the movie. This would be the first of several films featuring Hope and Raye. Their lives would take parallel paths in many ways.

Schooled in early life in the importance of timing and being punctual for vaudeville appearances, Maggie was well disciplined on the movie set. Her relentless good humor and joking repartee may have grated on the other actors as they arrived in the early hours of the morning for makeup sessions with Wally Westmore or one of the other Westmore brothers, so that filming could start at nine A.M. But Maggie's clowning enlivened things for everyone as the day went on.

Maggie was fascinated by the antics of W. C. Fields, as that portly gentleman rode a bicycle from his dressing room to the set and back again. For Fields's convenience, a martini shaker had been strapped to the side of the bike. Whether Fields felt the shaker was necessary to slake his thirst, or whether it was merely a part of his clownlike image enhancement as a heavy drinker with a bulbous nose, Maggie could not determine. Fields, she knew, had been a big name in vaudeville where he had appeared as a juggler who cracked jokes. The jokes, many of them stressing his professed hatred for kids and animals, were original with Fields, who wrote them. This had earned him the reputation for being a comedic genius.

When the film debuted in early March 1938, Frank S. Nugent's review in the *Times* contained few, if any, kind words for the movie, even though *Big Broadcasts* had been perennial box-office favorites. Even while acknowledging that the *New York Times* maintained tough standards, the cast of *The Big Broadcast of 1938* had to have felt abashed at the criticism. Most of Fields's performance was heralded by the *Times* as "sub-strata Fields." The producers and writers were categorized as "paralyzed from the eyebrows up." Bob Hope and Shirley Ross acquitted themselves "commendably" as they sang "Thanks for the Memory," which later would become Hope's theme song, but nothing else was commended. Raye "drubbed out 'That Moon Is Here Again,'" the review stated. Other reviews in other cities were probably much kinder, but it was the *Times* review that staked out important territory for the world of performers, producers, directors, and writers.

Today Steve Allen—talented comedian, writer, composer and pianist, whose measured opinions always have been taken very seriously in the entertainment world—commends *The Big Broadcast of 1938.* His book *More Funny People* advises students of comedy to see the movie "because there are so many important funny people in it." Allen praises Raye for performing "one of the most exciting song-and-dance specialties ever seen in films." He describes her, on the deck of a ship, "wearing a sort of Eleanor Powellish sailor-girl costume which exhibited her very attractive legs," singing "superbly, dancing up a storm," and being very funny.

The Big Broadcast of 1938, like its predecessors, was successful in ticket sales. Then Martha was moved quickly into *College Swing* starring George Burns and Gracie Allen. Hope took part in this movie, too, as did Betty Grable, the beautiful shapely blonde who would become the soldiers' favorite pinup girl in World War II. Hope rated fourth billing beneath Raye, who played the part of a professor of romance who advises a female student to be a bit coy, a bit demure to get her man.

Although a star-studded cast such as this one, including comedians Edward Everett Horton and Ben Blue, surely would attract fans to theaters, *College Swing* met the same unhappy fate at the hands of a *Times* reviewer as had Raye's previous movie. The reviewer suggested that studios should "stop trying to keep up plot appearances in musicals of this type and advertise them frankly as variety shows," noting that Betty Grable and Jackie Coogan shagged their way through the entire action, which consisted of several days. Raye and Hope were cited as "plumbing the depths of slapstick."

Disappointed by recent reviews, Maggie's secret yearnings intensified—yearnings to perform a dramatic role in a serious film. She was certain she could do it. She needed only a stroke of good luck to acquire such a role. Many other Hollywood actors were superstitious and searched their horoscopes for good luck. Unlike them, Maggie wore a cloth scapular, a token of devotion, beneath her clothing for good health and good fortune. She did not attend church, but she always insisted she was Roman Catholic.

Dorothy Lamour, whose trademark was the sarong, and Ray Milland were given the top spots in *Tropic Holiday,* but the Paramount Theater soon began billing the show as a Bob Burns–Martha Raye piece. "Intermittently, it is," agreed Nugent of the *Times.* He pointed out the "amusing high-jinks like those of Miss Raye's bullfight" (she battled a bull imported from Mexico), but said these highlights were spaced by the "trying romantics" of Lamour and Milland. He concluded that "the intermissions are the better part" of the movie.

The review was a sop to Maggie's pride in some respects, because she was tired of playing second-best to Hollywood's glamour girls. At such times of discouragement, she had blamed Westmore for what she saw as a decline in her popularity, because it was he who had made over the ugly duckling and turned her into a glossy facsimile of other Hollywood starlets. Now, however, she was beginning to look more objectively on her relationship with Westmore. He had been the first man to take a serious interest in her as a desirable young woman; he had made her feel beautiful and very feminine. And she had been flattered by the attentions of the good-looking and artistic young man with a promising future ahead of him. They had thought they were in love, of course, when actually they were infatuated with the idea of love and romance and with the glamour of life in Hollywood.

Moving on with her life turned out to be not that difficult after all, because by now there was David Rose, her music arranger at Paramount, to distract her. Maggie liked everything about Dave—his wavy blond hair and blue eyes, his skill as an arranger, composer, and conductor. He had an even disposition manifesting a stability and maturity that made him seem considerably older than his years. These were the qualities Maggie felt she needed in a man.

Maggie was happier with her next picture, *Give Me a Sailor,* because she had the glamorous starring role. Bob Hope had second billing, followed by Betty Grable and Jack Whiting. The movie "apparently was made without a script," wrote Bosley Crowther of the *Times.* In this Cinderella tale, Raye was the family drudge until she entered a national "Beautiful Legs" contest and won. ("Deservedly so," Crowther reported.)

After the picture debuted, Maggie was thrilled when she was invited to come aboard the USS *Pennsylvania,* flagship of the U.S. fleet, to be named the crew's official "sweetheart." She cheerfully shook hands with some five hundred sailors on her visit, and soon afterwards received a very special letter from one. "You don't remember me," the sailor scribbled, "but you autographed my cap. I've got a picture of you in a bathing suit and I'm taking it in town with me tonight. I'm going to have a tattooer paint your legs on my chest." Maggie was touched by the letter. She had very patriotic leanings, anyway, and both admired and empathized with men in military uniforms.

After her divorce from Westmore in September 1938, Maggie made an out-of-court settlement of her father's lawsuit from her earnings—earnings that were reported by the U.S. Treasury Department to have amounted to $81,958 the previous year. Then, even though both Peggy and the studio objected to another quick marriage, Maggie was ready to wed David Rose. Peggy kept preaching about "not so fast" and "taking time out to think it through, first," but the wedding took place in Einsenada, Mexico, in October 1938.

Maggie hoped that 1939 could be her big year. She quickly accepted the chance to star in *Never Say Die* with Bob Hope and the hoarse-voiced Andy Devine. Hope and Raye tried valiantly to make the best of the comedy, which lacked a solid storyline, but when the film went out to theaters, Maggie was hurt by some of the reviews. Hope and Devine were their usual funny selves, these critics said. But they wondered if Raye had delusions of being a dramatic actress. Bosley Crowther's review was more penetrating. He wrote of Hope and Raye just going in there and "swinging, throwing gags as fast as they can, sliding into and out of situations with the elegance of a roller coaster." And at the end, he concluded, "You can almost hear them panting anxiously, 'Did we make it?' They do," he admitted before diving into a description of the somewhat overdrawn plot.

Maggie tried to be objective about the critics' comments. Of course, she had enjoyed feeling pretty and desirable. What woman wouldn't? Still, she never had sacrificed an opportunity to make a funny gag still funnier with facial gymnastics, simply because it was her nature to do so. While other actresses and actors (in line with their studios' demands for physical perfection on-screen and off) fussed about being photographed only when their faces were posed at certain angles with their "best sides" featured, Maggie was too much of a natural clown and mimic to resist her impulses to mug, scowl, or contort her face or body in response to various situations.

And now if success meant relying on mugging and on the "rubber-mouth" image about which she was acquiring, under pressure, certain sensitivities, she vowed to overlook those sensitivities and give audiences the funny, awkward, bombastic Martha Raye they would accept and love.

"The size of Martha's mouth has always been exaggerated, for purposes of easy laughs and publicity," Steve Allen points out. "But because much of Martha's comedy was performed during the 1940s and '50s, writers and publicists who worked for her went for the easy jokes about her mouth. Martha, of course, cooperated by mugging and contorting her essentially quite normal face."

A new Paramount picture seemed an opportunity for Maggie to restore any lost popularity when she was offered a comic role with Joe E. Brown of "big-mouth" fame. But *$1,000 a Touchdown* turned out to be of such farcical quality that neither comic could spark the poor material. Frank S. Nugent described it as "a painfully witless football farce of almost fantastic unoriginality." He added that the movie ended with Brown "being thrown over the goal posts. They threw the wrong man: Delmer Daves, who wrote it, would be our choice—and we'd insist on a field goal."

If the comedies could have been as clever as some of the reviews, Maggie would have had some excellent material with which to work. Instead, the brightest spot in 1939 for Maggie was her popularity in a *Radio Guide* poll in which Bea Wain was voted the top female swing singer by *Guide* readers. Martha Raye rated second place.

Maggie was not the type to hide her feelings from those closest to her. At home, Dave endured her frequent mood shifts. Her noisy exuberance at the *Radio Guide* report. Her inconsolable misery over the failure of the picture with Joe E. Brown. She agonized, too, over Paramount's slowness to put her into another movie in a year when movies were popping out of Hollywood studios like flapjacks from a skillet. The eight biggest studios produced 376 motion pictures in 1939 (only two of them were Maggie's), spending more than a half-million dollars each on more than 100 films. To be slumping in such a mass-production year was an unbearable blow to Maggie's ego. She pushed aside her aspirations to be a straight dramatic actress and yearned now simply to get another comedy role.

Her spirits lifted again when Paramount cast her in *The Farmer's Daughter* early in 1940, but this film also turned out to be second-rate. It was panned by Bosley Crowther of the *Times* for being as "obvious and dull" as the oft-repeated jokes about "the farmer's daughter." When Maggie entered her dressing room one day after the completion of *The Farmer's Daughter*, she found a note that had been slipped under her door. She opened it and slowly read the several typed words. There was only one way to comprehend their meaning. She was no longer under contract with Paramount.

She had failed, and failures were outcasts in Hollywood. She had seen it happen to others who were no longer escorted to choice booths when they entered the Brown Derby. No longer invited to parties given by the motion picture elite. Stars who were paid $1,000 a week avoided the taint of mixing with those who had been reduced to $500. Money snobbery prevailed throughout the celluloid kingdom.

Was it possible, she demanded of her husband, that in three years she could have zoomed so close to stardom, then skidded back into nothingness? In less traumatic moments, Maggie admired her husband's even disposition. But there was no way now that he could calm her. She was voluble in her distress. But she hid the depth of her disappointment from others and insisted on throwing a party to celebrate her release from Paramount, a party at which Maggie was the most hilarious of celebrants.

Then, in another shattering blow, Dave admitted he was weary of her swift mood changes. Exhausted by her nervous energy. Annoyed by her clowning and noisy antics. She knew that he never had appreciated her clown image. She had come to realize that rather quickly and had tried to squelch her natural impulses to banter when he was serious, to laugh too loudly at a joke, to pantomime in her attempts to amuse.

Maggie had believed that Dave was totally caught up in arranging music for *The Tony Martin Show* on radio. No, not totally, she despaired now. She discovered that he was already involved with another woman, a teenager. The girl was Judy Garland, who had starred in *The Wizard of Oz* and won the hearts of an adoring American public as she sang "Over the Rainbow."

Maggie and Judy had much in common: both had big voices, expressive faces and eyes, and were short waisted with long legs. But while Maggie was vain about her shapely legs and svelte figure, Judy had a problem with her weight. Her neck was too short and she had a tendency to hunch forward. Maggie could take little consolation in recalling these deficiencies, however, because it was clear that Judy had stolen David Rose away.

Maggie and Dave had been married only one and a half years, so this second marriage had lasted just a little longer than her first when Dave left their home. The rejection and separation frightened Maggie because she had loved the music that her husband had created, soothing music of soaring strings and sweet rhythm, even as she had been awed by the fact that he had studied music at the Chicago Conservatoire and was an excellent pianist. She had also loved making their recordings of "Stairway to the Stars" on the Brunswick label and "I Walk Alone" and "Yesterdays" for Columbia. She had thought these recordings symbolized their closeness in marriage, his artistry complementing her own voice—not strident in the recordings but full-bodied. Her clown image was forgotten in the mellow harmonies of the music her husband loved. But now it was all ending in dissonance.

Concealing her hurt in public, she appeared in court in May 1940 to file for divorce. Her husband, she testified, had stayed away from home for days at a time. He had been sullen toward her and even abusive.

She realized, however, that she had learned a great deal from Dave about aesthetic values, even though she had stiffened frequently in her abashed awareness of his superior knowledge when he tried to explain some musical or artistic quality that he thought she did not, but should, understand. She made up her mind to be grateful for what she had learned from him and to try to forget her disappointment in love. From now on, she would concentrate totally on her career—or what was left of it.

Little was left of her convertible the night she hurriedly drove toward her mountaintop home to pick up Peggy and take her to dinner. As she rounded a sharp curve, the car went into a skid, brakes squealing as it hurtled off the road and slid 150 feet down the cliff.

Shocked, Maggie tried to climb out of the wreckage. But her right side felt numb from shoulder to foot. She reached for her scapular and discovered she had forgotten to wear it. Slowly, painfully, she crawled out of the car and began to pull herself with her left arm up the cliff and onto the road. After more than one car passed without stopping, Maggie managed to get to her feet and hobble the quarter-mile to her house.

"I'm okay. I'm okay," Maggie repeated as Peggy began to scream and cry. "Just scratched, that's all," she said as she washed blood from her face and arms, insisting that they could go on to the restaurant in her mother's car. Later, as she recalled the details of the accident and its aftermath for reporters, she told a tale of having gone with her mother to the restaurant where she promptly collapsed. Taken by ambulance for emergency care at a hospital, she was x-rayed to determine the extent of her injuries. She told reporters she had a broken ankle, broken kneecap, fractured hip, and cracked shoulder blade.

For a few days after the accident she did some serious thinking about her future. Then she was somewhat cheered when Universal Pictures phoned to offer her a freelance contract. Even though the salary was much smaller than her Paramount salary had been, she eagerly accepted the offer (despite the injuries she had reported) and quickly went into rehearsals for *The Boys from Syracuse*, in which she would costar with singer-actor Allan Jones.

When the Universal movie was completed, Maggie was off to New York for the premiere accompanied by her mother and by Maggie's Scottish terrier, Dinky. In a *New York Times* review, Bosley Crowther admitted that Jones sang rather well but that his acting was wooden. Raye was her usual self, he wrote, crediting the "tuneful numbers" sung by the actors but finding it disappointing that the producers "tossed away the lively musical score," which Richard Rodgers and Lorenz Hart had written for the Broadway musical comedy by George Abbott. In this kidding-of-the-classics story, Crowther wrote, "Modern slapstick and confusion only goes so far in ancient dress—and, in this case, it isn't far enough."

Maggie was not thrilled with her latest movie, but felt she was helpless to make changes in the kinds of scripts that studios presented to her. (Much later, she confessed to reporters that she should have refused some of the roles that were assigned to her in those early days. "But I was only nineteen years old," she added. "What did I know?") Her spirits lifted, though, when she heard from her friend Al Jolson. This time, his telephone call was not about his radio show. He had quit the show in a fit of anger when producers and directors urged him to imitate Bing Crosby's "crooner" style of singing.

Maggie understood Jolson's indignation. For years, the man had been a superstar on stage, radio, and screen. His distinctive voice had made popular such sentimental songs as "Mammy" and "Swanee," which he sang while kneeling, his face blackened with burnt cork. And now they wanted to change him into a crooner?

Maggie was surprised when Jolson began discussing his estranged wife, tap dancer Ruby Keeler, who had made it big in glitz movies such as *42nd Street*. Maggie knew that Jolson and Ruby were having problems in their marriage and that Ruby had sued her husband for divorce the previous December. The couple had been seen, more than once, arguing in their chocolate-colored Rolls-Royce. But now, Jolson was telling her, Ruby was going to have a good supporting role in a musical comedy that he was producing for the stage. Would Maggie like to play an important part in the musical?

If Maggie's injuries from the automobile accident were as numerous and serious as she had recently told reporters, it is unlikely that she could have accepted Jolson's offer. Her first question was, "When do rehearsals begin?"

"Rehearsals start right away," Jolson replied. "The show is scheduled to open in Detroit in a couple of weeks. At the Cass Theater. On June 30."

Maggie left at once for Detroit. There she joined the rest of the cast, the writers, and the music director, Al Goodman. Everyone except the star and producer, Jolson.

The three who had the main supporting roles—Maggie, Ruby Keeler, and Jack Whiting—rehearsed their parts as best they could in the absence of the star, who had an enormous stake in the production. Jolson had provided 80 percent of the financing and had made sure that the entire show centered around him. Everyone was asking why he wasn't in Detroit. But Keeler had little to say on the subject.

The musical comedy set was the scene of total confusion when Jolson arrived in Detroit on June 26, four days before the opening. The dude-ranch musical, originally titled *Silks and Saddles*, was renamed *Keep Punching*, then *Wahoo*, and finally *Hold On to Your Hats*.

The cast plunged into frenzied rehearsals. But each day, the star of the show cut off the rehearsal just before the finale. On opening night at Detroit's Cass Theater, the entire cast was nervous with good reason. The finale was still unrehearsed. Backstage, Jolson paced, worrying, as was his habit, whether he would be in good voice.

Then the orchestra was finishing the overture and it was time for Jolson to move onstage in his starring role as Lone Rider. Maggie, playing the part of Mamie, launched into her numbers in good style, whooping out "Would You Be So Kindly," "Life Was Pie for the Pioneer," and "She Came, She Saw, She Can-Canned."

The lack of rehearsal became apparent near the end of that first performance when a minor actor missed his cue to appear and Ruby Keeler stood alone on the stage, her face frozen with fear. Quickly, Al Goodman signaled the orchestra to swing into Ruby's dance number. The dancer responded with a furious tapping routine that covered the awkward moment.

For the show's finale, Jolson came back onstage to sing some of the songs that had brought him fame and fortune, and the audience applauded wildly. Backstage, the cast congratulated each other on the successful opening night. Then most of them headed for the Bowery, the popular nightclub where they had been invited to come for a party and where comedian Milton Berle was the main act. It was soon obvious to the rest of the cast that one of the gorgeous showgirls from the chorus of *Hold On to Your Hats* had caught Berle's roving eye. The egocentric Jolson never showed at the party, nor did Ruby Keeler, who likely was still upset that she had frozen onstage, even though the missed cue was not her error.

Despite the enthusiastic response from the audience on opening night, critics were not predicting that *Hold On to Your Hats* would be a hit. The show continued playing in Detroit for two and a half weeks while script changes were made. Ruby Keeler was not interested in the changes. She was interested only in getting released from her contract. Sensitive to the quips about marital problems that her estranged husband slipped into his monologues, Ruby finally forced Jolson to sign Eunice Healy as her replacement. By this time, the show was preparing to move on to Chicago where the Democratic Convention was in progress and the nomination of Franklin D. Roosevelt for an unprecedented third term was imminent.

Expenses for the show totaled $80,000 by the time the cast arrived in Chicago, where reporters pressed in on Jolson to ask about his relationship with Ruby. Jolson was morose and uncommunicative on the subject. He became even gloomier when he broke a bone in his foot during the second Chicago performance. But even on crutches, the star seemed as charismatic as ever to audiences.

The musical ran for six weeks in Chicago, raking in receipts of $22,000 weekly. Night after night, there were two high spots in the show. The first was a "slip of the tongue" that occurred as Maggie was supposed to thank the Lone Rider for "saving the jewels" and, instead, thanked him for "saving the Jews," a slip which was then incorporated into the show. The second highlight was the singing of the burlesque ballad "Down on the Dude Ranch" by Maggie, Jolson, and Bert Gordon.

The show then moved to Philadelphia where a tepid reception and lackluster reviews limited the musical's stay. The cast was nervous when the show moved to New York's Shubert Theater. This was the big test, the performers felt.

In New York, the show got off to a good start. Every night, Jolson would stand center-stage and alone in the spotlight to reign over an extended finale that seemed to the cast, waiting backstage in their costumes for the final bows, to run longer and longer. Audiences from every other theater on Broadway would have departed and arrived home while the Shubert's lights continued to blaze with Jolson, onstage, sparkling like a diamond in a brilliant setting.

The lengthy Jolson performances in New York did not continue long, however, because Jolson became ill with influenza. For several years, he had lived with the neurotic fear of losing his voice. Now his voice failed him, and the show closed. With 158 performances and more than four months of *Hold On to Your Hats* behind her, Maggie returned to California, only to begin moving about the country once again, doing a series of personal appearances while waiting to hear if *Hold On to Your Hats,* with a recovered Jolson at the helm, would open, as promised, in Atlantic City in the summer of 1941. When these plans were canceled, Maggie hoped that a Hollywood studio would offer her a role in another picture.

Nightclub dates kept her occupied in the meantime. One such

booking would be entertaining at the Royal Palm in Miami, following a gig, at that same club, featuring Milton Berle. Unrelated to Berle's act, a men's singing group also entertained at the Royal Palm. The singers wore uniforms, carried swords, and once had to put up with Berle's craziness as he had intruded, spontaneously, into their act, messing up their precise movements with his purposely clumsy stumbles and blunders. The intrusion was typical of Berle's ad lib comedy. He had been interposing himself into others' acts since his vaudeville days. The Royal Palm audience had found the comical intrusion so hilarious that the segment evolved into a nightly presentation before Raye was scheduled to arrive for her gig.

When Maggie duly arrived, she was not at all upset to find Berle staying on by popular demand. She simply joined in the riotous fun, since one of her major talents, like that of Berle, was the ability to ad lib, seemingly without ever running down. The result of the Berle-Raye liaison was overflow crowds every night.

At the same time, Maggie tried to fake indifference to reports that circulated about her estranged husband. David Rose, it was rumored, was eager to marry Judy Garland, who had recently received a special Academy Award for acting by a juvenile. Now, despite objections from Judy's mother, the couple planned to be married as soon as Dave's divorce became final.

In a fit of jealousy and hurt pride, Maggie decided that Dave's marriage to Judy would not precede her own remarriage. After the final Raye-Rose divorce papers were signed on March 19, 1941, reporters converged on Maggie to confirm reports that she would soon marry Neal Lang, a thirty-eight-year-old Miami Beach hotel executive. Yes, she confessed, but she did not know exactly where or when. (She did not tell them, as she would much later admit, that she was "still torching for Dave at that time.")

Five days later, friends gathered at the airport in Burbank, California, to see the Raye-Lang wedding party off to Vegas. Pete and Peggy Bouman were there, with Pete in the role of best man. Actress Ann Sheridan, wearing a beige outfit and a brilliant green hat, was to be the maid of honor. The bride, too, wore beige with brown accessories and a white orchid.

Maggie was beaming, aware that her friends saw Lang as a decent, likeable guy without any pretense. She had met him during one of her appearances in Florida only a short time ago, but he seemed so dependable and even tempered, not given to fits of brooding. And he was definitely not part of the Hollywood scene.

The plane took off from the airport at 8 P.M. At 9:45 P.M., March 24, 1941, Lang became Raye's third husband in a ceremony performed at El Rancho Vegas, a resort hotel near Las Vegas. The newlyweds returned to Burbank the next morning so that Maggie could report to work at Warner Brothers for the picture *Navy Blues* starring Ann Sheridan.

Three days later, Judy Garland's mother announced her young daughter's engagement to David Rose. On July 28, Judy and Dave eloped to Las Vegas. But Maggie took considerable satisfaction in having beaten them to the altar.

Maggie made new friends, fellow actors, as scenes for *Navy Blues* were filmed. Twenty-four-year-old Jackie Gleason, playing the role of Tubby, was new to motion pictures. At night, he and Maggie would make the rounds of bars, both vying to pay the check (often for everybody in the place), but Gleason usually won the battle because of his grandiose perception of himself, always, as that of a winner and a man who could stay on his feet while other drinkers were stumbling around.

In those early 1940s, drinking was a matter of pride in Hollywood. Movies invariably showed actors and actresses sipping cocktails and smoking cigarettes. There was no talk or information supplied about millions of brain cells being destroyed with every alcoholic drink, nor of lung cancer from smoking. But while Maggie visited bars with her pals, nothing was seen of Maggie's new husband, who apparently had returned to his job in Florida.

Gleason and Raye became very friendly with Jack Oakie and Jack Haley, who earlier had played the part of the Tin Man in *The Wizard of Oz* and now was taking the part of Raye's sailor-husband who ignores her need for love and companionship. Oakie would remain a pal, but ten years later, Maggie and Gleason would be competing for television viewers on Saturday night and definitely would not be considered friends.

Maggie no longer looked for *Times* reviews with any happy anticipation. The review for *Navy Blues* was no exception as it reported that "the worst to be said for *Navy Blues* is that it works hard without much to show." But then, of three more films reviewed on the same page of the newspaper, *Lady Be Good,* starring Eleanor Powell, Ann Sothern, Robert Young, and Lionel Barrymore, "deserved only a passing mark," while *Lydia*, starring Merle Oberon, Edna May Oliver, and Joseph Cotten, "could have done with much more restraint and good sense." And *Shors,* a Soviet film biography of General Suvorov, was dismissed as a "wordy, static film in which the actors can do no more than posture and declaim."

Still, Maggie took little consolation in being in the mainstream of films that received a thumbs-down from top reviewers. She did take consolation in the fact that her career was, once more, very busy in the year of her marriage to Lang as she went on to frolic through *Keep 'Em Flying* with Bud Abbott and Lou Costello for Universal. This film rated a few plaudits for the antics of Abbot and Costello and none at all for Raye, trapped in a "routine and sticky plot" in which she played twin sisters in love with Abbott and Costello. The entire movie was summed up in *The New York Times* with these words: "*Keep 'Em Flying* doesn't heed its own words. Too often it hits the ground with a dull, resounding plop."

Maggie hardly had time to be downcast between pictures. As soon as she finished one project, she moved on to the next. She soon performed in a Mayfair production released by Universal. The picture was *Hellzapoppin,* starring Ole Olsen and Chic Johnson, who had done the stage play. *Hellzapoppin,* the *Times* review would say, was "chockful of an anarchic collection of unfunny gags; it is not only insane, it is labored."

Movies kept Maggie so busy during the first five months of her marriage to Lang that the couple spent little time together. Maggie apparently forgot her promise to resettle with her husband wherever he might be managing a hotel. Lang, who never had promised to give up his employment or to become another of Hollywood's male "hangers-on" who lived off their actress-wives, had not realized the extent of his wife's dedication to her career. It was not what she had led him to believe. Nor did he realize that Maggie, despite her reputation for being "man-crazy" because of her three quick marriages, was not really a highly sexed woman. Once she had married a man that she sexually desired, she was quickly satisfied and had no driving need to be with him frequently. Or with him at all, it seemed, as far as Lang was concerned. In early November, a Los Angeles newspaper reported that Neal Lang, with Martha Raye's consent, would file for divorce in Miami. "Neal Lang and Nick Condos were the only ones of my husbands who didn't sue for big settlements," Maggie would say after she had been married and divorced many times.

On December 7, 1941, two and a half weeks before *Hellzapoppin* opened at Manhattan's Rivoli Theater on Christmas Day, Japanese warplanes had attacked the U.S. Pacific fleet at Pearl Harbor in a sneak raid that enraged Americans. As the United States became totally involved in World War II, Maggie's life—like the lives of many other American citizens—was to change dramatically.

5

In Love and War

Wartime draftees and recruits soon jammed induction centers and military bases as American troops were shipped to Europe. When her estranged husband, Neal Lang, was commissioned an army captain, Maggie, in a burst of patriotism, volunteered to serve in the first overseas entertainment unit formed by the army. Her show business career hadn't mixed any better with the hotel man, Lang, than with Hollywood matrimonial partners, but she was sure she could do a good job of entertaining soldiers.

On the evening of October 31, 1942, Maggie, along with actresses Kay Francis and Carole Landis and dancer Mitzi Mayfair, boarded a clipper headed for Ireland and England. Abe Lastfogel, president of USO-Camp Shows, Inc., herded the four women aboard the plane. Never mind complaining about the fifty-five-pound limit on each person's luggage, he warned. One costume apiece—that was it, he insisted, except for Mitzi, who was permitted to take two costumes for her strenuous routines.

Maggie knew the dancer from their 1934-35 *Calling All Stars* stint, and both girls were slightly acquainted with Carole. Neither Maggie nor Mitzi had previously met Kay Francis, the movie star whose classic beauty and regal demeanor awed the other girls into a subdued politeness. But as soon as the younger girls discovered that Kay Francis did not have any stuffy ideas about protocol, the tension disappeared. They began bantering and joking as the plane hop-skipped its way through the darkness across the Atlantic, stopping at various military bases. At each base, the entertainers staged their show for the personnel, dates and locales blanketed in military secrecy. Eleven nights from the evening of their departure from the States, the women were flown into London and driven to the Savoy Hotel.

With its windows heavily draped to conceal the lights within, the Savoy was just another shadowy hulk among the shrouded buildings in the city of blackness that wartime London had become. Inside, plush furnishings glowed under the muted light of chandeliers. But during the day, when the heavy drapes were opened, the nearsighted Maggie, who wore glasses offstage, looked out the window. The wounded city lay exposed, piles of rubble marking the most recent sites where Nazi bombs had exploded.

After their nine-day series of performances at military bases before arriving in England, the four troupers were tired enough to sleep around the clock. But there were other essentials to take care of in the two days of rest they were allowed. Since maid service was at a premium while English women manned factories and buses, the four American women washed and set their own hair, washed lingerie and stockings and dried them in the bathroom and bedroom, and pressed their costumes.

On Friday night they gave their first show in England in a high school auditorium that was being used as a children's barracks and mess hall. More than one thousand American soldiers from a nearby encampment crowded into the auditorium, cheering and whistling as the entertainers went through their fast-paced one-hour show, accompanied by a pianist and a drummer provided by the English volunteers' organization, American Overseas Artists.

This was the first in a six-week series of shows, six days each week, during which the four entertainers adapted their acts to a variety of stages ranging from 12' x 24' platforms in tin-roofed Nissen huts to velvet-draped theaters.

Sunday was their only day to rest as they returned to their London hotel to prepare for another week of furious activity, two or three shows each day. And after each show they signed autographs for servicemen crowding around to talk to the celebrities from "back home." In the midst of the camp tours, Maggie scored a triumph on a London radio broadcast by singing "Der Fuehrer's Face" for the first time in England, complete with robust Bronx cheers. Each night the entertainers were slowly driven some fifty miles or more along darkened country roads by a U.S. Army Special Forces officer who maneuvered his vehicle, headlights hooded, through the blackness to the next military camp. The tour continued for many hundreds of miles through England, Scotland, and Northern Ireland. Maggie and Carole continued with the rigorous schedule even when both Kay and Mitzi were hospitalized. Kay had a bad cold, and Mitzi suffered from a severely strained back and shoulder after being tossed around onstage by a hefty sergeant who had volunteered from the audience to jitterbug with her.

They were soon back in the show. At that point, the pressure of sustaining the entire show was removed from Carole, whose routine included a semi-striptease to the beat of "The Strip Polka," and from Maggie, who had filled in with jokes, rubber-legged eccentric dancing, and songs that ran the gamut from soulful to sexy. As she did at the end of every show, Kay read a "letter" from the folks at home to the audience of servicemen, and the entertainers and audience joined in singing "America" and "God Save the King."

The actresses' performances in England were canceled only once. This occurred on a night when they arrived at a centrally located air base where half the squadron's bombers had been lost that day. In a somber mood, the surviving pilots and bombardiers and the American women ate their evening meal by candlelight in a tavern with a wood-beamed ceiling. The survivors offered toasts in memory of their friends, then took candles and burned into the ceiling the names of those who had not returned from the mission.

Just as memorable, but not at all somber, were the actresses' preparations for a command performance for Great Britain's royal family. Coached by a British lieutenant ("a very proper 'Leftenant,'" as Maggie would describe him) in matters of protocol, the women practiced their curtsies and submitted their material for a decision as to its suitability for the royal audience. Although the lieutenant removed "Strip Polka" from the program, the rest of the format had few changes. Then the cast went to the barracks of the Grenadier Guards at Windsor Castle to perform for the young princesses, Elizabeth and Margaret, their mother, and their grandmother, the dowager Queen Mary. King George was unable to attend. After watching Mitzi dance, Princess Margaret asked if she could teach her to jitterbug. Mitzi did so, and quick-witted Maggie captivated Margaret at dinner with her humorous chatter while the older, more reserved Elizabeth looked on tolerantly. The pleasant conversation with the younger princess would pay off royally when, some years later, Margaret agreed to appear on Maggie's television show.

Before she left London Maggie, wearing a Victorian collar, had her portrait painted by one of the royal family's artists. Then with Christmas and the New Year holidays behind them in England, the four entertainers boarded a B-17 headed for the Allied headquarters in North Africa. As the big plane moved above the Bay of Biscay to Gibraltar, two German planes flew toward it, guns blazing. Shaking with fear, Maggie curled up into a fetal knot until the gunfire stopped. As the plane continued on its way, the performers learned that the B-17's tail-gunner had been killed.

At Algerian headquarters, American troops eagerly awaited the show. When the women arrived, soldiers crowded around them, pleased to hear the sounds of female voices speaking English.

"I'd rather be here than any place in the world," Kay Francis cooed into the microphone set up on the flatbed of a huge wrecking truck as the entertainers made their appearance at a desert airdrome. "There's no place else we could be the only women among several thousand men," she added in response to the servicemen's good-natured jeers as they squatted down to watch the show under the glaring sun. The men sighed over the blonde charms of the curvaceous Landis as she half-spoke, half-crooned her tantalizing lyrics. They whistled and wolf-called at the high kicks and shimmies of the skimpily costumed Mayfair. And they laughed and applauded at the antics and lusty songs of the boisterous Raye.

Apparently oblivious to the heat, the men called for encores, reluctant to return to the bleakness and terrors of desert warfare.

But the women had a tight schedule to keep. They closed their program by forming their usual line to sing the American, British, and French national anthems.

The strenuous tour they had made through Great Britain proved to be only a shadow of the exhausting North African tour. In Algeria, they ate army stew and beans, washed their clothes in small tin basins, and retired to the sounds of enemy planes overhead and guns booming.

One night, when the sounds of exploding shells and antiaircraft guns were especially violent, Maggie ran from her hotel room into the street—so frightened, she would later claim, that she forgot to grab her helmet. She told of staring up at a flame-lit sky and hearing a sharp whistling sound just as a sudden weight slammed her to the pavement. At the base hospital, she said, her head was stitched just above the hairline where a piece of shrapnel had cut her skull to the bone. Her description of the injury must have been exaggerated, if not entirely fabricated, however, because no discernible scar remained on her head. She soon moved on with her three companions, by truck and jeep, from one Arab village to another, entertaining air and ground units stationed in the villages where unrelenting heat, sand, and grit frustrated the entertainers' efforts to be glamorous. Soon the struggle for glamour was abandoned as influenza hit each of the women in turn while the act was carried on by the others. Influenza was not the only complication, although for Carole Landis it was a serious one because she had only recently undergone an appendectomy in England. Kay Francis tore a ligament in her leg; Mitzi suffered from an ulcerated tooth. Maggie would later recall that the four entertainers frequently wore mudpacks, not as beauty treatments but as the result of jumping into muddy slit trenches to cower down as German planes zoomed overhead on bombing raids.

At the scheduled end of the tour, though, when three of the women boarded a Flying Fortress to start the return trip to the United States, Maggie stayed behind. She had decided to continue trying to bring smiles to the faces of these boys and men who dodged bullets and bombs by day and who slept, in the cold of desert nights, in beds of blankets and sand under canvas shelters set up under trucks and gun carriers.

Life in Africa for the daring and determined Maggie turned out to be scarcely less arduous than the lives of the troops. She found a corporal who could play a small, tinny piano, and then traveled by jeep to the front lines. There, she sometimes gave as many as four shows a day, each show running an hour and forty minutes. And, after bombing raids, she began helping to carry wounded service-men on litters to the hospital tent, observing medics as they worked and helping out whenever she could. She would have liked to be a nurse if she hadn't gone into the entertainment field, she said. And yes, she told people, she had worked at one time as a nurse's aide at Cedars of Lebanon Hospital.

An eight-day bout with yellow fever temporarily ended her nursing chores as she, too, was hospitalized. Then, twenty-two pounds lighter, she returned to work. For three days and nights she was trapped in a trench with two hundred soldiers while Nazi planes bombed relentlessly. After another air raid, she hurried back to the building where she had left her suitcase to find only a pile of rubble.

Dressed in a khaki shirt and pants loaned to her by a soldier, her face shiny with perspiration, Maggie continued to sing and clown her way into the affections of the men who clustered around her. They wanted to touch the hand of the warm-hearted woman who repre-sented their sweethearts or wives back home, the women whose let-ters were the lifeblood of their endurance. And then there were the fellows who received no letters. Maggie sang for them most of all.

A letter from her mother arrived, bringing bad news. Maggie's younger sister, Melodye, had died in a Chicago hospital. Died, at age twenty-one, of tuberculosis, Maggie would tell friends. To oth-ers, though, she would say that alcoholism had caused her sister's death. Alcoholism was the curse of the Reed family. Pete Reed, drunk as often as he was sober, had claimed to be the "forgotten man." But Melodye had been the forgotten child, the one never trained to be in vaudeville. She was always on the sidelines as her parents occupied themselves with the training and advancement of Margie and Buddy.

Now Buddy was drinking heavily, unmindful of the needs of his wife and children. And there was Peggy herself—too weak to break her dependency on alcohol and likely drinking even more in despondency over her separation from Pete Bouman and over her youngest child's death. Maggie had her own guilt to deal with: the guilt she sometimes felt when she compared her own success with the failures of her family. But she had clawed her way to the top. She took satisfaction in that thought. And she had not succumbed to her fondness for hard liquor, not when it would interfere with her work. Her career meant everything to Maggie. But for her sister, Melodye, there had been no such goal. Nor had there been much attention or affection.

Returning to New York in March 1943, Maggie proudly displayed her treasures to reporters. A fifteen-foot tanned python skin, given to her by a soldier. The steel helmet she had worn for protection. A dainty blue bag with delicate embroidery work done by a courageous RAF pilot. And the honorary captain's insignia, awarded for bravery, that Maggie was entitled to wear only in Africa. The insignia was her proudest possession, as she became the first woman ever designated an "honorary captain" by the U.S. army.

As soon as she arrived back in California, Maggie enlisted Peggy's help in opening her Beverly Hills home to anyone in uniform. News of the offer spread fast. It was not unusual for two or three soldiers to be sleeping in her extra bedroom while another military man occupied a living room sofa. Peggy provided the extra food, knowing her daughter's compulsion to keep the refrigerator well stocked in compensation for the lean and hungry days of her childhood.

For Maggie, work was always a panacea for worry and depression. Once again she headed east to perform onstage at the RKO Theater in Boston, then the Palace Theater in Albany, but looking forward, in her dedication to the military, to beginning a new overseas tour in the South Pacific area.

But the strain of the past six months, the physical drain of yellow fever, and the loss of weight had depleted her energy more than she was willing to concede. At Peggy's urging, she went to see her mother's doctor, who expressed his concerns about her lagging strength and sternly advised her that, for now, an overseas tour was out of the question. Maggie was disappointed; her devotion to the military approached, if not surpassed, the intensity of her dedication to her career. But instead of heading back overseas, she started out on what was supposed to have been a six-week tour of army bases in the United States beginning in the Southeast. On the second day of the tour, fatigue caught up with her. She collapsed in New Orleans, too ill to go onstage, and was taken to La Garde Army Hospital.

A series of tests were performed while she was hospitalized. Anemia, a physician reported back to a subdued Maggie. She grinned wanly at him when he warned her that she must rest and build up her strength for the next several weeks. Camp shows, he said, were absolutely forbidden until her blood count improved.

Maggie returned to California to recuperate. Her gloomy spirits lifted, though, when Twentieth Century Fox offered her featured roles in two films. She willed herself to get well quickly so she could accept the offer.

Four Jills in a Jeep turned out to be a "quicky" movie based on the recent USO camp tour of England and North Africa. Betty Grable and Alice Faye starred with Maggie and comedian Phil Silvers. Its producers predicted a "surefire success." But the *New York Times* review was not kind: the film was a "claptrap saga" and "a raw piece of capitalizing upon a widely publicized affair." The clever and often biting humor found in various degrees in most *Times* reviews was found in this one, too, as reviewer Bosley Crowther commented on Carole Landis and her singing rendition of "Crazy Me": "This latter bit is the only one which rings remotely true."

It is quite possible that both the producers' expectations and the reviewer's opinions were correct. Certainly the film made money. Patriotism was running high, and audiences seemed to like the motion picture. But money-making films and quality films apparently did not have much in common.

The second film, *Pin-Up Girl*, followed quickly. Betty Grable had a leading role in this picture, too. Bosley Crowther's review began with either a halfhearted apology or a terse prediction of worse things to come: "The miserable report this morning is that the new Technicolored film at the Roxy is a spiritless blob of a musical, and a desecration of a most inviting theme." He went on to criticize the "Fox boys" for grudgingly doling out the music and restricting the dancing to a minimum. He concluded that "the picture came to the most abrupt and pointless end you ever saw" after he pointed out that "Martha Raye and Joe E. Brown open their big mouths often, but nothing amusing comes out."

Since photos of Grable showing off her shapely legs were already the favorite "pinups" of American servicemen, this film, too, was expected to be a box-office success by its producers, regardless of what Crowther had written. Martha Raye and her exuberant singing and antics were favorites with audiences, too. With Charles Spivac and his orchestra providing the musical background, the Condos Brothers, veteran "hoofers," had been signed for the picture to bolster Grable's dance numbers.

The duo had first been hired as "hoofers on skates" in a Sonja Henie film, and had performed so well that Henie became jealous. At her insistence, all but one of the brothers' intricate skating numbers were left on the cutting-room floor. They were brought out to the West Coast from New York again in 1941 to partner Grable in the lavishly produced *Moon over Miami.* Their dancing to the music of "You Started Something" was spectacular enough to assure Nick and Steve Condos of a follow-up job when they were hired to help Grable dazzle movie audiences in *Pin-Up Girl.*

In the movie, Maggie was teamed with comic Joe E. Brown. But she was actually attracted to the lithe and virile Nick Condos, whose background in vaudeville was so much like her own. From the time the Condos boys had been youngsters in Philadelphia, they had restless, rhythmic feet that led them out to sidewalks in the neighborhood of their father's Greek restaurant where they danced on street corners for pennies.

After the oldest brother, Frank, got a start in vaudeville, he had teamed up with the middle brother, Nick. The team struggled for recognition until Frank broke his knee. After Frank's accident, the youngest brother, Steve, took his place and the dance team that started out as King and King was renamed the Condos Brothers. Steve practiced every day, while Nick (more of a natural) rarely rehearsed. Returned only recently from entertaining in war-devastated London, the brothers were moving back and forth now from Broadway shows to nightclubs to Hollywood.

Maggie had met Nick Condos before she went overseas. One night, as she sat in a Hollywood restaurant, a drunk persisted in annoying her. As he leaned over Maggie, flicking cigar ashes into her hair, Nick Condos got to his feet and came over to the table, warning the drunk to leave. When the man blustered defiance, the quick-tempered Nick let go with a hard, fast punch. The drunk sagged to the floor and had to be carried out of the restaurant.

"I figured, then, that Nick Condos was a good guy to have around," Maggie was quick to admit.

6

A Child and Charlie Chaplin

Maggie never would learn to hide her feelings. As she became closer to Nick Condos, she openly admitted to friends that she regretted her quick marriage-on-the-rebound to Neal Lang. Maggie and Nick were spending most of their after-work hours together by this time, and Maggie made no secret of the fact that she was in love with the good-looking Greek dancer who had the sculptured body of an athlete. His lust for life was reflected in his magnetic personality and in his sparkling, almost black eyes. Even when he was drunk, the man was likeable. The problem was that Maggie's marriage to Lang was not yet dissolved despite earlier reports that Lang was seeking a divorce.

Regardless of the original reviewer's caustic criticisms of *Pin-Up Girl*, it, too, was a moneymaker for Twentieth Century Fox. Movie fans lined up at box offices to see the film.

After *Pin-Up Girl* had been completed in June 1943, the Condos Brothers moved on to Cincinnati for another engagement. Lonesome for Nick, the impulsive Maggie decided to go to Ohio to see him. Cincinnati newspapers soon carried reports that Martha Raye would marry Condos as soon as she divorced her estranged husband, now U.S. Army Major Neal Lang.

In late October, she was waiting to receive legal waivers from Lang, who remained in service in England. As the Christmas holidays approached, Maggie became deeply depressed because she suspected she might be pregnant. She always was reluctant to go to the office of any physician or dentist. Because of her own lack of formal education, she was intimidated by highly educated professionals. Only when she had been ill with yellow fever or the resulting anemia, or when the studio had ordered her to see its doctor, had she submitted to physicians' examinations.

Other movie stars were having near-perfect teeth filed down to nubs and capped with dazzling white porcelain into unnatural evenness. But not Maggie. She would use toothache gum and gin to deaden pain rather than make a dental appointment.

Her worries about being pregnant, however, could not be deadened; they tormented her day and night. She knew that many people labeled her "man-crazy" because of her three quick marriages. But the marriages (and the rapid divorces that followed) fit the creed of morality that she always expressed. Whenever she desired to sleep with a man, she married him as soon as possible for the sake of what she considered "respectability." Now Lang stood in the way of respectability.

With a string of personal appearances scheduled to begin in January, Maggie no longer could avoid facing reality. Again, she made an appointment to see Dr. Lloyd Tainter, to whom Peggy went when in need of treatment for any of her alcoholism-related ailments. The doctor confirmed Maggie's suspicions. She could expect her baby in July.

As much as she looked forward to marrying Nick Condos, Maggie had not anticipated a pregnancy. A child simply did not fit into her plans and certainly would hinder her career. The only alternative was to have an abortion.

Nick raged when she talked of an abortion. But Maggie pointed out the miseries of her own childhood. It was unfair for show-business couples to bring children into the world.

No, he would not allow it, Nick yelled, shouting threats. He had been drinking when he made the threats, she realized later. But then, he drank most of the time. Still, fearful of losing Nick, she backed down on the abortion issue.

But when she thought of her brother, Buddy, a former guitarist for Jackie Cooper's band who was now ill with tuberculosis and burdened by a wife and two children, Maggie must have wondered if she had done the right thing by continuing with her pregnancy. She knew that her brother's struggles to get ahead in the tough world of show business while holding his family together had proved so difficult that he found relief only in the fuzzy world of alcoholism. There, even the cruelest of disappointments became blurred around the edges.

It was obvious to Maggie that alcoholism was an inherited trait in the Reed family. Her sister had died at age twenty-one. Peggy's drinking had worsened since her divorce from Pete Bouman and the fading of her control over her daughter as now Maggie turned to Nick Condos for guidance. Only Maggie's father seemed to have an iron constitution; his heavy drinking had not weakened him in the way that his two younger children had been affected.

Maggie, too, often indulged in too much gin. But her career was much too significant to allow excessive drinking to push success out of her reach. Too important, also, to be spoiled by an unwanted pregnancy. But there she was—pregnant. And unable, as yet, to marry Nick.

Maggie's unplanned pregnancy spurred her to make a trip to Juarez, Mexico, where she filed a suit for divorce from Lang on January 13, 1944. Then Nick Condos went along as a member of Maggie's troupe as she started off on her January tour of theaters, beginning at the Golden Gate in San Francisco.

In early February, she returned to El Paso, Texas, and crossed the Rio Grande into Mexico, where, with the help of a Juarez divorce attorney, she appeared before Judge Javier Rosas Cevallos to charge incompatability in her marriage to Lang. The Mexican divorce was granted with no protests from Lang, and Maggie and Nick returned to the East Coast. There, they told reporters that they had married several months earlier in California. Actually, they had just been married in Newark, New Jersey, as quickly as possible after the Mexican divorce.

The newlyweds returned to the West Coast after the personal appearance tour ended. USO entertainment and movie making were pushed aside now as Maggie's due date approached. A movie magazine reported that Raye's doctor had said that she might have twins.

But when Maggie entered Wilshire Hospital near the end of July 1944, she gave birth after twenty-seven hours of labor, and with the help of some Guinness Stout stashed under her bed, to only one child. A six-pound, six-ounce, dark-eyed daughter. She named the baby Melodye, for her sister.

Maggie boasted of nursing her daughter in the first weeks of her life. Then she hired a nanny, Jean Mendola, to take over the child's care. On October 22, Nick and Maggie took the baby to St. Sophia's Greek Orthodox Church in Los Angeles, where she was christened Melodye Athena Condos. Nick's friends, Mary and Nick Pilafas, were the godparents.

Melodye was six months old when Mendola agreed to go with her employers and their child to Chicago where Maggie was scheduled to sing at a nightclub. As they came into the Chicago railway station, they were quickly surrounded by several young men who deftly stripped Maggie of her mink coat, money, and jewelry. The thieves were gone within seconds and the family moved on to its reserved rooms at the Spencer Hotel. A few minutes later, Nick's friend, restaurant owner Herman Prujansky, called the hotel and Nick told him about the ripoff.

"If it was my gang that did it, I'll have the stuff back in half an hour," Prujansky, who was reputed to be associated with Chicago's Purple Gang, promised. "But if it was the South Side gang, it's out of my hands."

A short time later, there was a rap at the door of the hotel room. When Nick opened the door, the coat and the rest of the loot were tossed into the room.

After the lackluster reviews given to the last several movies in which Raye had appeared, there had been no more offers from studios. So Maggie felt she had no choice except to begin another cross-country tour. As she left the stage of the theater where she was performing on March 17, she was told there was a message for her to call her home. The message was a shocking one. Her twenty-six-year-old brother, Buddy, had been found lying in the street the previous night and had been taken to General Hospital, where he died. His death from tuberculosis did not surprise Maggie. She was very much aware that those childhood years of deprivation, when the Reed youngsters often had suffered from hunger, had taken their toll on their health. Alcoholism had been a contributing factor.

Neither Maggie nor Peggy attended the funeral. Peggy was not well enough to make the trip alone, and Maggie had her theater engagement to finish.

No one could have been happier than U.S. Army Honorary Captain Maggie Raye Condos, who was still touring the country, when World War II ended in August 1945 with the Japanese surrender. Americans celebrated with joyous abandon as did the other Allies. People jammed the streets of Hollywood while servicemen crowded into the Hollywood Canteen to mingle with movie stars.

Maggie's little girl was crawling, standing, and taking her first unsteady steps now, supervised by the nanny who kept close watch over her. And although Jean Mendola was reliable and an excellent caregiver, Nick Condos was concerned. Maggie kept two or three dogs in the house. One of them was a black standard poodle that apparently was jealous of the child and occasionally snapped at her as she crawled along the floor.

Although, as his wife's personal manager, Nick wanted to be with Maggie on her tours, he was too concerned about the baby to leave home. They could not ask Peggy to come to the house and help oversee things because of her periodical bouts of drinking. Nor was Maggie willing to get rid of her beloved dog. So her husband stayed at home when Maggie headed for a Detroit engagement at the Downtown Theater in September. Their friends thought it was a funny situation. Laughable, really. Nick Condos, genial man about town and widely known as "the Greek," at home, baby-sitting. Unbelievable.

In Detroit, Maggie shared the theater bill with Ada Leonard and her all-girl band between showings of *The Phantom*. Still singing "Mr. Paganini," the song which had brought her fame, she also blasted out the popular "Manana" and "The Achison, Topeka, and the Santa

Fe." Detroit critics rated her humor as loud and rough, but lauded her "timing and comic posturing."

She had been staying at the Book Cadillac Hotel in Detroit for only a week when she was served with a subpoena as a witness in a divorce case brought against Herman "Turk" Prujansky, now owner of Turk's Bar in the downtown area. Turk's wife charged that he had been "associating with a Hollywood movie star." Instead of appearing in court, Maggie fled to Philadelphia to fill an engagement there.

Get out of the way and leave it to Nick to take care of any complications such as the contempt-of-court citation for failure to appear, issued by a Detroit judge. That was Maggie's credo. It was typical of her to ignore what was unpleasant or inconvenient and let someone else pick up the pieces. No one was better than Nick at picking up the pieces.

Regardless of the snapping dog, Nick left Los Angeles to catch up with his wife in Philadelphia. He was very much aware of Maggie's susceptibility to flattery, particularly when socializing over drinks in bars. Worse yet, he knew of Maggie's history of "picking up" men and even marrying them on short acquaintance.

In Philadelphia the two launched into a fierce argument, one of many recently. Condos objected to Maggie's generosity, which he thought she carried to extremes. Like Jackie Gleason, she spent money excessively on friends, casual acquaintances, and even street people. Helping Buddy's fatherless children, for example, would have been understandable to Nick. Strangely, though, Maggie seemed to turn away from the needs of relatives, except for her mother. But it seemed that Maggie was still trying to buy love and admiration from acquaintances in the same way that had impelled her, as a child, to share her precious "red hots" with neighborhood children in the hope of making friends.

"Maybe if I'd gone to school like other children did, I'd have learned how to work out better relationships," Maggie was to excuse herself, years later.

As she signed up for another tour, she could not escape her worries that, in early 1946, her career might be on the downslide.

She knew that the motion picture business was a roller coaster. Yesterday's celebrity could be today's nonentity. But she found herself unable to be philosophical about the possibility that, at age twenty-nine, her film career might be nearing an end.

There was no sign of her inner turmoil when she appeared at a popular New York nightclub, the Carnival. However, there was plenty of turmoil when, according to Milton Berle's entertaining autobiography written with Haskel Frankel, Berle walked into the Carnival, where he was slated to appear at the end of Raye's booking, and found her doing his act—the one he had begun at the Royal Palm in Miami several years previously and which he had worked on and performed frequently at the Follies on Broadway. There were Maggie's guys in their uniforms, and there was Maggie bouncing around, front teeth blacked out (à la Berle), and getting laughs from the crowd. Sure, Berle was peeved. But he got over it and even laughed about it later.

Gag theft had been a major problem among entertainers since early vaudeville days. Well-established vaudevillians stole gags from lesser-known entertainers almost with impunity. Berle, of course, was a celebrity by this time who would soon begin his spectacular television career. Fellow performers joked about Berle being a gag-stealer, and he accepted their gibes in good humor, often cleverly turning their accusations into new and better gags.

After Maggie's gig ended at the Carnival, Nick arranged for her to return to the Detroit area to appear on stage at the Bowery, the very popular nightclub featuring big-name entertainers. The Bowery was, in fact, located in Hamtramck, a densely packed city of some 50,000 working-class people, mostly of Slavic ancestry and largely employed by Dodge Brothers' automobile factory. But since Hamtramck was totally encompassed by the thriving city of Detroit, the Bowery drew most of its nightlife patronage from the Motor City and its surrounding suburbs, all of which were benefiting from the postwar boom and the resurgence of Detroit's automobile factories.

During Maggie's appearance at the Bowery, a young local dance team also appeared onstage, doing a Hawaiian number. They were not accustomed to having a celebrity prance onstage and join in the dance. But that's exactly what Maggie did, totally impromptu, like Berle. She fancy-stepped around the two dancers and pretended to imitate them "so comically," Doris Granata, one of the dancers, would recall much later, "that she had us laughing until tears ran down our faces."

The unrehearsed antics were typical of Maggie. Her lack of pretense and her down-home friendliness appealed to fellow entertainers and to audiences.

Although World War II was supposed to have broken down racial barriers between servicemen, Doris Granata recalled performing at the Bowery when the Mills Brothers headlined. "They were such fine gentlemen," she would say. The close, polished harmonies of the immaculately dressed black singers drew wild applause, but between shows, the famed entertainers were not permitted to enter the nightclub area. They had to stay in their small, hot backstage dressing rooms.

Soon after Maggie headlined at the Bowery, Charlie Chaplin telephoned. Thinking it must be a practical joker, Maggie almost hung up. But the caller told Maggie that he had selected her for an important role in a motion picture that he had written and was preparing to produce. Finally convinced that the caller was, indeed, Chaplin, Maggie eagerly absorbed the information he offered about the picture, *Monsieur Verdoux.* The information was sparse at this point, however. The film would be a comedy based on the life of a notorious French wife-murderer. Maggie would play the part of the only wife to survive. But Chaplin was so intent on keeping secret the details of the movie that Maggie had to promise, before signing the contract that Nick approved, not to discuss the script with anyone.

Chaplin, of course, had no idea that Maggie would have great difficulty reading the script, and that until it was given to Nick to read, Chaplin had little to worry about from the actress. And the promise of secrecy was not difficult to keep as far as the script's ending was concerned because Chaplin concealed the ending even from the cast. It was rumored that Chaplin had written the final scene in code.

Again, Nick was pressed into his role as dialogue coach. Paragraph by paragraph, he read Maggie's part to her so that she could learn her lines. Never was her dependency on Nick so apparent as when memorizing a script was necessary. But her ability to quickly memorize the lines, when Nick read them to her, was surprisingly keen.

Playing the role of Annabella Bonheur, Maggie worked under Chaplin for six months in Hollywood. Impressed by the genius image of the famous comedian who had starred in silent films, she worked quietly—almost meekly—under his direction for a time, addressing him deferentially as "Mr. Chaplin." Charles Chaplin Jr.'s book, *My Father, Charlie Chaplin,* tells of the metamorphosis in Maggie's behavior on the day she jauntily replied to an order from Chaplin by unexpectedly saying, "Okay, Chuck." The famous comedian laughed, and the two became friends.

To anyone who asked how she reacted to the temperamental Chaplin, Maggie replied carefully and consistently. Chaplin was always "pleasant and kind" to her, she insisted. And now she was more optimistic about her future than she had been in the past three years. As the clever and dapper Chaplin played the lead role of the French Bluebeard, Maggie admired his deftness in carrying out the murder scenes. Still, many of the clever ironies that sparked Chaplin's dialogue regarding politics were not clear to Raye, who did not read newspapers and was unaware of most of what was happening on the political scene. True, she listened occasionally to Nick's complaints or comments on governmental practices or absurdities, but for the most part she remained uninterested and uninformed about such issues.

In rehearsing the movie script, of course, Maggie learned of Bluebeard's complete lack of guilt for the murders he committed and how this was explained by Chaplin's remark that "numbers sanctify," a phrase that would have only confused Maggie. His references to "murders carried out by governments" in wartime were clearer to the patriotic Maggie and might have been more bothersome to her had she not been in total awe of Chaplin and his great reputation. So she concentrated on portraying Annabella exactly the way Chaplin was trying to mold her—as a woman so full of vitality that she remained alive despite his repeated attempts to murder her.

He buoyed her spirits by telling her that he had created the role of Annabella specifically with her in mind. Complimented, she accepted this as gospel. After all, Hollywood had tried to kill her, she thought, by offering her roles in substandard movies; writers had created unfunny dialogue for her to try to breathe life into with her comical antics. But she had persevered and survived, nonetheless, to play an important role in the great art movie that Chaplin's inventive mind had shaped.

When the picture was completed, Maggie began working at Slapsie Maxie's club in Hollywood. Things would change, she was certain, when *Monsieur Verdoux* debuted and was acclaimed as a classic film and the work of art that Chaplin, using words like "clever" and "brilliant," had convinced her it was.

As soon as the film began to play in movie theaters, Maggie anticipated that movie producers surely would be begging her to sign for roles in major films. She and Nick would be able to live at home with their young daughter instead of touring the nightclub circuit.

Maggie bought a home near Toluca Lake at this time. Then, to help secure the good roles that she expected might become available to her after *Monsieur Verdoux* was released, she signed a contract with the William Morris Agency where Abe Lastfogel, president of USO-Camp Shows, Inc. when Maggie had gone overseas to entertain, was now working. Raye would remain with William Morris for many years.

7

Roller Coaster

Maggie was on tour again when United Artists released *Monsieur Verdoux*. It ran in New York for six weeks, with good box-office receipts, until picketers, carrying large signs, began showing up at theaters. "Ship Chaplin off to Russia," the signs proclaimed. Or "Kick the Communist out of the country." The horrors of World War II were fresh in the minds and hearts of the American public, and protests and pressures from veterans' groups quickly helped to diminish the crowds at New York movie theaters, as did the protests from religious groups because of the ironic sidelights on Christianity that Chaplin had provided in his film.

This was the first real taste of defeat and failure that Chaplin had suffered in regard to movie making. Vainly he protested that his attacks on war, and on capitalism as a source of war, were intended only to shock people to their senses. People definitely were shocked, though, particularly by some of the film's charges against the "heroes" of World War II. Bookings from theaters in other parts of the country were canceled. A paternity suit filed against Chaplin by Joan Barry was just one more bit of sensationalism to arouse public animosity, even though the case eventually was decided in his favor.

Nor did the reviews help to sell the picture, although there were plaudits for Raye. Raye had given a splendid performance, several reviewers had agreed. Archer Winsten of the *New York Post* observed, "Only raucous Martha Raye holds her own with the . . . comedian.

Her bull-in-a-china-shop personality is a perfect contrast for Chaplin's very precision."

Almost fifty years later (1996) Joyce Milton would publish *Tramp: The Life of Charlie Chaplin,* in which she would write that Martha Raye was "a fine casting choice" for the role of Annabella Bonheur. But there were few other compliments for the film in the year of its debut. *Times* reviewer Bosley Crowther wrote that he loved the film, but other reviewers panned it, going so far as to indicate that it was an insult to the intelligence of the American people. Still, *Monsieur Verdoux* was selected best picture in 1947 by the National Board of Review Awards. Chaplin also was nominated for writing the best original screenplay, but he did not win.

Later, after Chaplin sailed for Europe for the premiere of *Lime-light,* the State Department barred his reentry to this country, where he had contributed so much to the world supremacy of the American film.

Deeply disappointed in her hopes for *Monsieur Verdoux,* which had slipped rapidly into never-never land, Maggie, accompanied always by Nick, continued to move from one nightclub to another while their child was cared for by the nanny who had become her mother-figure. Nick was in Boston with Maggie when she was entertaining at the Latin Quarter in October 1947. Just before showtime, Maggie received a telephone call from California. Her mother, she was told, had collapsed and had been hospitalized in critical condition.

Nick phoned the airport, but was told there were no planes leaving for Los Angeles for the next few hours. Maggie went ahead with the first floor show, then called home. "The hospital just called," the maid said. "Your mother passed away about ten minutes ago."

Maggie had faced deaths in her family before—and recently. The death of her sister, Melodye, three years ago. The death of her brother, Buddy, two years ago. But even with her alcohol-related health problems, Peggy had been a constant presence in her life—her mother, her sister, her closest companion, all gathered into one—who had shared the early deprived years as well as the triumphs of her daughter's life. "My mom's death nearly killed me," she would say many times in later years.

Calling the airport again, Nick reaffirmed that there were no flights scheduled to Los Angeles as yet. He offered to take his wife back to their hotel where they could wait for the next available flight. But Maggie shook her head. Tears ran down her face. Peggy had been a trouper all her life, Maggie sobbed. Now there was a second show to do and she had made up her mind to do it.

"You won't be able to carry it through," Nick warned. "It's better not to try. You'll break up on stage."

But Maggie was determined to try. She went onstage. Clowning. Laughing. Singing. She focused so intensely on her stage presence that she had the ability to recess the worst of disappointments and even tragedies into whatever pocket of oblivion existed within her that could contain and anesthetize shock and distress as long as she was caught in the glare of footlights. Then she came offstage, stumbled into Nick's arms, and burst into tears.

To friends and reporters, Maggie would say that her mother had died of peritonitis resulting from a ruptured appendix. But she had witnessed Peggy's rapid decline and knew that alcoholism had killed her mother.

Underneath her brash exterior, there was a vulnerability that spurred Maggie to throw up a protective shield rather than to expose the alcoholic weaknesses of the dysfunctional Reed family. It was the same kind of subterfuge that she continued to use to explain her younger sister's death, which Maggie now claimed had resulted from a kidney disease, nephritis.

After Peggy's death, Nick tried to distract his wife from brooding. Something new, he must have figured; something different for her career might be the best medicine. In early 1948, he made arrangements for Maggie to perform at the London Palladium in March. Their three-year-old daughter was left at home in the care of the nanny.

When the boat docked at Southampton at night, Nick had a Rolls-Royce and a chauffeur waiting to drive him and his wife up to London. Maggie's spirits soared as they came into the brilliantly lighted city. Its wartime rubble had been removed and many of its damaged buildings repaired.

Possessed by nervous energy, she was not yet ready to go to their hotel. So Nick ordered the chauffeur to stop at the Stork, where he introduced his wife to the owner of the club. Then Nick went on to take their luggage to the hotel, promising to return for Maggie. By the time he returned, she was singing along with the band and already had made arrangements to hire the pianist, Frank Still, to be her accompanist at the Palladium. The two got along so well that Still would stay on as her pianist for the next six years.

Maggie and Nick remained in London for four weeks. Her performances at the Palladium broke all previous box-office records and enabled Nick to arrange for a half-hour spot on British television. The raves given her television debut pleased Nick. "'Marth,' I just know you're going to be terrific on television," he predicted. "I'll bet that little box will take you right to the top."

The two went on to Glasgow, where Maggie performed and where, at her departure, Glasgow's famous bagpipe band turned out, with what was estimated as "half the town," to give her a sendoff she would not forget. But first, Maggie, dressed in kilts and beret, led the band in a short parade before she boarded the plane, while the bagpipes still played, and then flew with Nick back to their Toluca Lake home to consider what direction their lives should take next.

With no new movie offers, Maggie's spirits slumped. Nick, who could see more clearly the realities of his wife's relationship with the studios, tried to explain to her that much of the difficulty lay in her many talents, which did not fit easily into one of the typical genres that Hollywood studio magnates used to categorize their stars. They had glamorized Raye very easily, but this was a glamour girl who also sang blues, jazz, and ballads with equal skill and who could dance up a storm. And then there were the comedic talents. Every time the singer opened her mouth, audiences waited for a raucous "holler" or something funny. Hollywood was not accustomed to this combination.

Most movies in those earlier days were contrived to present stars as certain character types—the clown, the ingenue, the temptress, the hero, the villain. And the studios went all out to preserve the image presented. Even the publicity photos were carefully posed to fit the image. No blemish or deviation was expected or desired. Raye did not fit easily into a slot.

Maggie was not impressed by Nick's explanations. She realized only that she had been rejected by Hollywood. The consideration of what to do next was not a lengthy matter of discussion. They both knew that Maggie always did well in nightclub performances, and Nick was ready to set up a listing of gigs, even though they realized that following the nightclub circuit with Maggie's pianist, Frank Still, would be a tiring and difficult life that would keep them away from home for weeks at a time.

It turned out that many of the gigs were in Miami Beach, which was quite satisfactory to both Maggie and Nick because they had pals down there, including a few who had been in, or on the fringes of, the Mob. Miami Beach would be their choice for a new home, they decided.

By moving away from the Southwest, the Condos family would be bucking a trend that had been bringing millions of people to California since 1941 when jobs in the defense and defense-related industries begged for workers. After the war, the continuing availability of jobs lured millions more—all searching for the American Dream in the Golden State with the attractive sun-and-surf image. At the same time, the California governor was claiming that his state would have to build more homes, schools, and highways to avoid being overrun by the burgeoning population.

When Maggie and Nick listed their Toluca Lake home for sale, Doris Day bought it for $42,000. Shortly before the Condos family left for Florida in 1949, Maggie's ailing father, Pete Reed, came back into her life, and this time she responded to his needs. She moved him to Miami, too, and settled him into a nursing home. The move from California seemed to upset no one but Maggie and Nick's young daughter. She could not be consoled at being separated from the nanny who had mothered her for four years.

Maggie had little or no understanding of her child's trauma at the separation from her nanny. In the mother's view, Melodye led a protected and advantaged life in a pleasant home where her every want or need was met. The girl's life, Maggie thought, was near perfection compared with her own childhood—one of hunger, constant moving about, continuing exposure to seedy environments, stress, and frequent physical punishments when she or her brother had failed to meet their frustrated parents' expectations quickly enough.

Her young daughter was pretty, with Nick's very dark eyes and hair and Maggie's attractive features. It was time the child began to learn she would have to adapt to the life of a career-oriented mother, Maggie determined, because the entertainer had no intention of being diverted from the demands of the show-business career that made possible all their comforts and conveniences. Her career meant more to her than anything, or any person, in the world.

Shortly after the Condos family arrived in Miami Beach, Nick learned that back in Toluca Lake, Doris Day was converting his prized crystal bar into a milk and soda bar. He and Maggie were indignant; they decided to regard the renovation as a personal insult to their tastes and way of life.

Melodye Condos was enrolled in kindergarten classes in Miami Beach as soon as the family settled into the Ocean Creek Apartments on Indian Creek Drive. The apartment occupants were friendly and close-knit neighbors who frequently partied together. Two brothers, both of whom were doctors and personal friends of Maggie and Nick, also lived in the area.

On that first Christmas morning at the Miami Beach apartment, Maggie and Nick slept late. Only the maid was there to see Melodye creep into the living room. The maid knew it was likely that her employers would sleep for hours yet, and sympathizing with the little girl's excitement, she allowed her to rip apart the neatly wrapped packages marked for her under the tree. Discovering that many of the gifts were board games, Melodye looked at the pictures on the covers and at the directions that she could not read.

"Who am I supposed to play my games with?" she complained to the maid, who was busy picking up dirty glasses and filled ashtrays. "The dog?"

The question was solved the next day when she found that all the games had been removed by her mother, who had stored them (or given them away). One possibility was that Maggie may have been annoyed by the clutter. Or perhaps Nick had been drinking and gone Christmas shopping (without much discretion in his choices) for his daughter (a more likely possibility). A doll was the only gift remaining near the tree now.

Maggie frequently performed at one of the local nightclubs where she drew admiring audiences. But Miami Beach, too, soon became only a home base from which she departed for gigs in other cities, finding herself moving back onto the roller coaster that she had tried to avoid. When her daughter was almost ready for first grade, one of their doctor friends came to the Condos apartment to have a serious talk with Maggie and Nick. He pointed out to them that the partying, drinking, and even drug use that was going on around them created a poor environment for their young daughter.

Because both Nick and Maggie respected their friend's opinions, they decided to find a more protected shelter for their child. They finally enrolled her in a convent school, Academy of the Assumption in Coral Gables.

The young girl was apprehensive about the whole thing, but was quickly learning to do as she was told and not to moan about it. At the time of her September entry into the academy, Nick was busy making arrangements for Maggie to play the lead role in a television production of Cole Porter's *Anything Goes.* Maggie was thrilled to begin rehearsals for the show in New York that autumn of 1950.

In her early teens, Maggie had imitated her idol, Ethel Merman, for whom Irving Berlin had written the music in the original Broadway version of *Anything Goes* in 1934. Now, in the same starring role of a nightclub singer, Maggie became a bouncing bundle of energy at rehearsals, tearing into the lyrics of Cole Porter's "Blow, Gabriel, Blow" and exerting every effort to match Merman's stage success with the musical.

Unfortunately, just two weeks before the television performance, Maggie got into one of the scrapes that brought her the kind of notoriety she didn't need. While driving her Cadillac convertible in Boston, with Nick and her boxer dog beside her, she lost control and drove the car up onto a sidewalk. She was arrested and charged with drunken driving. Nick was charged with drunkenness, too, but was released first by police. Maggie, held for several hours in the Woman's House of Detention, raised more of a ruckus about her dog being taken away to Animal Rescue League headquarters than about her own jailing. She was finally allowed to leave after she sobered up and her husband provided $225 in bail money.

Forfeiting bond, Maggie did not appear in court on the date scheduled for a hearing. But she was in New York to make her debut on *Musical Comedy Time* with *Anything Goes* as its first offering in early October. And while a warrant was issued for her arrest in Boston, newspapers ran glowing reviews of the televised musical, especially of Maggie's inspired performance.

"Her singing, dancing and clowning topped anything she's done in the movies," one reviewer wrote. "She stole the show," another reported. None of them refuted Nick's claim that his wife "worked harder than a dozen Jackie Gleasons."

In an attempt to stabilize their lives, the Condoses decided to buy the Five-O'Clock Club, where Maggie appeared so frequently. This would make it possible for her to perform there regularly. She would leave Miami only when there was an opportunity to do shows in such top-flight spots as Las Vegas and New York's Latin Quarter, the couple decided. And, of course, she would travel for any television rehearsals and performances that might be offered to her.

Nick hired a manager named Casey for the Five-O'Clock Club and arranged for a variety of acts to complement his wife's routine and to lure customers. Dancer Roseanne for glamour. A snappy musical trio, the Nov-Elites. And Buddy Lester to back up Maggie in comedy takeoffs on Vaughn Monroe, the Lone Ranger, and Margaret Truman. When Maggie would get into her "blue" materials, one of the musicians would hit her on the back and her false boobs would pop out.

Maggie and Nick were well settled into the routine of running their own club when their daughter was sent home from the academy for summer vacation. As a part of that routine, every customer still hanging out in the club at five o'clock in the morning would get a free drink, in accordance with the name of the nightspot. At 5:30 A.M. the club closed, and it was not unusual for Nick and Maggie to awaken Melodye and to take her deep-sea fishing, accompanied by their dog, club manager Casey, and sometimes a couple of hookers—all the adults fairly tipsy.

After chartering the *Flying Cloud*, they would be three miles off the coast of Florida by 6:30 or so. But on one of these early-morning excursions, the boat began taking on water while they were far from shore. Although the captain, too, had been drinking, he had enough sense to use the radio for a Mayday call.

Everyone except Nick and the captain was soon thrashing about in the water, holding onto the partly submerged boat. Nearly seven years of age, Melodye already was a good swimmer and had the additional advantage of holding onto the dog while the captain yanked off his white shirt and frantically waved it in the air. Nick, the only nonswimmer in the group, held onto the mast and, with the blustering confidence of the thoroughly intoxicated, bellowed out the words of his favorite song, "It's Magic." Over and over. "It's Maaagic."

Before they had a lot of time to worry about barracudas, they were picked up by a small craft and transported to shore. While the captain arranged for the disabled boat to be towed in to a dock, Nick and Maggie asked about chartering another boat. A short time later, they were off on another fishing expedition.

When Maggie was asked to fill a summer theater engagement in Los Angeles, she was undecided at first, knowing that such a move might be a step back on the crazy and unpredictable entertainment circuit. She and Nick finally decided to go to Los Angeles, after returning their daughter to the academy and renting the Hollywood home of singer Mel Torme for themselves. After Maggie completed the summer theater gig, but before they moved out of the Torme residence, a fire started in the house when a smoldering couch burst into flame. The fire department responded to their call and firemen hauled the burning couch outside and extinguished the flames. Soon afterwards, the Condos pair returned to Miami and Torme returned to his home. Torme then sued for $3,906 in damages, claiming that the Condoses had gouged floors and battered furnishings in his house. Most of all, he said, he was peeved because they had tromped on his geraniums.

But by the time Nick and Maggie returned from Los Angeles, their fights had become more frequent and violent. Maggie also had financial problems. Floridian attorney Shirley Woolf had begun to advise Maggie and Nick and to prepare their tax returns, although she was not specifically a tax attorney. Earlier in the year, the Internal Revenue Service had filed a $30,922 lien on Condos properties to cover unpaid 1948-49 income taxes. It was not a good time to be in trouble with the IRS, Nick told Maggie. In Washington, Senator Kem of Missouri was demanding that the Justice Department should actively prosecute the many tax-evasion cases in its files.

There was better news for Maggie, though, when Milton Berle phoned and offered her a guest spot on his popular television comedy hour sponsored by Texaco. Berle was well known by this time as "Mr. Television" and "Uncle Miltie" because his comedy show, originating in 1948, before TV sets were fixtures in most average American homes, brought pioneer television onto the American scene. (Within a couple of years, hundreds of thousands, then millions of television screens would be bringing Berle's madcap antics into private homes.)

When Maggie made her first live televised appearance with Berle on *Texaco Star Theater*, bloopers and blunders were broadcast, as they occurred, to a fascinated, largely uncritical audience who also caught glimpses of stagehands at work and of microphones bobbing over performers' heads.

The television stage of the late 1940s and early 1950s was a natural setting for Maggie who, like Berle, could react to unexpected gliches with comical unrehearsed capers whenever necessary. Berle admired this ability and invited her back on frequent occasions.

In his captivating autobiography, Berle tells of the comedy episode on his show in which the very circumspect Basil Rathbone, performing his well-known role as the inscrutable Sherlock Holmes, was shocked when, after a blunder occurred, the result was near-mayhem. Raye and Berle raced around the stage, making up dialogue and chasing and shoving each other.

The two were accustomed to reacting to each other in this kind of frenzied way. And for Maggie, the guest spots on Berle's television show became almost a replay of her breakthrough experience at the Trocadero in the late 1930s. Soon after she had done a number of guest shots, and with Berle's generous recommendation, she appeared on *All Star Revue* in October 1951, with operatic bass Ezio Pinza. Then she was signed to make monthly appearances on the *All Star Revue* at eight P.M. on Saturdays, beginning in December 1951. Nick, still her personal manager, read each script to her so that she could memorize it more quickly.

"I'll never forget that Milton Berle gave me my break in television," Maggie often would say in later years. There was no hype in this statement. She had every reason to be grateful to Berle.

Maggie was a hit on *All Star Revue,* too. It seemed certain that 1952 would be a spectacular year for her as she clowned her way through a January show, supported by Robert Cummings. In a Cinderella segment, Cummings played the handsome Prince Charming. Maggie's Cinderella was a mixture of wistfulness and clowning that earned praise from reviewers. Her buffoonery was acclaimed as equal to that of Jerry Lewis or "Uncle Miltie" himself.

At this same time, however, Jackie Gleason was starring in his own television show on CBS, opposite the *All Star Revue* on NBC. For the first time, the *All Star Revue* faced competition that threatened to force it out of the top twenty most popular programs. Raye felt pressured to work even harder, if that was possible, as did Gleason. Soon Raye and the *All Star Revue* switched time periods to get away from Gleason. At once, the show's ratings rebounded.

Maggie's Miami-to-New York schedule was becoming increasingly rugged. After closing up their Five-O'Clock Club in the early morning hours, she and Nick would board a plane to New York. Maggie never had liked flying, and she would drink enough to lull her fears, then try to catch some sleep during the four-hour trip. Next would come rehearsals at the New York studio. The telecast. And then another flight south to headline shows at their Miami nightclub. This tough schedule must have taken its toll, but it didn't seem to affect Maggie's energetic performance at the nightclub or in her telecasts.

One of the more risqué numbers in Maggie's nightclub act was the skit she had adapted (borrowed? filched?) from Berle and in which she appeared with several uniformed men carrying swords. It remained a favorite at the Five-O'Clock Club and in other nightclubs where she agreed to appear. Now she added another off-color skit to her act, mocking the much-heralded Kinsey Report.

Her longtime friend and associate, Steve Allen, would recall that Martha "was notorious for frequent lapses of taste." But "in no way," he would insist, did these lapses "detract from the lavishness of her comic gift."

When her "blue" materials roused heckling from customers, Maggie grimly tried to hang on to her smile and to remind herself that all nightclub performers had to put up with that type of annoyance. But when the heckling became abusive, Maggie found it difficult to control her temper. Her control failed when a salesman at the Five-O'Clock Club called Maggie an insulting name as she circulated among the tables. Impulsively, Maggie raised her hand and slapped the man's face. The customer's reaction was just as swift. He punched her in the mouth only seconds before Nick and his friends pounced. Although Maggie realized that publicity of this kind was not good business policy, she was angry enough to go to the police station and sign an assault and battery charge.

The pressures of their lives continued to take their toll on Maggie and Nick. Their bickering became even more frequent and heated. Still, they shared happy excitement when, in 1952, Maggie was nominated for best comedienne in television. The other nominees were Lucille Ball, Joan Davis, Eve Arden, and Imogene Coca—an intimidating array of big names. Although Lucille Ball walked away with the Emmy, it was an honor to be nominated, Nick kept reminding his wife.

She got away from day-to-day problems that summer by having her daughter appear with her in the Miami summer theater production of *Annie Get Your Gun*. By her own admission, she learned at that time that her eight-year-old daughter had a mind of her own. While Melodye was supposed to be listening intently as Maggie read her a story, in reality, Maggie insisted, the child was "mugging at the audience." Laughing as she continued to talk to reporters, Maggie joked, "Can you imagine? Stealing the scene from her own mother?" It was typical Maggie hype, of course, and yet a decade later there would be a kind of prophetic significance found in those words.

The *Annie Get Your Gun* performances were only brief breaks for the child. Apart from an occasional deep-sea fishing trip, she could not spend much time with her mother. Nick was also frequently away from home, accompanying his wife and acting as her spokesman. Maggie felt much more comfortable when he was with her, regardless of their personal problems.

Maggie left again, during that summer of 1952, to travel to South Korea to cheer the American troops who had been helping defend the South against invasion from the North since June 30, 1950. Because Maggie was intensely patriotic, she felt that her celebrity status could and should be used in an unselfish way by bringing whatever entertainment and laughter she could provide into the lives of young men enduring the hardships of war in the bleakness and cold of Korea. She had felt guilty for neglecting the American servicemen in Korea because entertaining in her own Miami nightclub and performing in New York on the *All Star Revue* had kept her so busy. There was little fanfare for this overseas visit in 1952, because the tour did not last long. Maggie became ill and had to return home after only a few weeks.

Her visit was remembered, though, by the troops and by an army nurse who, years later, wrote to President George Bush to tell him of the nurturing that Maggie gave to a trainload of wounded marines during a three-hour trip from the Demilitarized Zone to Inchon where the marines were to be transferred to a navy hospital ship. Frances M. Liberty, an army nurse who attained the rank of lieutenant colonel before her retirement, told of how Maggie "went from bunk to bunk and spoke to each of the wounded, soothing their fears and distracting them from their pain." She described how overpowering was the stench in the train, but of how determined Maggie was to stay with the men throughout their ordeal. "There were a couple of young marines so severely wounded," her letter explained, "that I never expected them to last the trip, but they survived the train ride, I'm convinced, because of the tender care given them by Maggie."

By the time Maggie was ready to begin her weekly television show again in the fall, the Saturday night series was renamed *The Martha Raye Show*. When the season premiere was telecast on September 27, Maggie had actor Cesar Romero and opera star Risë Stevens as guest performers. She also invited her close friend, Rocky Graziano, to appear on the show. After having lost his title as the world's middle-weight champion to Chuck Davey, Graziano had been depressed, and he was thrilled to have a chance to move back into the spotlight. He had appeared on television, but only in regard to his boxing career and perhaps to say a few words about his next opponent.

When they put "this big script" in his hand, Rocky felt a few moments of terror, but he read a line that was pointed out to him. "Well, Marta," he began, "I tink I'm gonna go home."

"That's greaaat!" the director said. Rocky looked up in surprise. Hey, he had been talking that way all his life. Maybe this would be easier than he had thought.

Rocky became a regular guest on the show, and his loyalty to the star, whom he called "my gal, Marta," knew no bounds. In an early skit, Romero tried to get a date with Raye by intimidating her "boyfriend." But when he discovered that the boyfriend was Graziano, Romero took a sudden dive to hide behind a couch.

Graziano found that he could memorize his lines in acceptable fashion, but he also found that "Marta" frequently said and did crazy things (ad libs) that at first disconcerted him. Once she suddenly addressed him as "Goombah." Rocky did a double-take, then realized that he was the Goombah to whom she was referring. From that time, Rocky became known as Goombah on the *Martha Raye Show*.

In another popular skit, Maggie and Rocky portrayed a gauche couple visiting Risë Stevens's home for a sophisticated social event. Later in the program, Maggie and Romero did a burlesque of the antics of two chimpanzees who also appeared on the show.

"She was always bouncin' around, kiddin' everybody," Rocky

would recall to a *TV Guide* reporter, "burnin' up more energy than a guy in a 15-round fight." Most of all, though, he admired her for her generosity to people who were "down on their luck," and the way she would talk with writers, producers, or directors to try to get an out-of-work performer a spot on a TV show.

Good reviews pushed *The Martha Raye Show* off to a glittering start. Later in October, Maggie decided that she needed a brief vacation. With an acquaintance, Mimi Marlow, Maggie was off again—aboard a plane headed for Jamaica. But she was jolted out of her sleep in her hotel room the next morning by a flame of pain searing her internally. Marlow immediately called for a doctor, who supplied pain killers. Then Maggie was carried on a stretcher to a plane headed for Miami, where Nick and a physician awaited her arrival.

At St. Francis Hospital, doctors treated the entertainer for an intestinal infection. When transfusions of rare O-RH negative blood were needed to save her life, many of the loyal employees from her nightclub offered to donate blood. An entire marine battalion stationed near Miami also volunteered to give blood.

Transfusions were nothing new to Maggie. She had been receiving them, she said, since "I went to North Africa during the war and fell so deeply in love with a million or so GIs that I wore myself out trying to entertain them, with the result that a yellow fever bug so poisoned my blood that I'll be borrowing corpuscles from cops, actors, and U.S. Marines as long as I live."

As the intestinal infection subsided, Maggie was grateful for the skill of the doctors and the attentiveness of the nuns who cared for her. She fingered the scapular she wore around her neck for luck and made up her mind to get back in front of television cameras as soon as possible.

8

Shangri-la

As soon as Maggie was discharged from St. Francis Hospital, she moved back to the grueling Miami-to-New York round-trip. At the same time, Nick promoted a series of plays he planned to stage in Miami. Despite heavy promotion, ticket sales lagged and the actors performed in a nearly empty theater.

Under these pressures, Maggie and Nick quarreled even more fiercely. Still, both were pleased when Maggie was nominated for an Emmy again in 1953. The other nominees for outstanding television personality were men—Bishop Sheen, Arthur Godfrey, Jack Webb, and the winner, Edward R. Murrow of the popular show *Person to Person*. It was an honor simply to be nominated, Nick kept reminding his wife. But defeat of any kind always was difficult for Maggie to accept because of her low self-esteem and her insatiable need for admiration. Maggie filed suit for divorce that year after a violent argument with Nick while he was drunk. She also asked the court for a restraining order and custody of their daughter.

Actually, Maggie was afraid to break off her business partnership with Condos. Although Nick had only a sixth-grade education, Maggie knew that he was as quick with his mind as with his rhythmic feet. And his fists. Without him, all of Maggie's self-doubts about her own abilities rose to the surface. As far as Nick's failure in his recent efforts to promote legitimate plays was concerned, Maggie figured that everyone was entitled to one flop. For the rest, she could dump all her mail, her contracts, her scripts, and her problems into

Nick's lap and he would straighten everything out. She was convinced that he deserved the generous 25 percent of her income that he collected from her.

Moreover, she panicked at the thought of trying to get along without him. It was Nick who had bolstered her confidence and helped her to develop a whole line of strategies to disguise her reading deficiencies, a shield that she feared might crumble without Nick's constant sheltering presence. For example, she often placed an open newspaper next to her chair, as if she had been reading it, or left a word game, cover removed, on a nearby table.

Nonetheless, she continued to have her lawyer pursue the divorce proceedings, even though Nick did not want a divorce. He could scarcely believe that Maggie would persist with the separation process. The thought of going back to dancing for a living did not appeal to him. He had never done as much practicing as his brothers, and now he faced the unpleasant fact that he was out of shape; he was not at all sure that he could meet the rigorous demands of "hoofing" after nine years of marriage and easy living. Had the 25 percent he had been collecting from Maggie made him soft? Dependent? For "the Greek," who despised weakness in a man, these had to be stinging questions to ask himself.

Nick had often spoken of what he called the "deal history" that he claimed he had pioneered in the 1940s as Maggie's business manager. According to a contract he had arranged first at the Paramount Theater and thereafter at many other theaters, Maggie would receive a percentage of the box-office returns because Nick strongly believed in his wife's popular appeal. The agreement invariably worked out better for Maggie than the usual prearranged salary, he pointed out. And it worked out better for Nick as well.

Now, although there had been job offers from other talent agencies and he could have gone to work for one of them, he felt that employment with another agency was beneath him. Or he could have begged Maggie to forgive him and made wild promises to control his drinking and to stay away from hookers, but that was not the Greek's style. With Maggie asking for custody of their daughter, the divorce and its consequences were troublesome to contemplate.

Still, as he admitted to friends, his kid was actually in the custody of the nuns at the academy.

By the time the divorce decree was granted, Maggie and Nick had come to terms with their inability to get along harmoniously in their marriage. Nick asked for no alimony or property, and agreed to continue as Maggie's personal manager. And he and Maggie amicably decided not to change their life insurance policies.

When Maggie returned to her new season's television scheduling, she spent most of her time in New York at a leased apartment. Her daughter already had returned to the Academy of the Assumption in Florida and, Maggie told friends, she did not want to disrupt Melodye's life by switching schools in the middle of the academic year. Since Nick was still in Miami, Maggie confided to reporters that she was not worried about their daughter because the girl's relationship with her father was a close one.

There was no doubt that Melodye Condos loved her father very much. Still, she often felt deserted by both parents. When other students went home for special occasions, Maggie's daughter would ask one of the nuns to find out if her mother would allow her to come home, too. The nun would call, and Maggie would explain to the nun why her daughter must stay at school. Invariably, these explanations entailed citing the various cities in which Raye had commitments to entertain. And the nun would agree that the care of a child and the demands of a successful entertainment career posed many difficulties.

When Melodye stayed at school through one or the other of these holidays, she usually was the only student there with just the nuns and the novices moving about ever so quietly, the occasional clicking of rosary beads or their muted ripples of laughter echoing in the silent corridors. It seemed very clear that Maggie had no intention of relaxing the rule she had set that her daughter could come home for either Christmas or Easter break, but not for both.

For the most part, it was a quietly scheduled kind of life for a child at the academy except for certain festive occasions. One of the nuns must have felt sympathy for Maggie's daughter when, shortly before the girl was to take part in a ballet recital, she sprained her ankle. Knowing that the girl had visions of becoming a dancer, the nun took matters into her own hands and broke at least one of the strict rules that governed the convent school. Calming the girl with talk of her mother and father and the "show must go on" kind of thing, the nun escorted her into the infirmary and asked for a pain shot. The shot worked very well, making it possible for Melodye to perform.

Although Maggie and Nick had chosen to have their daughter baptized in the Greek Orthodox religion of her father's family, Maggie told the nuns that she wanted the girl to be confirmed as a Roman Catholic when she was nine years old. For Melodye, it was a comfortable arrangement; being confirmed would help her to fit right in with the other girls at school. The nuns happily fussed over her and made her feel special for a while as she was prepared for confirmation. So the entire process seemed kind of charming to the girl, although Maggie was not present to witness the actual religious ceremony.

Like the other homes in which Maggie had lived, her New York apartment was not a lonely place. Because she made a habit of collecting people who were temporarily down on their luck, it was not an unusual thing for her to do when she offered the use of her apartment to Pat Ward after Maggie met the young woman in a New York nightclub and learned she needed a place to stay. Ward's stay ended abruptly, however, when she tried to commit suicide in the apartment and had to be taken to the hospital.

Soon afterwards, Pat Ward was called to testify in a highly publicized court suit charging Minot "Mickey" Jelke with procuring. Heir to millions made in oleomargarine, Jelke was convicted on the testimony of several call girls. Pat Ward testified that Mickey had collected the money she had made as a prostitute.

The publicity surrounding the trial could taint the career of any performer who was even remotely connected with the participants, and Maggie was mentioned by newspaper columnists who looked for even the most fragile connections.

Nick reminded Maggie to be more cautious because of the "morals" clause in her television contract. But the warning didn't seem to penetrate; Maggie simply fluffed it off. She had signed the contract without worrying about its contents. Nick had advised her to sign, and that was enough reason for her to do so. She had divorced her husband, but she retained absolute faith in him and in his ability to straighten out any scrapes in which she might get involved.

The hourlong *Martha Raye Show* debuted on December 26, 1953, under Nat Hiken's direction with Norman Lear as writer. Herb Ross choreographed for Martha as well as for the Martha Raye Dancers. Rocky Graziano returned as a regular. Actress Irene Dunne appeared on the show, as did singer Perry Como, comedic duo Sid Caesar and Imogene Coca, and Maggie's old friend from vaudeville days, Donald O'Connor. The guest list was studded with names that attracted viewers who were amused by Maggie's rollicking humor and boisterous energy.

With her gorgeous legs and thighs molded in the fishnet stockings that had become a kind of trademark for her, Maggie pranced tirelessly around the set. Torch songs, rhythm numbers, blues—Maggie did them all with equal skill. "That Old Black Magic" and "Blues in the Night" were favorites of her fans. She continued to close each show with a fervent thank-you to the nuns who staffed St. Francis Hospital at the time of her recent collapse. "Good night, Sisters."

Never had Nick been more accurate than when he had predicted, five years previously, that television would be the medium in which Maggie was destined for success. She was now earning $150,000 for the season, which was apparently a good financial arrangement at the time, although television stars' salaries would soon spiral to unanticipated heights.

Although Maggie and Nick had fought violently for nine years, Maggie confided to acquaintances that since their divorce they got along beautifully. What she did not confide was that if Nick displayed any affection for their daughter, complimented her appearance, or praised her for her grades, Maggie flew into a rage. Nick invariably retreated in the face of what seemed to him to be such unjustified anger. He did not grasp the reason for this jealousy. But it was clear that his praise for the excellence of his daughter's school-work touched a nerve because Maggie had never attended school. She had felt inferior to her mother, because of Peggy's superior knowledge, and now could not bear that her only child—as much as she loved the girl—would also grow up to be superior to her. "There's only one star in this family, and that's me," she frequently would declare to her daughter, and even to Nick, who knew her so well, as a scarcely veiled reminder that his support was entirely dependent upon her talent.

In 1954, Maggie suddenly decided to change her image and lifestyle completely by buying a house in a picturesque town in Connecticut and making a home there. A real home, "for myself and Melodye," she told an interviewer.

Now that Raye was known as television's number one female clown, leading magazines sent reporters to interview her. *Look* was one of the first to run a major piece on her after she had settled into a colonial-type home near Westport, Connecticut. The article described Maggie as a woman who finally was "living like people," doing her own marketing and cooking, driving a station wagon, and looking forward to taking her daughter with her to the Catholic church in Westport on Sundays after Melodye came home from Florida. In reality, Maggie had never visited Connecticut before deciding to move there. But she had heard that a number of motion picture producers and stars had moved to the Westport area to enjoy country life in the small town where artists and writers lived alongside "regular people."

Only recently, the magazine *Photoplay* had reported that Joan Crawford had publicly scolded Marilyn Monroe for "not behaving like a lady." It was quite possible that Crawford's criticism of Monroe, plus Maggie's own desire to legitimize her lifestyle in view of the "morals" clause in her contract, had motivated her move to Westport. It may also have motivated her newly adopted "living like people" way of life with a priority of "getting acquainted with her young daughter."

Later, when Melodye did live with her mother in Westport, the two were rarely, if ever, seen in church on Sundays. Maybe once a year, on Christmas.

Still, seized with an airy sense of euphoria stemming from the success of her television show and the sudden fawning attention of magazine interviewers, Maggie's self-esteem began to inflate; her self-doubts gave way to a wonderful sense of indestructibility. For the first time, she told the truth about her lack of education. "I never went to school in my life," she admitted, throwing caution to the proverbial winds and adding that the most important accomplishment in her life had been "having and nursing" her own baby girl.

Asked about her child and the move to Westport, Maggie told one magazine reporter that her daughter would have "all the love that one small girl can use" when she came to her new home. But when another reporter asked if she wanted more children, she replied emphatically, "No. One 'Mel' is enough."

Nick Condos was living in a Fifty-eighth Street apartment close to the West Forty-sixth Street Ziegfeld Theater where Raye spent countless hours rehearsing in a large, drab room containing a piano and a few essential props with steam pipes looming overhead. The room looked no more like a television set than Maggie, in jeans and moccasins, looked like a glamorous star. But for eight hours at a time, Maggie clowned, mugged, and, with Nick always close at hand, went through a rigorous routine of acrobatics and dance steps. Even when she was not a participant in the scene that was being rehearsed, she did not relax. Instead, she paced on the sidelines, impatiently awaiting her cue.

At the close of rehearsal, it was time to head for Grand Central Station. Still tossing wisecracks like confetti, sometimes in her lisping "Baby Snooks" kind of voice, Maggie headed for the bar car on the commuter train and tried to unwind with cigarettes and drinks during the trip back to Westport. Evenings at home were busy, too, when Maggie would ask Frank Still to come to her home and entertain at the piano for selected "show-biz" friends who were invited to join Maggie and her secretary-companion, Anne Russell. If people thought of these musical evenings as open-house affairs, they were mistaken. If any invited guest brought along an extra person without permission, he or she was soon informed that "extras" were not expected or welcome. Despite the drinking that was going on, Maggie remained in control. She wanted to be sure that when she went upstairs to bed, there was no one still roaming around her home and that no one had fallen asleep in a corner. Her caretaker and maid, whom she trusted implicitly, also helped keep things (and visitors) under control.

Always a creature of many moods, Maggie was also a woman of changeable appearance. In jeans and a sweatshirt for television rehearsals, she could have been mistaken for a teenager. Her body was slim and firm, her movements quick and agile. Dressed for dance numbers on her show, she became glamorous in sequined and spangled costumes that flattered her legs. But offstage, with eyeglasses in place, she was not too concerned with her appearance. Often wearing a sweater and jeans, her hair brushed straight back, she walked about the town of Westport or strolled into one of the Westport pubs.

Years later, a Connecticut entertainment columnist would recall Raye's careless clothing about town and would say that it was customary for her to have "a woman friend living with her." It was hard to tell if she was "AC or DC," he concluded. But his conclusion likely was faulty. It was true that Maggie often did have a woman living with her—someone who also took care of her employer's mail, bills, and schedules. A secretary who wrote notes and letters for her. Someone Maggie could depend upon to do the things she couldn't, and wouldn't, try to do for herself. Maggie did have some very attractive and stylish clothes, most of them selected by Nick, who had excellent taste. In Nick's absence, Maggie depended on her friend and secretary to advise her and to shop with her, or for her, when she needed something new to wear for a special event. On the set, of course, she had no need to worry about the suitability of her attire; there were dressers and wardrobe people and designers, when necessary, to see to it that she was beautifully dressed.

J. Fred Muggs, the chimpanzee trained by Charlie Ruggles, made several appearances that year on Maggie's show. While rehearsing one skit in which she and the chimp were supposed to take intelligence-quotient tests with the chimp tallying up the higher score, the animal nipped the star's left arm as they sat at a table. The usually redoubtable Maggie fled from the set. As much as she loved animals, she insisted that an empty chair had to be placed between her and the chimp at the next rehearsal.

The blank look of stupidity she assumed for the act with the chimpanzee vanished, though, as Maggie got into a brief costume, black net stockings, and high-heeled pumps for the dress rehearsal of a colorful dance number. Backed by a line of male dancers, their chests bared, Maggie was pushed and pulled about, then tossed into the air as the dance became a comedy routine.

Maggie's attention suddenly was riveted on a new male dancer in the chorus, Edward T. Begley. (This was not the Ed Begley who would later become a well-known actor.) Begley, like the other dancers on the show, was not large or tall. Maggie was petite, and her dancers were carefully chosen not to overwhelm her in size, so that she would look taller. Why she was attracted to Begley so quickly, she herself possibly could not have explained. There was nothing about him that resembled the charming, but explosive, Nick Condos. And nothing about him, she would discover later, to suggest the sensual maleness that Condos projected to women.

Becoming quickly infatuated with a man was now a habit. As she took a pratfall in her dance-comedy routine, she stared up at Begley with lustful interest. And lust, to Maggie, was synonymous with love; therefore, it meant marriage as soon as possible. Everything else in her life was being done under pressure and in a hurry, so why not marriage?

Following an April show, Maggie chartered two single-engine planes to fly her and the thirty-year-old Begley, never previously married, and their attendants (Maggie's neighbors, the Carl Eastmans) to Elkton, Maryland, known for quick marriages. After landing in Maryland, the planes left. But the wedding party was disappointed to learn that regulations had been changed and a forty-eight-hour wait now was necessary. The impetuous Maggie then chartered two more small planes to fly them to Alexandria, Virginia, where they were able to get a license and to be married on April 21, 1954, without further delay. By this time, Maggie's bouquet of violets was as wilted as her marriage soon would be. Nonetheless, within minutes she and Begley were husband and wife.

Returning to Westport, the newlyweds settled into Maggie's spacious home on East Meadow Road. In May, neighbors on Old Hill Road gave them a reception. But no one could outdo Maggie in this kind of generosity. In return, the Begleys invited neighbors and friends to a lavish party at their home. Nick Condos was on hand for the party and, according to a Connecticut newspaper columnist, "he passed out from nervous exhaustion." It was more likely, though, that he passed out from drinking.

At the academy, Melodye Condos was notified of her mother's new marriage. The marriage was simply one more unknown (since she spent so little time at home) for the girl to accept. She was growing fast, and it was becoming clear that she was going to be much larger than her mother. And it seemed that her hands and feet were growing faster than the rest of her body. The last time she had gone home on a break, Maggie had said nothing at all about her daughter's good grades, and certainly nothing about the girl's desire to be a ballet dancer, but had pointed out to visitors, "I think Melodye's going to be a truck driver. She's got such big hands and feet."

Maggie finally noticed, too, that her daughter's toes were crossing, one over the other, and could not be straightened. When she had been away at school for long periods of time, acquiring a pair of new shoes had become a complicated problem for the youngster. No one at home had thought of ordering new shoes for her, and so the child had continued to wear outgrown shoes and, as a very little girl, had considered it a normal thing to do. Later, letters asking for money for new shoes would arrive at the house. But Maggie might have been out of town when a particular letter arrived, and then might have forgotten all about it after her secretary brought it to her attention. Even when Nick received a letter explaining the need for new shoes for his child, there usually was a delay. He, too, might have been out of town when the letter arrived, or he might have been drunk when he read the letter and simply forgotten all about it. So another letter would be written, and finally someone would send a check. Then the housemother would have to find time to take Melodye to a store to get the shoes. The result was that years later, as an adult, Melodye would have to wear shoes fitted with orthopedic inserts to separate the crossed-over toes.

Dancing as a career seemed no longer a possibility. But the girl did possess a very good, rich singing voice, and she already had aspirations to become an actress. After all, her parents were entertainers. It was quite reasonable for her to anticipate that she, too, might succeed in show business.

Not long after Maggie married Begley, her daughter completed her boarding school term and came to Westport. To stay, her mother said. And in many ways, that first summer in Westport at the house Maggie called Shangri-la was a pleasurable summer for Melodye as she enjoyed a kind of freedom that was very different from the totally structured life she had had at the academy.

Maggie's home was built of stone and surrounded by several acres of land. And even though Maggie took off for Las Vegas to fill an engagement and frequently left for other destinations, the young girl found various ways to amuse herself. She enjoyed romping on the rolling lawn with the two-year-old boxer, also named Maggie, that had become one of Raye's pampered pets along with a white pekinese, Bluford, and a basset puppy named Humphrey.

Now and then the girl ran on, up the incline behind the Raye property, where the Gabors lived. Soon she was invited into the kitchen by Jolie, the mother, who seemed to like what she referred to as the girl's outgoing, spunky personality. The young visitor thought it odd, though, that Jolie Gabor was always wearing what she thought of as a nightgown, even in the afternoons. And whenever she caught a glimpse of any of the three daughters—Zsa Zsa, Eva, or Magda—they, too, were wearing nightgowns. An adult Melodye would relate this story to Geraldo Rivera on his afternoon talk show many years later when Francesca Hilton, Zsa Zsa's only daughter, also was a guest.

"Waiting for men?" Geraldo queried.

Zsa Zsa herself phoned in to assure him that the Gabors "didn't have to wait for men."

In July, Maggie was happy when a contract for an upcoming 1954-55 television series was offered to her by Hazel Bishop, Inc. Under Nick's watchful eyes, Maggie signed the contract for the next season, guaranteeing that she would have her own weekly show. The following month, she was off to Bimini with Begley and a group of friends to celebrate her thirty-eighth birthday.

The celebration turned into a nightclub brawl, and a nightmare as far as bad publicity was concerned, after Maggie's party argued with a man named Barton and his friends. Newspapers told of the argument flaring into a fight during which, Maggie claimed, she was punched, then hit over the head with a bottle. Her husband, Begley—no Nick Condos, for sure—did not get involved in the fight. But as others approached Barton to seize him, Barton grabbed a fire extinguisher and sprayed them and then the room with foam.

Maggie sued for $400,000 in damages, stating that the attack caused blurred vision, fainting spells, and insomnia. She needed neither the bad publicity nor the so-called injuries to add to her problems. Her recent marriage was already in trouble, threatening to explode. And she was having serious trouble with her teeth. Refusing to see a dentist, she continued to use beeswax to make her own repairs. When, as she entertained at a nightclub, one of the "repaired" teeth flew out of her mouth, she began making this part of her act, deliberately spitting out beeswax teeth from time to time. Anything for a laugh.

After enrolling her daughter in sixth grade at Bedford Elementary School in Westport that fall, Maggie's professional life flourished with the arrival of the new television season, despite the publicity about the fight in Bimini. The ailing director, Nat Hiken, left the show, and Norman Lear stepped in. Rocky Graziano returned, and feature articles and photographs of Maggie were published in leading magazines including the *Saturday Evening Post* and *Life*. There was scarcely a reference to husband Ed Begley, the invisible man, in any of the articles. However, there were frequent references to an incident involving Nick Condos, with whom Maggie was seen, accompanied by another couple, in nearby Bridgeport at the Cafe Howard.

When Nick got up from their table at the cafe and went into the men's room, he saw three husky young football players writing their names on the wall above the urinal. To keep out of their way and out of trouble, Nick urinated into a sink—a procedure that became second nature to many entertainers who had traveled the vaudeville circuits. Cramped dressing rooms, where quick changes had to be made, usually had no toilets. Rather than take time to go down the hall, vaudevillians sometimes relieved themselves into industrial cans set out for such emergencies or into sinks if necessary.

"Slob!" One of the young men spat out the accusation as Nick zipped up his pants. The word might as well have been a red flag waved in front of a bull. Nick charged and the three hulky young fellows jumped him. The fight burst through the door of the men's room and into the dining room. Maggie screamed and began swinging her purse, hitting Nick's attackers as the four men threw punches and wrestled Nick to the floor, knocking dishes and glasses from the tables. The fight ended only when the attackers, getting the best of the tough and seasoned Condos, heard someone yell, "The cops are coming!" All four men and Maggie escaped through a back door, got into their cars, and roared away into the night.

After that unsavory episode, Maggie and Nick stayed away from Bridgeport where there was supposed to have been a warrant issued for their arrest. "She divorced me, but I still love her," Nick replied when questioned about his relationship with Raye.

9

Threats in the Night

Shortly before Christmas 1954, Maggie was gratified to be asked to appear on *Dateline,* a ninety-minute NBC special hosted by John Daly and sparked by the dedication of the Memorial Building in Manhattan in the name of those who had given their lives in the cause of the free press. Thrilled to be one of the few women to appear on the program, along with the famous black contralto, Marian Anderson, Maggie was equally thrilled to meet poet Carl Sandburg.

Less than a month later, Maggie was admitted to a Norwalk, Connecticut, hospital for what was termed a "physical checkup." She was taken to the hospital after she quarreled noisily with Edward Begley in a Westport restaurant where, a local columnist said, she slapped a coconut cream pie into her husband's face. Her frequent hospitalizations were now referred to in print as "flakeouts . . . mental rather than physical."

Some of her associates whispered that these hospitalizations were caused by alcoholic blackouts, both mental and physical. Although there was no doubt that personal problems were responsible for much of her mental anguish and her increased reliance on alcohol and sleeping pills, it was also true that she was still pacing herself too fast. This was risky because of the chronic anemia that had plagued her ever since she had gone to Africa during World War II.

But she had gathered herself together enough by February to perform with typical clownish abandon, along with Ray Bolger and host Milton Berle, on *The Big Time*, a ninety-minute variety show on NBC.

The "king of television," Berle had had his crown knocked a bit askew recently when his sponsor, Buick, had turned to Jackie Gleason and offered the "Great One" an $11 million contract. Gleason's popular show was now scheduled on Saturday nights, and the star, who claimed to be involved in every aspect—writing, directing, whatever—of his show, had introduced many innovations, including the June Taylor dancers, to attract viewers. The dancers always completed their routines by positioning themselves on the floor like petals on a flower and performing in synchronized movements reflected onto viewers' television screens from two overhead mirrors.

Berle really didn't have to worry. His own thirty-year contract with NBC guaranteed him a generous salary regardless of whether he was actually performing or was producing or consulting. But for most television entertainers, competition was frightening. They watched the ratings with trepidation—up a few decimal points one month, down the next. And there was Gleason to measure up to. Buick was so anxious to keep him that the company had given the entertainer a free hand in designing his own car, which Buick promised to build for him.

At this time, Maggie was worried about more than ratings for her show. She was receiving threatening telephone calls, which she believed were coming from Begley, who had moved out of her house. The threats were ugly and terrifying. Nick suggested that it might be wise to hire an off-duty policeman to stay overnight at the Westport house. The cop could listen in on the calls and protect Maggie and their daughter.

Still, she should keep the whole thing low-key. Off the record, Nick warned. A poor public image could be disastrous to her career. When Maggie impatiently brushed aside his warnings, he pointed out the unhappy fate of movie star Ingrid Bergman. Look how quickly such a star could plummet into disfavor. Bergman was the darling of the motion picture industry until she had gone to Italy to make a movie directed by Roberto Rossellini and had fallen in love with him. Deserting her husband and daughter back in the United States, she bore an illegitimate son to the Italian director and later had twin daughters whose legitimacy was questionable because the legitimacy of their parents' marriage-by-proxy in Mexico also was questionable. The Bergman-Rossellini affair, lavishly publicized throughout the world in the 1940s, resulted in Bergman being barred from reentry into the United States. Maggie's only concern about the Bergman affair seemed to be the stigma of the illegitimate children. Such a disgrace, she complained any time she spoke of the Swedish actress, to bring illegitimate babies into the world.

Despite the furor over Bergman, times were changing in the American movie industry. Actually, things had begun to change as early as the 1940s when European films, particularly the Italian cinema of Vittorio DeSica, Roberto Rossellini, and Luchino Visconti, began depicting real people with real problems (poverty, war, desperation). Hollywood had begun to pay attention to these films and, in the early 1950s, to make films of its own, such as *On the Waterfront* and *Rebel without a Cause,* featuring troubled characters trying to eke out a living.

Tennessee Williams created characters who had problems with alcohol and sex, and reality began to set in as Hollywood made pictures based on his dramas. No longer would a major film star have to be pigeonholed into one type of public persona. Maggie, a multifaceted woman, had been a film star caught in a previous period when people like her were very clearly in the minority. She had allowed herself to be photographed, candidly, in natural poses that were not encouraged in earlier years. Now, the maturing of Hollywood was bringing a new visage to the industry.

After Maggie had been released from the hospital, she had returned to her East Meadow Road home where reporters were waiting. She gave surprisingly casual answers when they asked about Ed Begley's whereabouts. "Oh, he lives with neighbors," she replied airily. And yes, she expected him back and she hoped it would be soon.

Unable to wheedle any definitive answers from Maggie, the reporters got in touch with Nick, her spokesman. "I can neither confirm nor deny that Miss Raye is separated from her husband," he told them.

By this time, Nick Condos was in love with a twenty-one-year-old woman, beautiful Barbara Caplin, although, as yet, his daughter did not know about their relationship. She did know, however, as did most of the country, that her mother seemed to have no sense when it came to men. And now there were rumors that Maggie already had fallen in love with the muscle-man policeman, Bob O'Shea, whom she had hired as a bodyguard.

When a photo of the two, seated at a table in the Stork Club, appeared in some of the country's larger newspapers, Maggie lied to protect herself. "It's a phony," she claimed to press people who promptly printed her protests. The truth of the matter was, she said, that there were five or six people in the group that night, including her "real" boyfriend, Al Riddle. O'Shea happened to be in the picture, she added, only because she hadn't wanted to leave her bodyguard waiting outside in the cold while the others were in the restaurant.

Club owner Sherman Billingsley had sent a copy of the picture to everyone in the party, as was his custom, she pointed out. But the others in the party had been cropped by the media, leaving only O'Shea and herself. To make sure that Riddle would back up her story, she called him in Las Vegas where he worked as a pit boss and explained her problem.

Although big-city papers in other parts of the country carried many items on Maggie's personal problems, the local paper in Westport printed few of them. West Coast and Miami papers both ran stories on a burglary that netted thieves $1,000 in cash and $15,000 in furs and jewelry in February while Raye was telecasting a show in New York. And they ran a story on a fire that started in Raye's bed at her Westport home after she had fallen asleep with a cigarette in her hand. The bedding smoldered until Olivia, the maid, smelled smoke and called the fire department. Then she ran upstairs to Melodye's bedroom and awakened her. If it hadn't been for Olivia, Maggie would have burned to death in her own bed. She had been sleeping heavily, and Olivia had trouble waking her. But firemen had even more trouble rousing O'Shea, who was sleeping in the guest room. They had to pull him out of bed.

O'Shea was listening on another telephone the night that Maggie received one of the anonymous calls. This time, the caller threatened to throw acid in her face. "You've got to report this to the police," O'Shea advised her. "There's only so much that I can do on my own."

Maggie went to the police station with her report and her suspicions that her ex-husband was making the threats of disfigurement and kidnapping. She was worried for the safety of her child and herself, she said. Suspicions were not enough, she was told. Proof was needed before much could be done. But the police chief assured her that his men would make extra runs near her house and keep watch as much as they could. The Raye house was not on the main road, however, and after a short time, the extra runs dwindled. Then O'Shea arranged for Maggie to hire a second policeman to help watch the house when O'Shea was working his police-run and could not be at Raye's house.

The Westport paper, protective of the genteel community's image and wary of sniping at the many celebrities who lived in the town, gave coverage to Raye's problems only when the local fire department was called again in April to save the house from destruction. This fire had started with a short in the electric range and spread to the kitchen, breezeway, and garage. Everyone had run from the house—Maggie with her boxer dog in her arms—by the time the firemen arrived. Everyone, that is, except for Maggie's daughter.

Melodye was asleep in her bedroom, just above the kitchen, with the door shut. She awakened only at the approaching sound of sirens and the smell of smoke. Then there was the sound of someone pounding at her window, which had been painted shut. At the sound of breaking glass, she ran to the window and into the arms of a fireman who helped her scramble down a ladder to safety. Olivia had told the firemen, "Miss Melodye is up there," pointing up at the bedroom window. Maggie, it seemed, had not yet become accustomed to having her daughter at home during the school season and, in all the excitement, had forgotten her.

The police chief estimated that damages would run between $5,000 and $7,000. In gratitude, Maggie announced that she would throw a big party for the firemen who had come to her aid once again. But the party never took place.

The daughter had questions for her mother. So what if Maggie didn't like questions? The girl was upset. Why had there been so many fires at their house? And what terrible thing was going to happen next?

The series of misfortunes on the home front seemed symptomatic of more dramatic problems in Maggie's life that year. It also seemed clear that she wasn't risking any more questions from her daughter because, in the fall of 1955 and with the beginning of another television season for her, she informed the girl that she would be going to Mrs. Beard's School in East Orange, New Jersey, for the coming term.

Quite surprisingly, Barbara Caplin had been appointed to take care of all the details of getting Nick's daughter enrolled in her new school, taking her to register for seventh grade and shepherding her to the school store to be fitted for uniforms. Melodye was sullen through the whole procedure; she was tired of being passed around like a football, and now she was being given into the care of a total stranger. But Barbara remained calm and pleasant. She was capable, too. Even the sulking daughter had to admire her for that.

Nick Condos's sudden marriage to Barbara Caplin in November 1955 surprised many people. Even Maggie confessed that she had not expected him to actually remarry. Not Nick Condos, who seemed to glory in his "wild playboy" image. Not "Iron Man" who would later be described by Barbara, in her book *Hard Candy,* as the "best action in town for spongers."

But Maggie had too many other things to concern her at that time to brood about Nick's marriage. Her show was drawing less than enthusiastic comments from reviewers this season. In a September show, Rocky Graziano's "dese, dem and dose" had contrasted strangely with the husky elegance of Tallulah Bankhead's voice as, together with Maggie, they satirized *The $64,000 Question,* the television quiz show. The skit was weak compared with a more biting satire on the same subject done the previous week by Martin and Lewis. "Unfunny script," said *Variety.*

Obviously, Maggie was not to blame for the script. But a week before a late October flood hit Westport, washing out roads and bridges, her show also turned out to be a kind of disaster when guest Douglas Fairbanks Jr. filled the role of a man madly in love with her. *Time's* critic reported that Raye had proved that "slapstick can be tasteless" in an "interminable skit" with Fairbanks.

The knowledge that every performer must expect to take a few lumps from reviewers did not relieve Maggie of her worries that her show might be losing its viewer appeal. Her meteoric rise to success in Hollywood, followed by near obscurity in the movie world, was still vivid in her mind. And her feelings of insecurity were compounded when she read or heard the commentary of others on her lifestyle: that she drank to excess, that she was a loner as far as the so-called elite of the entertainment world were concerned, and that she mixed, instead, with unsavory characters, even "mobsters," in whose company she may have "felt superior."

Sensitive to criticism, Maggie was especially hurt by the charge (not totally new, but stronger now) that she relied on "blue" materials for her success. As far as television was concerned, off-color materials were taboo. Actress Faye Emerson was pilloried by ministers and priests from their pulpits as she exposed "cleavage" as a panelist on the popular and inoffensive program *What's My Line?*

In Maggie's nightclub act, true, she frequently used double entendres and suggestive skits. But there were many successful male comics who used even more risqué materials in nightclubs and were not castigated for doing so. Why the double standard? Maggie complained.

So, concerned about her television series and about the complications in her love affair with O'Shea, Maggie wasn't too distressed about Nick's marriage. But her daughter, like most other teenaged daughters of remarried fathers, must have had mixed feelings. It was not surprising that the girl appeared to be on guard when her stepmother tried to reach out to her.

When Melodye came home for the Christmas break in December, her mother had just returned from attending a luncheon at the Sheraton-Astor Hotel to which she had been invited by the National Nephrosis Foundation of New York and New Jersey. The Foundation officers knew that she had claimed to have experienced intermittent kidney problems. Now Maggie informed them that her younger sister had died from nephritis several years previously. Then she had graciously accepted the chairmanship of the 1956 Nephrosis Fund Campaign. She also promised that she would appeal for donations toward the campaign at the close of each of her television shows—which she did.

A "first" for *The Martha Raye Show* occurred in early January when Bill and Cora Baird and their puppets were Maggie's guests. As they practiced for the telecast, Maggie abruptly interrupted the rehearsal. Her daughter was the one who had suggested having the Baird puppets on the show. Why not have Melodye introduce the puppets to the television audience? The writers immediately began making changes in the script as Nick sent a car to Westport to pick up his daughter. During the ride to the studio, the girl carefully brushed her long, dark hair, which now reached past her waist, and fastened a clasp to hold the hair in its usual ponytail.

Melodye's debut with the puppets sparked the Raye telecast at a time when Maggie's show still was not drawing the rave notices of past years. Maggie's remedy for less than top-flight shows was to work even harder at rehearsals and to bring in more "regular" people as guests. Regular people, she believed, provided an important link to viewers who easily related to the noncelebrities featured on her show. In January 1956, Maggie had a twelve-year-old black schoolgirl, a spelling champion, make a guest appearance. The child, who had previously said she wanted to be a school teacher when she grew up, was asked if she still had the same ambition. "Naah," Gloria Lockerman told Maggie. "I wanna be a movie star." The answer may have been rehearsed, of course. But it came across to the audience as a natural and hilarious response as Maggie hugged the little girl.

The $64,000 Question (which also used "regular" people as contestants) was very popular and supposedly unrehearsed. It made a big name of Dr. Joyce Brothers. The audiences of the 1950s did not question the authenticity of the program and were totally unprepared for the furor that eventually developed when it became known that answers had been furnished to some of the winning contestants.

In early February, NBC honored Maggie for her thirty years in show business (although it really was almost thirty-six years, because she had begun performing at such a young age). It was her night to sparkle and to become just a bit teary-eyed, too, as more than 350 people came to her party at Danny Stradella's nightclub, including singer Johnny Ray (who was even better known for tears and crying) and comedians Jack Carter, Jack Leonard, Sam Levinson, and Buddy Hackett. Also in attendance were Tennessee Williams, Rocky Graziano, and actresses Nanette Fabray, Jayne Mansfield, and Dagmar. And from the many people who could not come, Milton Berle and Sid Caesar among them, there were floral tributes to embellish that night of triumph when Maggie was acclaimed a "Comedian's Comedienne."

A week later and despite her demanding schedule, Maggie was off on another of her patriotic tours, heading for Greenland to entertain American servicemen stationed there. She soon returned to travel her Westport-to-New York route. Almost always, twenty-eight-year-old Bob O'Shea—tall, well built, and dubbed "Nature Boy" by fellow police officers because of the hours he spent boxing and lifting weights—was at her side.

Shortly before Easter, Maggie learned that her daughter had to return home because, unlike the convent school in Florida, the New Jersey school closed its doors for the Easter break. The girl could not have suspected she was walking into the proverbial "hornet's nest." O'Shea's family was no longer trying to hide its concern over the amount of time that Maggie's bodyguard was spending at his employer's East Meadow Lane address and away from his twenty-year-old wife, now in the final weeks of her first pregnancy.

Maggie was plainly jittery, making a lot of telephone calls from behind closed doors, then, in a loud voice, demanding to talk to

Bob. She informed her daughter that she would be away on Easter Sunday and for the following few days. O'Shea, too, had told his family that he had to escort his employer to the Catskill Mountains to fill an engagement on Easter Sunday. But the trip was not to his family's liking. They protested—his very pregnant wife, his mother, and even his brothers.

Three days after Easter, one of O'Shea's brothers called the Catskills resort, ordering O'Shea to come home at once. But another three days elapsed before he returned with Maggie, at which time Melodye returned to school.

Only nine days after the bodyguard's return from the Catskills to Westport, and while Maggie returned to New York and to rehearsals for her show, O'Shea's wife gave birth to a girl. A few days later, Maggie telephoned O'Shea's mother's home, offering to be the child's godmother and to gift the baby with a $500 bond. Apparently Maggie felt she was doing a good acting job in the role of a generous employer extending a gift to the family of her employee-bodyguard, in line with the many protestations she had uttered that she and O'Shea were employer and employee—nothing else. Once more, Maggie was in denial, completely ignoring the newspaper publicity and choosing to believe that her role-playing of a benevolent employer would eclipse reality.

The O'Sheas must have been stunned by the totally unexpected offer. They refused to accept it.

By this time, O'Shea's wife was ready to come home from the hospital with her newborn child. She arrived to find her husband packing his clothes into suitcases and preparing to leave the home.

Still, Maggie made another attempt to build goodwill with the policeman's family when she returned to Westport by going into the little shop where O'Shea's mother worked. Trying to be very polite, Maggie inquired about the new baby and the family as she bought a two-piece ensemble for herself. To the O'Shea family, the entertainer's overtures must have seemed unbelievable, even ridiculous. But Maggie didn't see it that way. She had convinced herself that by pretending that there was only a business relationship between herself (threatened with danger from a vengeful husband)

and the policeman she had hired to protect her, she could avoid another explosion of bad publicity that might, she finally realized, wreck her television career. And so, for a very short time, she played out her role of respectability with a remarkable amount of self-control for a woman with such an impulsive nature, as if she were onstage where actors were being maneuvered by the firm hand of a director.

The explosion happened anyway. On the heels of O'Shea's departure, his distraught wife filed a $50,000 alienation-of-affections suit against Maggie. That same night, O'Shea, under pressure from local officials, accepted a leave of absence from the Westport police force.

Within hours after the suit was filed, a deputy sheriff arrived to serve papers attaching the Raye house and property to back up the suit. Overwhelmed by the collapse of the role that she had been playing as newspapers printed details of the alienation-of-affections suit, the damage suit, and O'Shea's resignation from his job, Maggie found her problems compounded when her estranged husband, Ed Begley, sued for divorce on the only grounds valid in the state of New York: adultery.

Devastated by the quick turn of events, Maggie phoned Nick, her troubleshooter, who had advised her on the role she should play. It hadn't worked, she sobbed, knowing that he was thoroughly disgusted with her for getting involved with another younger, married man even before Begley had sued for divorce. Nick, temporarily hospitalized in Miami, could do little more than send Maggie's lawyer, Shirley Woolf, to Westport "to straighten out this ridiculous mess," as the lawyer told reporters.

Under Woolf's guidance, Maggie did a disappearing act, leaving her Westport home and going into seclusion at the home of friends. Unable to locate Raye, reporters converged on her attorney. "O'Shea has not been seen by Miss Raye since the suit was filed," Woolf told the reporters, "and Miss Raye does not know where he is."

"There seems to be a new trend," Woolf added. "Start the month of May by suing Martha Raye." Then she began to read what she said was a prepared statement from Raye. "'I don't know whether to be flattered or not,' Miss Raye says. 'A beautiful 20-year-old girl accuses me of stealing her husband. I am sorry Mrs. O'Shea is having marital difficulties, but I don't know what it has to do with me. All I did was hire four bodyguards to protect my life when it was threatened, and he was one of them. I have no new romance and have no intention of marrying again.'"

Still unprepared to face reporters, Maggie quietly moved into a Brooklyn hotel. But rehearsals for her May telecast, the season finale, brought her out of seclusion. At that time, forced to respond to reporters who were trailing her again, Maggie spoke firmly: "If there were one single bit of truth to the charges, I'd settle the suit for the full $50,000 right now—in fact, long ago. I don't go around stealing the husbands of nice little girls, and I want to prove that."

The statement sounded as if it had been prepared by someone else and memorized by Maggie, who added that she would fight the court suit no matter how long it took and that the whole affair was absurd.

Regardless of Maggie's disclaimers, many of the stiff-necked residents of Westport were dismayed by the garish publicity. They complained about the attention and notoriety that actors and actresses such as Kirk Douglas and Joan Blondell and their children were bringing to their community. And they complained especially about Martha Raye and her husbands and lovers.

It would have been better if Maggie had remained silent. But she had self-destructive tendencies that prodded her to deny the obvious. Quotes, printed in various newspapers, simply added fuel to the fire.

When reporters caught up with O'Shea, he claimed that he had tried to reconcile with his wife. But both his wife's family and his own family were influencing Mrs. O'Shea not to talk with him, he explained.

O'Shea's mother, however, confided to reporters that everyone in the family had tried to influence her son to remain at home with his wife. He had left, "saying that he was in love with Martha Raye."

O'Shea's wife claimed abandonment. Martha Raye had "captivated" her husband, she pointed out, by showering him with money and costly gifts. This last claim was brushed off by Maggie's lawyer, who pointed out that the gifts given to O'Shea were only Christmas gifts of the type regularly given to employees by the generous Miss Raye at her annual Christmas party.

The entire affair, Maggie complained, had been a "bombshell" in her life—a bombshell that was driving her out of Westport. She wanted to sell the Westport home, but the lien that Barbara O'Shea had placed on the house was limiting what Maggie could do. Still, before she left town, Nick managed to make a deal for her to sell the house to actor David Wayne once the lien was lifted.

Reporters clustered around the beleaguered entertainer at Idlewild Airport in early June as she waited to board a Miami-bound plane. She very much wanted to sell the Westport house she had once called Shangri-La, she told them. "I just want to get out of the state of Connecticut. It's not lucky for me." So quickly had her Westport-house-in-the-country dream expired.

In Miami Beach, Maggie temporarily settled into an Alton Road home owned by the Richmans, friends of Shirley Woolf. Her daughter was still in New York, sent to her father's apartment on Madison Avenue when school closed for the summer. Barbara tried to make the girl feel welcome when she came to visit, but she could sense the resistance. Melodye had experienced rejection too many times to be able to accept the unconditional friendship that her young stepmother seemed to offer. Barbara understood that, even when her patience was tested to its limits. "You're not my mother," the girl insisted stubbornly soon after the marriage had taken place. Still, Barbara remained invariably gracious and kind, even when gently but firmly pressing Melodye to do something she preferred not to do.

Sometimes only Barbara and Melodye were staying at the apartment. Still employed as Maggie's personal manager, Nick frequently accompanied his ex-wife on gigs to various cities or visited her in Miami Beach to boost her morale.

Maggie's morale was at a low ebb. Her television series—the show that had given the entertainer the biggest boost of her entire career—was not being renewed for the upcoming season. The conditions of the "morals" clause in her TV contract had not been met.

Maggie had another reason to be despondent: she was desperate to get a divorce from Begley so she could be with the man she loved, Bob O'Shea. She had tried to file her own divorce suit against Begley in Miami, she told Nick. But a Miami judge refused the suit because the applicant's length of residency, less than two months, did not meet the requirements of Dade County.

While Nick was away, trying to bolster Maggie's spirits, Barbara and her stepdaughter began sharing confidences—tentatively at first, then more freely as Barbara talked about how much she had loved her adoring father, boxing promoter Hymie Caplin, who had been "framed" and sent to Sing-Sing. Barbara was only ten years old when her mother had died, one year before Hymie was released from prison.

Five years after her father's release, he, too, had died, leaving three orphans. Soon there were only two: Barbara and the younger Janice. Barbara's brother had died of Hodgkin's disease shortly before Barbara married the swaggering, cigar-smoking Nick Condos, who reminded her of her beloved father. But her father had not been a heavy drinker. Nick customarily drank a fifth of Dewar's White Label every night, then got up in the morning without a hangover.

Barbara had not had a happy childhood. That was clear. But she had moved ahead, nonetheless, graduating from the Fashion Institute of Technology and Design. She read books of all kinds, viewed art films, and visited museums. Barbara, still in her early twenties, was a cultured lady, in the rapidly changing opinion of Nick's daughter.

Barbara took the girl to skating rinks, concerts, movies, and, best of all, clothing stores. For the first time in her life, Melodye could go into a store, with her stepmother, and select a skirt or sweater that she liked. Clothes that fit her properly. Up until the time that Barbara came into her life, Nick's daughter had been grateful that the girls at boarding school had worn uniforms. Conformity had been fine when the alternative would have been to look dowdy compared with the other girls. But things were changing for her now. She had a friend, someone she believed she could trust: her stepmother, Barbara.

10

Imperfect Balance

Maggie remained despondent in Miami Beach after a judge rejected her divorce suit. Her television show had expired, and her personal life was in a shambles. Begley was demanding a divorce settlement, and lawsuits were threatening her properties.

Discouraged, Maggie returned to Westport, where she and O'Shea talked again about his plans for establishing his own detective agency. He had an experienced partner willing to go in with him, he explained, but the partner had no more financing than did O'Shea. Maggie finally agreed to back the business venture, even though Nick warned her she was making a big mistake. But she was troubled, wondering if she had done the right thing, and this uncertainty, added to the recent humiliations she had suffered, had left her extremely vulnerable to the slightest criticism, the least suggestion of rebuff or ridicule, real or imagined.

In this heightened aura of suspicion and paranoia, she and O'Shea found plenty of things to argue about. They were arguing intensely when Melodye, who had come from her dad's apartment to stay in Westport that summer, walked into the middle of a quarrel. Maggie wheeled around to face her daughter, ordering the girl to go into the kitchen and get drinks for them.

With her long, full ponytail swinging, the girl turned and hurried into the kitchen where she reached into the refrigerator for a container of grapefruit juice. As she nervously poured the juice, the container slipped from her hand. The screams of the maid, upset at having a sticky mess spreading over her clean floor, brought Maggie and O'Shea to the kitchen.

"Go get the pinking shears!" Maggie shouted at her daughter, who shrank back. But there was no backing away when her mother turned the fullness of her fury and her urge to humiliate someone else from O'Shea to the young girl. "Right now. Go."

And then there was the terrible slashing sound of the shears, relentlessly chopping off the glossy dark hair right at the rubber band that held the ponytail at the side of her head—the long hair that the girl prized; the distinctive, side-swept ponytail that gave her an identity in her own mind. But she refused to cry as jagged shafts of hair fell to the floor. Finally Maggie's fury was spent and the side of her daughter's head was a slanted, saw-toothed mess. O'Shea stared, saying nothing. But the girl was sure he was glad, glad to see her humiliated.

In August, Maggie went back to Yvonne Richman's house in Miami. Soon after her 2:30 A.M. arrival, Yvonne's maid found the entertainer lying unconscious on the floor of her bedroom. The maid phoned for an ambulance, which took the drugged woman to St. Francis Hospital. When doctors learned that she had swallowed twenty sleeping pills, they pumped her stomach and placed her in an oxygen tent.

By this time, Nick and Barbara were convinced that Maggie, thwarted by the courts, was desperately seeking attention. Nick immediately flew to Florida. A week later, apparently revitalized by his presence, Maggie celebrated her fortieth birthday at a Miami Beach nightclub where, under Nick's watchful gaze, she clowned as if she had no major problems. But Nick had learned, long ago, that his ex-wife's volatile moods shifted quickly from dejection to euphoria and vice versa.

Still, as important as her career was to Maggie and despite frequent arguments with O'Shea, her relationship with the younger man seemed just as important. Within a week of celebrating her birthday, Maggie became very upset after she resumed her court action to divorce Begley—this time in Sebring, Florida. This judge also dismissed her suit, saying that he wanted to avoid "friction" among judges after a Dade County judge had previously denied the divorce.

With the new television season beginning in September, the best that Maggie could hope for was an opportunity to guest on other stars' shows. When such opportunities did not immediately present themselves, she was very depressed. Even her good friend, Rocky Graziano, who, she heard, was trying to market his own television series, would soon appear now and then as a guest on Jack Paar's show.

Returning to the nightclub circuit, Maggie appeared in Philadelphia in late September. Onstage to sing "That Old Black Magic," the entertainer got as far as the words "Down and down I go" when she sagged to the floor. A doctor, called to her dressing room, checked her vital signs and said that she had fainted but could return to the stage to finish her performance.

Was the incident "staged" by Maggie, seeking attention? Nick and Barbara were not the only ones to wonder about this. It seemed "too pat," too coincidental, to collapse at the very moment she sang, "Down and down I go," entertainment columnists wrote.

From Philadelphia, Maggie went back to Westport where her attorney filed with the town clerk a statement signed by Barbara O'Shea. The statement released the attachment she had placed on Maggie's Westport home and property. But the alienation-of-affections suit was still pending.

On October 6, 1956, Maggie was once more a single woman after she was divorced by Ed Begley on grounds of incompatability in a suit filed in Juarez, Mexico. It had cost her a considerable amount of money to be rid of Begley, her fifth husband, but she was elated to be free to marry O'Shea.

The trouble was that O'Shea was not yet free to marry her. In December, she finally closed the deal for the sale of her thirteen-room Shangri-La and its three and a half acres of land in Westport for $50,000. Then Maggie rented a beautiful home in Kingspointe, Long Island, and told Nick that she was being more cautious now. She would stay in the rented house until she found an appropriate home to buy, to invest the money she had received from the sale of the Westport house.

She was wiser now, Maggie told Nick. When she married O'Shea, things would be very different, she declared, trying to convince her personal manager who was thoroughly disgusted with the cavalier manner in which Maggie would pay off former husbands so she could marry another "loser," as Nick would say. And their daughter? Well, Melodye was going to be enrolled in yet another boarding school for girls in East Islip, Long Island. True, it was another change of schools, and in the middle of the year, but the new school was much closer to Kingspointe. Her daughter was a good student (it was the closest Maggie came to a compliment regarding Melodye's scholastic abilities—she certainly did not want the girl to think of herself as more knowledgeable than her mother) and could quickly adjust to new surroundings.

By January 1957, Maggie was alone in her Kingspointe home, except for brief visits from O'Shea when he could spare time from the demands of his detective agency. He tried to explain to Maggie that it took a lot of hard work and long hours to get a new business off the ground. So between gigs on the nightclub circuit or occasional guest appearances on television shows, Maggie often returned to her midtown apartment to be with O'Shea. She chafed at his inability to speed along his divorce and join her in Kingspointe.

Once again, Maggie was staying at her New York apartment when, in the middle of May, she became very upset at the news that *Studio One* planned to televise a drama titled *The Mother Bit* on CBS. The drama would center on a troubled relationship between a television singer and her young daughter, who had ambitions to become an entertainer. June Havoc was to take the lead role.

Maggie rushed to the telephone to call her attorney, Shirley Woolf, in Miami. The attorney immediately wrote to CBS and to McCann-Erickson, Inc., the advertising agency associated with the program. Woolf's letter pointed out similarities between the proposed television drama and the life of Martha Raye.

Denying that the play was modeled after Raye's life, a spokesman for CBS explained that the drama was only under consideration, with nothing officially scheduled. Still, Maggie was worried. Nick went to her apartment and tried to calm her, but she was still upset when he left. When O'Shea arrived later, she had been drinking and was ready for a confrontation. At 5 A.M., she was carried on a stretcher to a private ambulance, which moved her to Doctors' Hospital.

Newspapers reported that Martha Raye had been admitted for treatment and placed in an oxygen tent. Some papers announced that she had suffered a heart attack. But Nick Condos denied this. He had spent the previous evening with Miss Raye, he said, and because she complained of feeling "run down" they agreed that she should check into the hospital. "Simply for a checkup," he insisted.

Reporters asked, Why would anyone go to a hospital in such a fashion for a routine exam?

"'Miss Raye is an extraordinary woman who may enjoy being taken to the hospital this way," Nick answered, running out of more logical explanations. Still, further comments by Nick appeared to link the furor over the proposed television drama with Maggie's collapse.

"It's amazing," he said angrily. "If writers are being paid to write, why don't they create instead of going after somebody's life?" But it soon became apparent that plans for the telecast of *The Mother Bit* had been dropped.

Later in the summer, Maggie went back to her nightclub gigs. She entertained at New York's Copacabana Club in October. Soon afterwards, she began making plans to celebrate the Christmas holidays in a home she was arranging to buy in Great Neck, Long Island.

On Christmas Day, the hype deliberately circulated to reporters was that Maggie was entertaining an unfortunate cab driver and his family as dinner guests in her new Great Neck home. The cab driver's family had just lost their house and belongings in a fire, Nick Condos explained. "She's always doing nice things for people," he pointed out.

There was no doubt that Maggie could use some positive public relations and that Nick was good at manufacturing them. But the reality was that there was no cab driver and family at the Raye home on Christmas. Instead, the guests—apart from Melodye and Bob O'Shea—were Maggie's longtime friend, comedian Bernie Allen, and his family. The only connection to a cab driver seemed to be that Allen frequently had done a comedy skit as a taxi driver.

The other two guests on Christmas Day were Herb Blaund and his wife, owners of a furniture store. The Blaunds were helping Maggie select new furnishings for her home and Maggie, dependent as always on others' advice, appreciated their assistance.

Soon after the Christmas holidays, Maggie moved her daughter from her boarding school in Long Island into the freshman class at Great Neck North High School, which meant that she would be coming home each afternoon to her mother's new house. Then Maggie went on to Manhasset, New York, to rehearse for the lead role in *Annie Get Your Gun,* slated for a two-week run in New York City Center. When she collapsed during a rehearsal, she was taken to a hospital. The hype this time was that the entertainer needed an emergency appendectomy. Actually, the collapse appeared to be another blackout.

The O'Shea divorce was still moving too slowly for the impetuous Maggie to accept. When she supposedly "recovered" from her emergency "surgery," she moved back to the nightclub circuit. Keeping busy was one way to help reduce tension.

For Melodye, living at home was not easy—not when her mother, obviously upset about her relationship with O'Shea, was drinking to ease her anxieties. The girl was aware, too, that her mother sometimes relied on downers and uppers—especially now when she was so edgy, waiting for O'Shea's divorce. She had never seen her mother sniff cocaine, though, despite its popularity as a recreational drug with the Hollywood and New York celebrity crowd. But she had seen Maggie sniff amyl nitrate capsules (later called "locker rooms"). Amyl nitrate was the drug considered the "in thing" for the gay crowd. And Maggie liked to be "in" with the gays.

Almost fourteen and of an independent and spirited nature, Melodye resented having to ask her mother's permission for everything she wanted to do, even attending something as innocuous as an afternoon birthday party at a schoolmate's home. She was home alone one day after school, lying on her bed and reading in her second-floor bedroom, when she heard O'Shea's voice downstairs as he came into the house with a pal. A drunken pal, it soon became clear, as the man opened her door and came into her room, a stupid grin on his flushed face.

The girl jumped up from the bed and reached for the baseball bat she kept in her closet, warning the unwelcome visitor to get out. But the man had no intention of getting out. He clumsily tried to grab her. She jumped up on the bed and started swinging the baseball bat.

At the same time, she could see that O'Shea had come upstairs and was standing in the hallway. "Get your pal out of here," she shrieked as the other man, still grinning foolishly, hunched over and moved to the side of the bed closer to the footboard. Melodye took a couple of steps toward the footboard and swung harder. There was the sound of glass smashing, and then the man was backing away, out into the hall. The bat had broken the full-length mirror at the back of the door. Shards of glass lay on the floor. *It could have been the man's head.* Melodye shuddered at the realization.

She was still picking up smaller pieces of glass when she heard her mother and O'Shea talking downstairs. Then Maggie came into her daughter's room, demanding to know what the hell was wrong.

"I need a lock for my room. That's what's wrong! I want my privacy."

"There aren't any locks in this house," Maggie declared, her face set in an angry mold. The argument escalated when the daughter complained again about having no privacy and told her mother that she knew her telephone had been bugged by O'Shea. Maggie had to have known about it. There was no way that O'Shea would have bugged the girl's telephone unless Maggie had asked him to do it because of her suspicions of what her daughter might be telling Nick or Barbara in their frequent conversations. Still arguing, the mother and daughter moved downstairs into the living room where, as O'Shea listened, Melodye tried to explain what had happened up in her room. But the mother was not listening, shutting out the sound of her daughter's voice as if the words were stones hitting the protective facade that Maggie had built around herself,

Right, A 1936 publicity photo of Raye distributed by Paramount Pictures to promote *Rhythm on the Range.* Courtesy of Detroit Public Library, Performing Arts.

Left, An equally glamorous publicity photo taken later shows the rapidly rising star with a different look. Unless otherwise noted, photos courtesy of Academy of Motion Picture Arts and Sciences.

Left, Raye as a matador in Paramount's *Tropic Holiday* (1938). Her costume is a replica of the one Rudolph Valentino wore in *Blood and Sand.* Courtesy of Detroit Public Library, Performing Arts.

Right, Raye takes a break with former vaudeville comedian Bob Burns after roller-skating around the Paramount lot. They appeared together in several movies, including *Rhythm on the Range* and *Mountain Music.*

Raye isn't worried about the studio's "be glamorous" edict when she and her mother, "Peggy" Reed, pull this stunt at the 1939 housewarming party Raye gave after completing the film *Never Say Die*.

At a homecoming party for her husband, songwriter Dave Rose, Raye (top) enjoys a hearty laugh with friends (clockwise from lower right) Joe E. Brown, Benny Rubin, Charlie Ruggles, Joan Davis, and Alan Mowbry.

Above, With her dog, Dinky, Raye and her mother, Peggy, arrive in New York for the 1940 premiere of Universal's *Boys from Syracuse. Right,* Martha and Nick Condos with their daughter, Melodye, in 1944.

Raye made a number of appearances on *The Steve Allen Show. Above,* Raye, with Tom Poston at her side, waits for her cue to sing as Mel Torme plays the piano. *Right,* Raye and Allen perform a dance number in matching outfits. Courtesy of Steve Allen.

Above, Raye, who broke a lucrative engagement in 1969 in order to perform in Vietnam, waves as she leaves for one of her many trips. *Below*, Returning to Vietnam in 1970 as the star of *Hello, Dolly!*, Raye is greeted by Patricia Krause, Director of Public Information, USO-Vietnam. Courtesy of USO.

Right, Raye on stage in 1970 as she entertains the troops in Vietnam. Courtesy of USO. *Below,* Honorary Lieutenant Colonel Raye mimics Lieutenant (j.g.) Russell McMurdy, USS *Coral Sea*'s public affairs officer, to the amusement of her "boys."

fearful that the stones would smash the remnants of her dream of marrying O'Shea and living happily together in this lovely Long Island home.

And then Maggie suddenly was out of control. "You're a piece of shit. Get out of this house. Pack your bags and get out." Her face was livid. "Right now. I don't want you here any longer, you liar. I'm sending you to your father."

Nick and Barbara were living in a thirty-first-floor apartment on Central Park West. The girl had to take a train and two buses to get there, repeating the same phrase over and over to herself on the way. *Thank God for Barbara.* And Barbara, warm and sympathetic, was waiting for her when she arrived.

Her dad welcomed her, too, and seemed genuinely happy to see her. But it was clear that some things hadn't changed. He really didn't want to hear her side of the story. As much as Maggie irritated him at times—her infatuation with O'Shea was one of the worst irritations at present—he remained loyal to her. He knew that loyalty (and his livelihood) would be threatened if he were forced into supporting his daughter in any altercation between mother and daughter. Maggie simply would not allow it.

Only later when Barbara was alone with her stepdaughter did she learn about the attempted rape and about Maggie's refusal to believe her daughter or to confront O'Shea in any way. She knew that while the girl was living at the apartment, she would have a long daily trip back to Great Neck North High School five days a week, unless she chose to switch schools. But her stepdaughter did not want to switch schools again until she had completed her freshman year. She preferred to get up at 4:30 A.M. and, because of her love of swimming, to go to the nearby YMCA to use the pool, then catch a bus and transfer to a train and another bus to get to school. After school, the reverse trek awaited.

At the apartment, the young girl observed her stepmother's patience in dealing with her husband when, as happened frequently, he drank too much. One night, when Barbara was away, Nick invited some of his cronies, including Jake LaMotta, who had once been a guest on Maggie's show, and Jack Dempsey, to the apartment. The living room was thick with smoke and alcohol fumes when Nick opened the window and stepped up on a radiator, then to the narrow window sill, and over the casement to a ledge. He would show these champion ex-boxers what a dancer could do. He stood there, teetering delicately and urinating down thirty-one stories, while bellowing, "It's Magic. It's Maaaagic." His drunken cronies looked uncomfortable with the situation as they watched Melodye plead with her father to come back inside. But Nick, the dancer, was in no hurry. He was proud of his perfect balance. He came back in through the window only when he was ready, not because of a daughter's pleadings.

The liaison that existed between Nick's daughter and Barbara included an agreement that each lived up to religiously. The girl was to tell her stepmother everything that happened when she was away. Barbara, in turn, would never let Nick know that his daughter had squealed on him. So everything was reported to Barbara when she returned home. Barbara was sympathetic to Melodye's terror at seeing Nick dancing on the window ledge because Nick had made a previous excursion out the window in Barbara's presence. The woman and girl were allies. Both loved Nick. But now Barbara was giving up on her commitment to "reform" her husband. She had been so certain she could do it when she married him.

The excessive drinking was not the only reason for her discouragement. On a couple of occasions when Melodye had come to visit, Nick had said that Barbara was visiting a spa. Much later, it had been disclosed that the spa excursions had really been trips to Cuba for abortions—abortions that Barbara had not wanted. But her desire to have children had been overruled by Nick, who was so set against his wife giving birth to a baby that he had threatened to leave her if she did not have the abortions.

There was an important contradiction here, even if Nick failed or refused to recognize it. He had threatened to leave Maggie when she had wanted to abort Melodye. Yet now he forced Barbara to have abortions. The change in attitude surely had to result from the guilt Nick felt in yielding to Maggie's insistence not to show any affection to his daughter.

Nick's gambling also was hard to live with. Ever since the mid-1940s, he had been accompanying Maggie to Las Vegas for summer engagements. At that time, Vegas had been in its infancy with regard to its gambling casinos. Kirk Kerkorian, son of Armenian immigrants, had just set up a charter airline service from Los Angeles to Las Vegas. And Nick had arranged for Maggie to entertain at Bugsy Siegel's ninety-seven-room Flamingo Hotel, a state-of-the-art gambling emporium in those early years. The flamboyant gangster-owner of the Flamingo seemed to be sensitive on only one subject—that of the nickname Bugsy, used consistently by the media. Nick and Maggie, Siegel's pals and girlfriends, the hookers, pit bosses, and all other Flamingo employees were obligated to defer to the boss's excitable sensibilities and always called him Ben.

In the same year that Bugsy Siegel was murdered by the Mob, Nick and Maggie had taken their three-year-old daughter with them to the fledgling Flamingo. Many years later, the daughter would recall sitting on top of a grand piano while Tony Martin sang. Later, their daughter went only rarely to Vegas, sharing a room next to Maggie's suite at the Sahara with her mother's maid.

From the time Nick first began to go to Las Vegas with Maggie, he would be found at the gaming tables. Sober, Nick could handle the gambling problem. But he was rarely sober on those Las Vegas nights.

Aware of his weakness, Nick made an agreement with the pit bosses at whatever hotel where Maggie was performing not to allow him to run up a gambling debt that would total more than Maggie's salary at the particular casino. Invariably, however, Nick would be indulging in his Dewar's White Label when a pit boss would inform him that he had used up all his markers and had better quit for the night. Then Nick would start complaining to the pit boss, sometimes so loudly that he could be heard in the main room, where Maggie was entertaining.

Everyone knew Nick Condos and knew that he had friends in high and low places. And so no one really wanted to get rough with him. Sometimes, though, there was little choice in the matter. After being escorted out of one casino, Nick often would cross the street and go into another to try to start gambling all over again. Occasionally, when Nick was in better shape, Maggie played along with him at the craps table. But not for long. She would roll the dice and then someone would have to inform her when she won. And how much. It wasn't much fun when you couldn't interpret what was happening.

After Nick's marriage to Barbara Caplin, he continued, as Maggie's manager, to go to Vegas with his famous client. Sometimes Barbara went along, too, in attempts to keep her husband on the straight and narrow, but she was successful only as long as she stayed at his side. She was with him at the Sahara, but not at his side, the night he ran up a $65,000 gambling debt at the craps table, exceeding his credit line. When the pit bosses demanded $12,000 to cover his losses, Nick began to shout because the bosses had failed to protect him from himself. But this time his was a losing battle. The sheriff ejected him from the casino where he had been advised to come back, as soon as he was sober, with the money he owed. Nick took the advice as a warning, left town, borrowed $12,000 from his attorney, and then returned, pronto, to Vegas.

There was little hope that Nick Condos would change. But how long would it be before his young wife would come to the absolute end of her patience with him?

11

The Marriage Merry-Go-Round

Nick's daughter registered to enter another school, Rhodes High School in Manhattan, for her sophomore year. Now there would be no more need for the long bus-train-bus circuit each school day. Before the semester began, though, Barbara took her stepdaughter on a shopping expedition for skirts, sweaters, and matching shoes.

In October 1958, a jubilant Maggie announced from Las Vegas that she would marry Bob O'Shea soon. He had just been divorced, she told reporters, after Barbara O'Shea's suit was "settled out of court for a substantial amount." The amount, it was reported in newspapers, was $20,000. Early in November, Maggie and O'Shea appeared in Teaneck, New Jersey, to apply for a marriage license. Maggie asked Nick if he thought that his friend, Pepsi-Cola president Alfred Steele, and his wife, Joan Crawford, would be their witnesses at the ceremony. Crawford, who had married Steele three years previously, now lived in her husband's New York apartment, which he redecorated for his bride at a cost of a half-million dollars. But the couple traveled extensively across the country and in other parts of the world, publicizing Pepsi-Cola.

There were many similarities in the lives of Crawford and Raye, although the two knew each other only casually. Both actresses loved dogs and kept several in their homes. Crawford invariably carried her favorite white poodle in her arms when she traveled. Maggie's relationship with her only daughter was often strained while Crawford's relationship with at least the older two of her four adopted children was even more strained; the older girl would accuse her mother of cruelty. Both women did considerable drinking; Crawford was accustomed to drinking 100 proof vodka and Maggie, who had switched to Pim's No. 1 Cup for a while, now drank 100 proof vodka, too. Crawford, though ultrafeminine in her dress (she clung to high platform shoes with ankle straps, suits and dresses with padded shoulders, and large picture hats—all of which she continued to wear for years after they were no longer high fashion) was widely rumored to be bisexual, although she, like Maggie, had been married several times. The same kind of rumors still surfaced occasionally about Maggie. But Hollywood people "in the know" placed Maggie in what was inelegantly referred to as the "fag-hag" group—people who were not gay but were socially attracted to gays. Judy Garland also was reported to be in this group.

The Steeles said they were delighted to serve as witnesses at the wedding, and Maggie was delighted to have them. She was sure that the Steeles, admired for their promotional travels worldwide, gave an air of respectability to a wedding that had been preceded by such a lengthy blitz of bad publicity. Wearing a straight skirt and a beige satin camisole veiled by a beige lace blouse with dolman sleeves, Maggie wept throughout the brief ceremony as she and O'Shea exchanged wedding bands in the home of Mayor August Hannibal on November 7, 1958. Maggie had her daughter appear on the scene. The girl's appearance may have been for the same reason: to add to the aura of respectability and family solidarity that Maggie was desperate to create at this point.

The newlyweds quietly settled into the beautiful Great Neck, Long Island, home that Bob O'Shea would soon claim Maggie had promised would be his when they were married. Life, too, settled into a quietness to which Maggie was not accustomed. Each morning, her young husband left for work at his detective agency and Maggie found herself alone with her two basset hounds, Bridget and Bernie. There were no television offers. She feared that the bad publicity which had shadowed her for so long had finally taken its toll on her career. Perhaps if she lived quietly for a while, the public would forget her attempts at suicide, her marital problems and divorces, and the court suits that had created lurid headlines. But it was not in her nature to live quietly. And would her career fade away entirely? she wondered.

Her career would not fade away if Steve Allen had anything to say about it. He had begun doing a weekly comedy series for NBC on Sunday nights, in a difficult time slot, opposite the very popular *Ed Sullivan Show*. Allen would recall that he was "startled" when, at his first suggestion to book Raye for his show, he was told, "She's dead in the business. Forget her." But at his insistence, Raye was booked a dozen times as his guest. "In each case," he says, "the writers—all Martha Raye fans—wrote brilliant sketches tailored especially to exhibit her talents," with "stimulating results." Allen already had introduced comedy sketches done in what he refers to as the "Right Way/Wrong Way" formula. In Maggie's first appearance in one of these sketches, written by Don Hinkley, Leonard Stern, and Bill Dana, Allen says, the audience could see "a truly original, funny, likeable, vulnerable, imaginative artist at work." To know that she was appreciated by the talented Allen and his crew meant a great deal to Maggie at what had been a time of discouragement for her; and to know that Allen wanted her back on his show again, very soon, gave her a tremendous psychological boost.

On weekends, Maggie's daughter came to visit. Mother and daughter circled each other warily at first, neither wanting to renew the hostilities that had provoked Maggie's previous ultimatum: "Pack your bags and get out." Early in February 1959, no one could have been more enthusiastic than Maggie to take part, as she had the previous year, in a nineteen-hour telethon presented for the benefit of the Association for the Help of Retarded Children wherein $352,000 was received in pledges. Shortly after the telethon, Maggie phoned Nick to complain that the government was filing a tax lien of some $40,000 against her properties for 1957 taxes, still owing. Nick shook his head and said he didn't understand the tax mess, either. He would send a check for Maggie to her attorney and hope that would be the end of the matter. Forty thousand dollars was a lot of money, Maggie groused. At the same time, what was much worse, she found that the glow of married life was beginning to fade as she became suspicious of her husband's motives for having married her. Her husband was so rarely at home. And here she was, rattling around in her large house with too much time to brood. Bob O'Shea, she realized by now, was not at all like Nick Condos, ready to shield her from the press and to soothe her when she felt irritable or angry or simply very lonely. Perhaps she had made another mistake in marrying for a sixth time. Perhaps her career had finally fizzled out because of it. As usual, she confided in Nick.

Recalling the success of her earlier visit to London and her first appearance on television at another low point in Maggie's career, Nick suggested a trip to Europe. It was possible that he could make arrangements for Maggie to give a command performance in Monaco, he said. They could take their daughter with them; it would be a treat for Melodye. Maggie eagerly seized upon the idea. It would be the honeymoon that the O'Sheas never had, a new start for their faltering marriage. Nick knew that it would cheer Barbara, too. Barbara had never been to Europe. But she dreamed of going there. If he could arrange the command performance, transportation and other expenses would be covered by the royals.

In June 1959, the oddly assorted five "family" members—the O'Sheas, Melodye, Nick, and Barbara—boarded the *Queen Mary*. Three first-class staterooms had been reserved for them—the O'Sheas in one, Nick and Barbara in another, and a separate stateroom for Melodye. Except for O'Shea's seasickness, the ocean voyage aboard the luxurious ship was a happy, pleasurable experience for each of them, and particularly for the teenager who found herself free of parental supervision much of the time. After all, the girl was safe aboard ship, Maggie assumed. Where could she go? When Barbara visited the girl's stateroom, she ran her hand over the fine mahogany desk in one corner of the room. "It's Chippendale," Barbara told Melodye, "and we've been invited to have dinner with the captain tonight." O'Shea was feeling only slightly better as they boarded a train at Le Havre that took them to Cherbourg, then boarded another train to go on to Monte Carlo.

At the Hôtel de Paris in Monte Carlo, Maggie and Nick's daughter had her own beautiful room again, right on the circle Monte Carlo.

It was a thrill to see the Mediterranean sparkling below. It was also thrilling to get ready for the command performance for Prince Rainier and Princess Grace. Barbara loaned Melodye an olive-green chiffon dress that the girl absolutely loved. And because she was almost as tall as her stepmother by this time, the dress was the right length— just above the knees. With it, she wore gold shoes. She looked quite adult, Barbara assured her, admiring her chic beehive hairdo and bangs. The sun was still shining when they arrived at the palace. The two men sat quietly, waiting for the performance to begin. But Barbara and her stepdaughter could not resist looking around at the others who had been invited.

Trying not to stare, they stole covert glances at women, with elaborately sculptured hairdos, wearing low-cut dresses that seemed designed to show off the diamonds and emeralds encircling their necks and nestling between their breasts. Barbara nudged the girl, and both turned their heads to see Ari Onassis entering the room. He was a short, stout man with flashing dark eyes and heavy brows who entered with the commanding presence of great wealth and the knowledge that he was instantly the center of attention. The thick brows lifted slightly when he caught sight of beautiful Barbara Condos. Soon after the arrival of the prince and princess, Martha Raye became the center of attraction as she sang, danced, and clowned around the stage. The four family members watched with what must have been varying degrees of pride, the young girl quite aware that Maggie wanted her to feel proud of her mother. Proud and adoring. Always. Every moment of the day and night. And it just wasn't possible.

Maggie didn't want to even hear about her daughter's own ambitions to be a singer and an actress. The daughter had hopes now of attending Juilliard to study music and composition. Melodye had never taken piano lessons, even though Maggie's own interests had always centered around her grand piano. Maggie adored pianists, and her first thought was to bring in a pianist each time she had a group of friends in her home. So the puzzle was, why had Maggie not allowed her daughter to study piano? Was it because she did not want the daughter to read music when Maggie could not?

The spotlight was centering on a triumphant Maggie now as

she finished her performance to a burst of applause. People were rising from their chairs and lifting their arms to clap wildly. Melodye and Barbara looked about in amazement. They could see that some of the women, many of whom wore sleeveless or cap-sleeved gowns, had thick, dark hair growing under their arms. For the girl, that would be her outstanding memory from the command performance. That was the norm for southern European women, Barbara told her the next day as they shopped for mementos in Monte Carlo. Southern Europeans thought it sexy for women to have underarm hair and unshaved legs. Barbara had known that and yet had been fascinated to observe it for herself. The two shopped together in Paris, too. And then Barbara and her stepdaughter were on their own as the other three returned home at the end of two weeks. But Barbara had not been able to bear the thought of leaving Europe until she had seen more of the cities about which she had read. Both Barbara and Melodye were quite aware that Nick was trusting his daughter to be his pretty young wife's companion-sentry.

They spent two marvelous days at the Louvre, and then moved on to Rome, Venice, Capistrano, Sorrento, Pompeii, and to Naples where Barbara happened to meet one of her father's old friends—"Lucky" Luciano, long since deported from the United States because of his Mafia activities. There he was, sitting at a small table in a piazza, using his influence as a good citizen to distract a street urchin away from a tourist's automobile where the boy had begun to detach one of the hubcaps. He would buy ice cream, Luciano promised, if the boy would leave the car alone. "Hello, Uncle Charlie," Barbara said in greeting as she and Melodye approached the man and the boy, both sitting at the table now. Luciano looked up, surprised to discover that the beautiful American woman was the renter of the car whose hubcaps he had protected. But Luciano's exuberance at meeting Hymie Caplin's precious "Babsie" faded quickly as he asked about her mother, about Hymie, and about her older brother. Dead. All dead years ago, he was told. The young boy looked in awe from the American tourists to the lined face of the man everyone knew had been a "big gun" in the Mafia, surprised to see that lined face, usually expressionless, mirroring sadness at the words of the pretty American woman.

Soon after they left Naples, Barbara and Melodye boarded the *Ile de France* for the trip home. When they disembarked in New York, they discovered that their trunks had been lost. Barbara tried to soothe her tearful stepdaughter. "Maybe they'll be able to recover the trunks," she said. "Anyway, we'll go shopping again soon, in New York," she promised. The girl knew she could trust Barbara to keep her promises. Her stepmother was the only one she could really trust. The only one.

For Maggie and Bob O'Shea, the European trip seemed to have been just a lull in a series of arguments that now grew more threatening. The detective agency was losing money and the partner had abandoned the business. It was clear that Maggie was stuck for the money she had invested—not only for O'Shea but even for his partner. Even more important than the money, there was little companionship between husband and wife. O'Shea was not at home much of the time. While Maggie rehearsed for the summer theater production of *Bells Are Ringing* at the Carousel Theater in Framingham, Massachusetts, she reluctantly considered initiating divorce action. In August 1959, less than a year after the long-anticipated wedding, Nick Condos admitted to reporters that his client, Martha Raye, was ready to shed her husband.

One month after this admission hit the newspapers, Maggie appeared again, as she did intermittently, on *The Steve Allen Show*. She enjoyed performing with regulars Don Knotts, Louis Nye, Johnny Carson, Andy Griffith, Gabriel Dell, and Pat Harrington Jr.— all of whom knew that her marriage was in trouble. In *More Funny People*, Allen would write that "a large part of the explanation for Martha's personal difficulties as an adult is that, because she started entertaining so young, it was never possible for her to have a normal childhood. Childhood is the time during which we learn to be mature, responsible adults." He added, "Because she had no early training or preparation for the roles of wife or mother, it can hardly be surprising that she had difficulty performing them. What seemed most important to Martha was the expression of her gifts." The expression of her gifts was never easier for Maggie than when she appeared on Allen's show. She felt a true bond with Steve because each had performed in vaudeville as children. She also felt a great respect for his many talents.

Even before Maggie filed for divorce, O'Shea quickly took legal action for a separation that would award his wife's plush home and furnishings to him. Again, he claimed that she had promised to give him the house and its contents as a wedding present. At this point, Maggie could no longer conceal the mental anguish she was experiencing. Near collapse from alcohol poisoning (a "kidney ailment," the press was told), she was hospitalized again and forced to withdraw from *Bells Are Ringing*. Her role was handed over to Peggy Cass while Maggie underwent another "dry-out" procedure.

A month after Maggie left the hospital, her father, Pete Reed, died in the Venetian Nursing Home in Miami where he had spent the last ten years. Maggie never had been close to the man she called the "Old Gent," but she had seen to it that his needs were met because she felt some guilt that she had succeeded in show business while her father, the only remaining member of her birth family, had met failure everywhere. Now that he had died of a cerebral thrombosis, she felt saddened, and somehow threatened, by the thought that she was alone in the world except for her friend and personal manager, Nick Condos. And her daughter, of course. But the mother-daughter relationship had always been a strange kind of push-pull link that stretched very thin when Melodye rebelled against what she saw as arbitrary controls; that stretched to the near-breaking point when the girl exhibited her superiority in reading and math. But Nick remained as loyal and supportive to Maggie as any ex-husband or manager possibly could be, even though he was married to Barbara. True, Nick became furious at her sometimes, but that was usually because of something foolish that she had done.

Maggie acknowledged that she had made many foolish mistakes. The affair with O'Shea had likely been her biggest mistake, an embarrassing mishap that had ripped apart her pride and further damaged her public image, as Nick had pointed out. And now O'Shea wanted her home and furniture. O'Shea's attempt to claim the Raye home and furnishings was countered, however, by the argument given by Maggie's lawyer. A 1938 state law prohibited breach-of-promise suits in New York, the attorney pointed out. The judge agreed with the Raye lawyer, and O'Shea's claim was declared illegal.

Soon after this court decision, O'Shea went into the armed forces and Maggie toured the country. O'Shea filed a suit against her for separation and for $21,000 in services, including bodyguard and secretarial duties. Shortly before she learned that he was scheduled to be sent to Germany, she was informed that someone had gone into her Long Island home and removed its contents, including the carpeting and a chandelier. Strips of wallpaper were pulled from the walls. Tiles had been lifted up from the floor. Maggie was sickened by the destruction. From the Beverly Hills Country Club near Cincinnati where Maggie was performing, she announced to a reporter that she was tired of paying O'Shea's ex-wife's alimony and of paying "for his many extravagances." "I can no longer afford him," she said. And she was suing him, she told the reporter, for the contents of her home, "which he raided." It was not the kind of publicity she wanted, but she felt she could no longer allow O'Shea to take advantage of her.

By this time, Barbara was considering leaving her husband, whom she had foolishly thought she could "tame." She loved "the Greek." She admitted that. But he continued to drink heavily even though the excessive drinking had begun to trigger epileptic seizures. His doctor had prescribed Dilantin, twice daily, as a preventive medication. "Guess I forgot to take my medicine," Nick would say after he recovered from a seizure. Not that he remembered the attack. Hell, no. But Barbara would tell him about it and he got the picture. It wasn't pretty. Barbara felt that she could no longer put up with her husband's mad capering about on the window ledge, nor could she put up with the fear that she would arrive home to find him lying on the floor, possibly bleeding to death from striking his head during a seizure. He had already fallen and hit his head on a marble table, cracking the marble and cutting his head so badly that he had been taken for emergency care at the hospital. And still he was careless about taking his medication. If he remembered to take the Dilantin, he often washed it down with a shot of Dewar's or vodka, whichever was handy. Sober, Nick was considerate of his wife. Proud of her. And fun to be with. Above all, he was a generous man. But drunk, he could—and often did—turn vicious.

Maggie had another opportunity to star in a summer theater production of *Bells Are Ringing* in Atlantic City in June 1960. She then appeared in *The Solid Gold Cadillac* at Drury Lane Theater in Chicago. Her daughter completed her junior year at Rhodes High School and was wildly excited to be invited by her uncle, Steve Condos, to come to Las Vegas and sing with the trio in which the former dancer now played trumpet. Barbara helped her select a couple of gowns, with matching shoes, for her appearances at the Riviera Lounge in Vegas. It would be the last time that Barbara would be on hand to help her stepdaughter. Melodye did not know that the woman she had learned to love and trust was leaving New York. Nick was busy coaching Maggie for her summer theater role in *The Solid Gold Cadillac* and arranging for her to appear in *Wildcat*. Thrilled with the anticipation of performing in Las Vegas, Melodye was hardly aware of her stepmother's problems.

When she arrived in Vegas, Melodye, who would not be sixteen until late in July, found that she and the trio were to be the opening act at the Riviera. Buddy Greco headed the bill. Melodye received a warm reception that first night as she and the trio swung into the melodious "Misty," "I'm Old-Fashioned," and "Am I Blue?" Afterwards, Steve Condos assured her that she had done a great job. Each night her confidence grew. Then, after a performance, one of the bosses approached her. They were sorry, he told her, but she could no longer work at the Riviera. The law in Vegas was that performers must be at least sixteen. Her mother had phoned, complaining that her daughter was only fifteen. If they didn't stop her daughter from working in their lounge, Maggie threatened, she would go to the press. In fact, she already had talked to her friend Ralph Pearl, reporter for the *Vegas Sun Times*.

Melodye was very disappointed. She was sure that Timi Yuro was not yet sixteen, but was working at the Tropicana. Still, Steve's trio stayed on at the Riviera while she had to leave because of Maggie's interference. Convinced that Maggie had not acted out of a protective concern for her daughter's youth, the girl must have wondered if having a daughter entering into the entertainment business had made Martha Raye jealous. Had it given the older woman a sense of competition that was unacceptable, coming from her own daughter?

12

Separate Lives

During her stepdaughter's senior year at Rhodes, Barbara left Nick and went out to the West Coast. Even Maggie, who trusted Nick and depended on him for so many things, couldn't blame Barbara for the separation. It was a difficult matter to be married to Nick Condos. Maggie knew that.

Many of the girls in the senior class at Rhodes were already registering for college. But Maggie made it clear that she had no intention of sending her daughter on to Juilliard. Maggie already had built up a wall of resistance to her daughter's every mention of "my education." Why should she contribute to any more of it?

By the time Melodye graduated from Rhodes at age sixteen, Barbara had been granted a legal separation from Nick. The estranged couple agreed to leave the divorce on hold until such time as one or the other wanted to marry someone else. The agreement actually served as a protection for Nick—so that, while on a drunken spree, he could not plunge into another marriage. Barbara promised to keep in touch with her stepdaughter, and the two continued to correspond and to talk by telephone.

Surprisingly, Maggie came up with an idea for her daughter to get a job that summer in the same theater production in which the older woman expected to perform. As Nick arranged for Maggie to play the lead in *Separate Rooms,* he and Maggie also arranged for Melodye to take the part of a newspaper columnist.

In the role of Pamela Barry, a beautiful actress who metamorphosed into a devoted housewife, even Maggie with her keen "ad lib" ability could not breathe energy into the insipid lines of what turned out to be a dreary production. To revitalize the bored audience, Maggie adopted a familiar Jolson technique and gave a half-hour cabaret show as a piano was rolled onto the stage at the end of the three-act play. The cabaret show transformed audience boredom into enthusiasm.

The tour already was giving Melodye a taste of what it was like to perform in summer theater with her mother. Never before had the girl been so nervous onstage as now, when she was interacting with Maggie. For the daughter, it was like walking on eggs.

Wearing moccasins and tight toreador pants that molded her still firm, curvaceous legs, and with a floppy denim shirt "borrowed from Melodye," Maggie talked with a reporter about her daughter after one of the early performances.

"Although her father and I were divorced," Maggie explained, "Melodye has never known the bitterness of a broken home. That's because Nick and I have always been close, cordial friends," she concluded with her marvelous ability to euphemize.

The reporter wrote nothing about euphemisms after the interview with Maggie, but managed to refer to Raye's "outsized mouth." It was the kind of cheap joke that writers of the 1940s and 1950s had relied on for celebrity identification, which, in later years with the arrival of "political correctness," would sink into near-oblivion. But Maggie had long ago become accustomed to frequent references to her "rubber mouth" or "Grand Canyon–sized mouth" and claimed no longer to be sensitive on that subject.

Regardless of the sluggish material in the play, Melodye was thrilled by the chance to perform. She threw herself into her role with an enthusiasm that overcame her nerves and drew hearty applause from the audience, possibly because of her youth. She made it through Cincinnati and Fayetteville and was still drawing extra applause from audiences when Maggie pounced. "How dare you upstage me!" she hissed after they had taken bows at the close of a performance.

It was a repeat of the *Annie Get Your Gun* performances about which Maggie had joked with reporters ten years previously. "But I fixed her. I fired her," Maggie had said in 1952, laughing about her daughter making eyes at the audience. It had been funny then. But it was not funny to Maggie now. The firing was for real, so it was not funny to Melodye, either. This was the end of the tour for her. With a replacement for the columnist, *Separate Rooms* moved on to the next city. "It would be better for you to be on your own," Maggie said.

Nick advised his daughter to go to Glenview, Illinois, to stay with her godparents, Mary and Nick Pilafas, who recently had opened a new restaurant, the Tiffany. Melodye began working days at the restaurant, but since she really wanted to work as a singer, she began looking for a gig at night.

When she found a job singing jazz in a Chicago club called the Nocturne, she was elated. When that gig ended, she found another at Mister Kelly's. But she knew her father was right in saying that finding singing gigs was a chancy affair. So she continued working days in the restaurant.

That fall, the William Morris Agency (with which Maggie still was affiliated) gave her daughter a job in its New York office as a "floating secretary." (It is possible that Nick had used Maggie's association with the agency to procure the job offer; certainly the parents did not oppose it.) Melodye found a small apartment and took pride in her independence. Soon she began taking evening classes at the Actors Studio in Manhattan and at an Uta Hagen workshop.

Maggie was now touring with *Calamity Jane.* She received good press notices until, while feeling fuzzy after several drinks, she failed to appear for a scheduled interview with reporters. If she had not previously realized how harmful it could be to alienate the press, she began to realize it now as critics became increasingly hostile to the "deliberate flubs" and "planned ad libs" they claimed that Maggie incorporated into her lines. These were techniques she had found effective back in the days of Jolson's *Hold On to Your Hats* when occasionally she had forgotten her lines. Now she forgot her lines more often, especially when she had been drinking, at which times she embellished some of the tired "ad libs" that appealed only to the unsophisticated in current audiences.

In early 1962, Maggie was heartened at the offer of a role in Billy Rose's movie *Jumbo*. Playing opposite her old friend Jimmy Durante in the MGM musical starring Doris Day and Stephen Boyd, Maggie took the role of the daring circus girl Lulu. When she was interviewed about her *Jumbo* role, Maggie tossed off a remark that added another twist to the assorted and imaginative tales she told of her early life. Her entertainment career, she said, had begun in the circus where her parents had performed in an acrobatic act.

Always crazy about animals, Maggie loved the female elephant, Jumbo, much more than she loved Doris Day, whom she and Nick had never forgiven for converting their beautiful crystal bar to a milk and soda bar after Doris had bought their Toluca Lake home. Now Doris was having her own problems on the set because she could not cry on demand. The director, Chuck Walters, had to deal not only with assorted animals but with a star who could not spout tears when required. Walters became so upset at Doris when her eyes remained dry that instead of spritzing her with movie tears, he raised his hand and slapped her. The actress started to cry. But they were not appealing tears.

At age forty-five, Maggie energetically attacked her role of Lulu—dancing with a bear, getting shot out of a cannon, and performing other demanding stunts. Her daughter came to visit at Maggie's rented apartment in Malibu while the film was being made, and one evening she brought along a young Oriental fellow, whom she had dated a couple of times. Upset by the appearance of her daughter with the young man, Maggie voiced her objection and slapped her daughter's face. Reacting quickly, Melodye returned the slap and walked out of the apartment.

Later, when Melodye returned, the apartment was empty, but there was an empty Tuinal vial sitting on the kitchen counter. Alarmed, the daughter went next door to her father's apartment. Then Nick and his daughter set out to look for Maggie and her French poodle.

It was not necessary for them to go far. There was Maggie, lying on the beach with her dog, Conkie, curled up beside her. The poodle leaped up as the daughter knelt down beside her mother to feel her pulse beating slowly and slightly irregularly. Nick scooped up Maggie in his arms and hurried to the closest home to call for help.

Minutes later, as the fire rescue squad arrived, Melodye told the paramedics that her mother had overdosed on sleeping pills. Quickly, the paramedics went to work, trying to revive the woman with oxygen. But the oxygen brought on vomiting. Vomit spewed over Melodye's hands and shirt as she tried to help her mother. She then rode to the hospital with her, still confused by her mother's reaction to her Oriental friend. Maggie had never been known to express any racial biases.

At the hospital, Maggie's stomach was pumped. "Exhaustion," the doctor said, refusing to say that it was a suicide attempt. His patient would remain hospitalized for a couple of days, he told reporters. "One of these days, it's really going to happen," Nick Condos predicted, shaking his head. "She'll go too far."

Later, after the hospital psychiatrist had tried to talk with Maggie, he reported back to Nick and his daughter. His efforts to talk with Miss Raye were unsuccessful, he told them. The patient was in denial.

Caught up in her enthusiasm and hopes for a renewed movie career as the filming for *Jumbo* finally was completed, Maggie bought a home in Bel Air, California. She hired a decorator who began to equip the home with modern furnishings and decor. When Jimmy Durante sent her a housewarming gift, an electronic life-sized Santa Claus that would do the twist at the press of a button, Maggie stationed the Santa outside her front door and told friends that she "kept running outside every five minutes to look at him."

Jumbo premiered at Radio City Music hall on December 1, 1962, with accompanying hoopla. In Bosley Crowther's review in the *Times*, Maggie had to search carefully to find positive comments. In the clowning of Raye and Durante, the reviewer wrote, "limited though it is, may be found the few bright and solid nuggets of fun and frolic in the film." He also admitted, "There's a certain graphic glamour and innocent, nostalgic charm in the setting of a small circus, with its rollicking characters, its serenely casual elephant and its modest performing acts." But the movie, he wrote, was being presented ten years after *The Greatest Show on Earth*, "which is far and away superior as a film about circus life."

Nonetheless, Maggie was encouraged by Crowther's positive statements, and she told Hollywood gossip columnist Louella Parsons that Bel Air was going to be her permanent home because she was finished with nightclub appearances. No longer would she have to put up with heckling from drunken patrons or struggle to be heard over the noise of clattering crockery.

Regardless of her statements to Louella Parsons, Maggie, with Nick at her side, was still moving back and forth between her Bel Air home and the New York area. Occasionally, there was news of their daughter—first that she was taking acting classes at the Actors Studio, and later, when Nick and Maggie were staying at the Summit Hotel in New York, that she was seriously ill with peritonitis in Sinai Hospital. Since Maggie was still registered with the William Morris Agency and her daughter was still employed there, it was to be expected that someone from the agency supplied the information to the parents. But neither Nick nor Maggie visited her at the hospital, nor did they phone. Melodye knew that they had been informed of her illness and its gravity, and she felt totally rejected when they did not respond in any way.

Maggie was grateful to be asked to guest on the *Bob Hope Show* in April 1963 with Dean Martin and Lucille Ball. Maybe this was the breakthrough she had hoped for. Perhaps living quietly for a while had finally paid off. Soon afterwards, she was playing the part of Sally Adams in *Call Me Madame* on the Guber-Ford-Gross circuit when her daughter used her connection with the Morris Agency to talk to the manager of a club called the Apartment and received a contract for a two-week singing gig at two hundred a week.

There was a maturity about the eighteen-year-old Melodye that belied her years. Because her flashing dark eyes mirrored an intensity that gave her a commanding presence in front of an audience, she projected confidence when she debuted at the Apartment. Her act was reviewed by Dorothy Kilgallen in *Variety*. "A singer of merit and promise," reported Kilgallen, a popular panelist on television's *What's My Line?* The singer had performed "with conviction and strength," and the reviewer predicted a promising future in the entertainment world after the novice entertainer had more experience and exposure to the public. The two-week contract turned into sixteen weeks of appearances.

By this time, Melodye was steadily dating a saxophone player she had met recently. Ed Lancaster, who was working in a band at the Round Table, seemed to share her goal of making it big in the music entertainment field. Tentatively, they made plans. If he could organize his own band, she could sing with it. They could start out in nightclubs.

While Nick Condos was staying in Manhattan, he had gone to a nightclub where his brother Steve was entertaining. Nick had also met Ed Lancaster, who happened to be working at the same club. When Nick heard that his daughter was planning to marry Lancaster in June, he got in touch with her to voice his protest. He did not like Lancaster, he said emphatically.

Ignoring her father's protests—after all, he hadn't as much as phoned when she was so ill in the hospital—she went ahead with plans for a small wedding. An elopement, really.

The couple drove to Dillon, North Carolina, to get married, but found that city hall was closed in honor of Jefferson Davis's birthday. The wedding was delayed until Monday. Then the couple headed for Secaucus, New Jersey, and spent their wedding night in a hotel located next to a garbage dump. It was not an auspicious beginning for a marriage.

Although *Jumbo* had enjoyed a much heralded premiere at Radio City Music Hall the previous December, the movie had not attracted large audiences. Nor were any motion picture contracts offered to Maggie after *Jumbo* languished on the movie circuit.

Maggie had no patience for waiting another year or two to perform in another movie. She sank back into a depression. "I thought success in show business was the answer to everything," she told columnist Sidney Skolsky. "It isn't. I don't know what is."

It was back to the nightclubs of Las Vegas for Maggie that summer of 1963. Even her precious poodle, Buddy, got her into trouble. A visitor at the Sands Hotel filed a $100,000 damage suit against the entertainer, claiming that Maggie's "vicious gray poodle" had attacked him and bitten him several times on the leg in the hallway of the hotel. It was just another of the many "nuisance" suits in which Maggie had been involved over the years, some of them filed by her. Most of them were dismissed, withdrawn (as were the charges resulting from the Bimini brawl), or settled out of court for much lesser sums.

That fall, Bob Hope again invited Maggie to appear on his show, this time with Andy Griffith and Jane Russell. At the same time, Maggie's daughter was happy to be invited to guest twice on Garry Moore's show. Then she flew to Hollywood near the end of November to appear in two skits on Red Skelton's CBS show. In the first skit, Melodye both sang and danced. In the second skit, she performed with her mother and Skelton.

Perhaps Maggie felt that her daughter's career, which might be successful, was already threatening her own sagging career. Only days after Melodye returned to New York, the telephone rang late at night in the Bel Air home of bandleader Les Baxter. Maggie told him that she had swallowed a handful of sleeping pills. A lot of them; she didn't know how many. By the time Baxter had summoned an ambulance, Maggie had slipped into unconsciousness.

At the hospital, attendants worked with a stomach pump to save the actress's life. And once again, Maggie recovered from an "accidental overdose of sleeping pills," as reported to the press by police who were not notified of the "accident" until almost eight hours after Raye was admitted to the hospital. The nurse in charge "forgot" to notify authorities, reporters were told by a hospital spokesman.

"She has this terrible liver or kidney thing, and normally takes sleeping pills," Les Baxter explained to reporters.

Maggie's daughter soon learned of her mother's latest emergency hospitalization. It seemed to her, as well as to Nick, that almost everyone was busily occupied in making excuses for Maggie's suicidal behavior. By this time, Melodye was having her own problems because of her husband's insistence that she should not contract for any more gigs or out-of-town appearances. He did not want her to work at the agency, either. He was very firm about it. No work, period.

Early in January, Maggie's guest appearances on television began to pick up with her participation in *Hollywood Palace* on ABC. That spring, she appeared again on *The Bob Hope Show* with Tony Randall, Groucho Marx, and Jack Jones. Soon afterwards, she learned that her daughter was expecting a baby.

While Melodye was in the early stages of pregnancy, Gene Kelly got in touch with her about the possibility of doing a film for Universal. The film would star Sandra Dee as a ditzy blonde, he told her. There was another role. Would she like to try out for it?

Her husband had firm objections. He was determined that she should forget about the audition. She was expecting a baby and he wanted her to stay at home and take care of their child. What about her own experiences as the neglected child of a mother interested only in a career? Did she want a repeat performance for her own child?

Reluctantly, Melodye deferred to her husband's wishes. She had not yet realized that what her husband really wanted was control. When she finally did realize it, she would file for divorce.

On July 4, 1964, a review of *Monsieur Verdoux* ran in the *New York Times*—seventeen years after the film had been withdrawn from release in this country. The comedy had been part of a series of Chaplin films being shown at the Plaza Theater. Bosley Crowther referred to it as a "superior sardonic comedy . . . an engrossing, wry and paradoxical film" with Chaplin in the role of *Monsieur Verdoux*, supported by a good cast "headed by Martha Raye. Miss Raye, as the most obnoxious and indestructible of the wives, is howlingly funny. You shouldn't miss *Monsieur Verdoux*."

Maggie's grandson was born on January 28, 1965, and Maggie, always attracted to babies, was quite excited. But her son-in-law did not arrive at the hospital to see his wife or the infant until the following day. It was, after all, the story of Melodye's life. But now she had a son and she would be close to him always, she told herself as she brought the child home to their Brooklyn apartment.

Both Maggie and Nick were in New York when it was time for the christening of Nicholas Lawrence Lancaster at the Greek Orthodox Church in Manhattan. Afterwards, Sherman Billingsley threw a christening party at his 21 Club. It was a gala affair, and Joe E. Lewis was among the celebrities at the party. With his big cigar angled in his mouth, the drunken Lewis stuck his head into the bassinet where Nicholas Lawrence had been sleeping peacefully. Rings of smoke encircled the baby's head as Lewis kept puffing while talking loudly and cracking jokes. When the baby continued to sleep, Lewis lost interest.

Maggie and Nick did not lose interest in their grandson, but 1965 would mark the beginning of several years when Maggie would be out of the country a great deal of the time, devoting herself to a patriotic cause that would take priority for as long as she would live.

13

Under Fire

Maggie, grandmother of four-month-old Nicholas, was energetic enough at age forty-eight to fly to Manila in May 1965, accompanied by two musicians, to entertain servicemen there. She knew that Bob Hope had arrived in South Vietnam some months earlier, and his stories of seeing courageous American young men "being baptized in guerrilla warfare" in places with such exotic names as Dong Tam and Pleiku had prodded her to set out on a similar journey. So, after a short stint in Manila, she flew on to South Vietnam.

Like Hope, she entertained at a great number of the military bases, then was practically mobbed by young soldiers, lonesome for home, when she began taking telephone numbers from them—numbers of their parents or sweethearts. She promised to place personal telephone calls to the numbers when she returned to the States, at which time she would pass along the messages these boys wanted to share with those who were dear to them. This was a time-consuming promise that Maggie definitely would keep.

By the time she returned to California from that first trip, Maggie was hooked on Vietnam and the young soldiers toughing it out in the unrelenting heat of the jungles and rice paddies. She made up her mind to go back as soon as possible. In the meantime, though, her Bel Air home was threatened by one of the raging fires that periodically destroyed forests and properties during southern California's dry seasons. This fire blazed out of control at the top of the hill behind the Raye house and worked its way down the hillside as firemen fought to save luxury homes from the flames. When the fire was finally restrained and then reduced to smoke and embers, only the Raye house remained standing near the bottom of that section of the blackened hillside.

As if it had taken a near-disaster to convince Maggie to get rid of the modern furnishings that she never had really liked, she decided to keep only a few things that had been selected by her interior decorator. The wall entertainment unit that held the television set was among the furnishings that would stay. For the rest, Maggie chose to return to the Early American style that she had always favored.

That fall, Bob Hope invited her to guest on his show again, shortly before she was scheduled to leave the country for a second three-month tour of South Vietnam military bases. Five days later, she appeared in an hourlong special hosted by Danny Thomas and featuring Bill Cosby, Tim Conway, Spike Jones Jr., and others. Then she was off to South Vietnam.

On this tour, Maggie soon left the larger bases with their canteens and small comforts and went on to Special Forces camps and to deep-jungle outposts where frequently fewer than a dozen American soldiers might be stationed. She asked for no special accommodations—indeed, there were none—and she went into the bush to relieve herself, as did the few fellows occupying the outpost. The soldiers coming under fire there seized Maggie's imagination in a grip that would motivate her to return and to try to do more—and to return again and again.

When she came home from Vietnam on January 21, 1966, she wore a ring that GIs had given her as a Christmas gift. Beneath the U.S. Special Forces beret that had been presented to her at one of the camps, her blue eyes smoldered when reporters asked for her opinion of antiwar demonstrators whose protests were becoming more vociferous as the war progressed.

She had a message from American soldiers for the demonstrators, she said fiercely. "The guys told me to try to put some sense into those kooks when I got here. They're pretty bitter about it. They feel badly. And I don't blame them."

Maggie was in a "let the chips fall where they may" mood. She was quite aware that regular USO-sponsored personnel were encouraged to refrain from talking politics; that they were warned that they were not sent to Vietnam to make political statements, either in Vietnam or on their return to the United States. But Maggie was not exactly a part of the regular USO-sponsored personnel. She went her own way, actually "thumbing airlifts from remote base to remote base," as Bob Hope later recalled in his book *Five Women I Love*.

Hope would remember, too, encountering Raye at Tan Son Nhut Air Base and noticing her combat boots, ill-fitting fatigues, and the old brimmed hat she wore as protection from the relentless sun. Shaking his head in wonderment, he marveled, "God help the Cong." And when the seemingly indefatigable Raye returned to Los Angeles and Hollywood, she was often seen there, too, dressed in jungle fatigues and combat boots and with her prized green beret at a jaunty angle as she moved about town, saluting smartly whenever she encountered a military officer. Then it was back to nightclubs and some summer theater until her next junket to Vietnam.

Near the end of June, the B'nai B'rith Eddie Cantor Lodge presented Maggie with its Suzie Award because of her treks to Vietnam. It was a sentimental occasion for her in Los Angeles that night, not only because of her dedication to American soldiers but also because of her many happy memories of Eddie Cantor and of the opportunities he had given her to perform on his radio programs. She had worked with Eddie as far back as the 1930s when Cantor hosted the *Chase and Sanborn Hour* and the *Eddie Cantor Pabst Blue Ribbon Show*.

At the close of the awards ceremony, Maggie flew to Las Vegas to perform at the Sahara. But now, even in the nightclub arena where besotted fans wildly applauded her singing and antics, she experienced a curious sense of marking time. It was paradoxical that Maggie, always geared toward her goal of career enhancement, now felt that the real world existed only in the Vietnamese jungles where U.S. troops were shouldering a terrible burden of which most Americans seemed unheeding as they went about their self-absorbed lives.

In October 1966, she was performing in the steaming Mekong Delta when the Vietcong suddenly attacked. As casualties were hauled into the dispensary at Soc Trang, Maggie began working alongside doctors and nurses—helping to carry litters, cleaning wounds, changing bandages, and comforting the wounded. She refused to stop and rest for what turned out to be a seventeen-hour stretch during which the overworked hospital staff struggled to keep up with the needs of battle casualties. At such times, Maggie, reaching the end of her endurance, gulped a speed pill for a recharge of energy when, and if, she found the opportunity. It was one way to keep going.

Not long after her stint at the Soc Trang dispensary, Maggie began moving from one jungle outpost to another, sometimes punching out her songs and gags, if she was lucky, to the accompaniment of a guitar, but at other times performing alone. Then it was a relief when she approached a larger base where she could catch an honest-to-God shower and where there would be some kind of stage with a piano and perhaps a makeshift dressing table where she could use hair curlers and makeup as she prepared to perform with musical accompaniment to hundreds, instead of a handful, of military personnel.

She was preparing to give one of her shows as soon as there was some relief from mortar fire during what she would refer to as the "Battle of Attleboro," when a chopper churned over the tree tops and landed in a small clearing. Open-mouthed with surprise, Maggie recognized the man who leaped from the helicopter and, bending forward, ran out of range of the whirling chopper blades. Nick Condos! Here in the jungle, looking for her.

Only recently, producer David Merrick had offered her the title role in his stage production of *Hello, Dolly!* And she suspected that was why Nick had come to Vietnam. She did not need Nick's prodding to recognize that the role would be a good opportunity for her, because she hadn't done a Broadway show since 1940 when she had appeared in *Hold On to Your Hats* with Al Jolson. Nick soon pocketed the signed contract and headed back to the States. "I signed for *Dolly* under mortar fire, with the Vietcong for witnesses," Maggie would joke to reporters later.

Since her contract with Merrick specified a January 1967 date to begin rehearsals for *Dolly*, Maggie stayed on in Vietnam for another two months. On November 10, she came to Saigon where General Westmoreland, commander of American forces in Vietnam, presented her with a U.S. army certificate of appreciation "for patriotic civilian service."

In late January 1967, Maggie returned to her Bel Air home before flying to Washington D.C. to receive the Distinguished Service Award from the Women's Forum on National Security. Then she came back to Hollywood and to CBS where she rehearsed with Red Skelton and Mickey Rooney for a program that would be televised the first week of March. While she was in Hollywood, she also began rehearsing with Gower Champion, choreographer for *Hello, Dolly!*

The role of Dolly previously had been played on Broadway by Carol Channing and Ginger Rogers, but Maggie had not yet seen either actress's interpretation. When she flew to New York to begin two weeks of frantic rehearsals, she managed to see Ginger Rogers's final New York performance.

Maggie also made time to meet reporter Sheila Graham for lunch at Sardi's West. Enthusiastic about her *Dolly* role, Maggie hoped this assignment would lead to other Broadway roles. She confided to Graham that she "would like to live in New York again." There was, she went on, "something very cold about working in films for someone raised in the theater. In Hollywood, they're so wrapped up in themselves. They don't believe anything exists anywhere else."

Since only a few years ago she had expressed her intention of living permanently in Hollywood, it was obvious that the entertainer was bitter about her rejection by filmmakers. Her preference as to a permanent residence was clearly based on opportunism. But her loyalty to American soldiers in Vietnam was unshakable. She told Graham she would play in *Hello, Dolly!* no longer than six months because she intended to return to Vietnam in October for five or six months.

Once Vietnam was mentioned, Maggie was eager to tell the reporter about the servicemen she referred to as her "family." She told Graham of her recent experience while doing her show on a truck, describing her surprise at suddenly being flung down by a marine who leaped up to the truckbed to save her from sniper fire after two servicemen in the audience were wounded. "Six weeks later that marine was killed," she added somberly.

Regardless of fallout, Maggie had no qualms about voicing her criticism in regard to the filming of the John Wayne movie *The Green Berets*. "How can they do this while it [the war] is still going on?" she demanded to know, pointing out the dangers of revealing any Green Beret secrets but choosing to ignore the considerable cooperation that had been provided by the government to the filmmakers to boost the reputation of the Green Berets.

Graham had a final question for Maggie. Would she ever marry again?

For Maggie, of course, there were as many different answers to questions as there were sides to her personality. Not too long ago, in response to the same question by another reporter, Maggie had admitted that she probably would remarry. "Only cowards give up the search for happiness because they're afraid of getting hurt." Now, she told Graham that she hoped she would never remarry. She said that her one big romance was the love she had "for my family over there," meaning American troops in Vietnam.

On opening night of *Hello, Dolly!* Maggie was a glittering and glamorous Dolly Gallagher Levi in an off-the-shoulder hourglass gown, flashing her firm, shapely legs as she danced across the stage. Later, as she pasted up congratulatory telegrams in her dressing room, she interspersed them with photos of soldiers she had known in Vietnam. Reserving a conspicuous spot on her dressing table for the photo of her grandson, Nicholas, she placed another snapshot next to it—a snapshot of an orphaned teenage Vietnamese girl Maggie had met in a field hospital.

Much of the warmth of Maggie's *Dolly* audiences was generated by their appreciation of the actress's devotion to the American forces in Vietnam. On many nights, groups of servicemen, some newly returned from Vietnam, were in the theater. In her star's dressing room, with fresh flowers on a table and maids and makeup people at her command, Maggie was aware that her accommodations were a world apart from the backstage quarters of the shabby, moldering theaters where the Reed family had often worked in those precarious earlier years when Pete and Peggy had relied on the talents of their children to attract the applause they craved.

Now, in the midst of the pampering given the *Dolly* star, Maggie took the time and trouble to make sure that all her personal house seats were set aside for Vietnam veterans. She left orders with stagehands to see to it that veterans were allowed backstage to visit with her after the shows. Women who informed stagehands that their sons were overseas with the American forces also were invited backstage, where Maggie offered whatever hope and comfort she could to the mothers with whom she felt such empathy. And every time she saw a television report of antiwar demonstrators in the United States, she raged against the protesters. "An illiterate minority," she called them. "Even if you don't believe in the war, instead of degrading your country, back up the men over there."

Since she had given her first performance as Dolly after only two weeks of rehearsal, Maggie had been very worried about forgetting her lines on opening night. But the nervousness was only temporary. Her audiences remained enthusiastic, and reviewers were complimentary for the most part. A mixed review by *New York Times* theater critic Dan Sullivan complimented Raye by stating that she lent a sense of pathos to her role of Dolly. The reviewer wrote: "Someday someone is going to write a great role for Martha Raye. Just as Miss Raye's face at times suggests a haunting combination of the Greek masks of comedy and tragedy, so her force, as a performer, stems as much from her sense of pathos as from her rowdy, slapstick sense of fun." Sullivan added that there was "piteousness in her plea [new to the show] when her Dolly Gallagher Levi character is summoning up the ghost of her late husband to ask his permission to marry again." He complimented her "Hello, Dolly" number in act two and pointed out that she had "something special going for her—the admiration of her audience for her stints in Vietnam." He felt that the audience was welcoming Raye herself back to New York and that there was "a warmth between the actress and the audience."

Despite Sullivan's compliments, his negative comments needled Maggie. He charged that she and Dolly had nothing in common.

"Dolly—the lady. Martha—the hoyden. Martha with the elbow in the side; Dolly with the iron hand in the velvet glove." Sullivan noted, "Martha scurries where Dolly would glide, jabbers where Dolly would elocute, mugs where Dolly would sweetly smile." He concluded that "Martha belongs on Broadway, but in a different kind of show than *Hello, Dolly!*"

Nick and other friends consoled Maggie by pointing out that critics had to find something to criticize. Her full, resonant voice overwhelmed Channing's baby-squawk and Rogers's tiny voice, they told her. And they reminded her that Sullivan had complimented her sense of pathos—the sense of pathos which had motivated Charlie Chaplin to select her for the lead female role in his art movie, *Monsieur Verdoux*. This was the kind of reinforcement that Maggie needed in her incessant craving to know that she excelled. And Nick was there to supply those needs, aware that her self-esteem rose or fell with his and others' approval or disapproval.

Maggie swept onto the stage with confidence the next night. She sang "If You Ain't Got Elegance, You Can Never Carry It Off" with the self-assurance she felt only onstage where she could assume the persona of a character far removed from that of little, uneducated Margie Reed. Still, she freely admitted to reporters that she was basically a clown. "Clowns are singular," she said. "To be a clown is a gift. There are no schools for clowns. Take Chaplin, Keaton, W. C. Fields. Do you think any one of them minded making fun of himself?"

Letters began arriving daily from servicemen in Vietnam, wishing her luck in the musical. The letters were a poignant reminder to the entertainer of what she considered of utmost importance: Vietnam and the American soldiers slogging their weary way through the jungles of that torrid country of the monsoons.

When twenty members of the 173d Airborne Brigade came to St. James Theater, Maggie held a reunion with them after her performance. On every possible occasion, she continued to refer to the fighting men in Vietnam as her "family." In Vietnam, she claimed, "There are no boys—only men. The boys arrive, and two days later they are grown up. Instant maturity."

In recognition of her dedication to American soldiers in Vietnam, honors and awards accrued to Maggie during the months she continued to perform in *Hello, Dolly!* A plaque presented by the American Legion. The Silver Helmet special award given by the American Veterans of Foreign Wars. Her selection to serve as honorary reviewing officer for the VFW parade in New York in April. The Franklin D. Roosevelt Humanitarian Award given by Brooklyn's Midwood High School after Maggie was selected for the honor in preference to Senator Robert Kennedy and U Thant of the United Nations.

In the middle of May 1967, Maggie gave a special performance of *Hello, Dolly!* at St. James Theater, at which time she received the Woman of the Year Award from New York City's USO. Afterwards, Maggie attended a glitzy supper-dance at the Rainbow Room of the RCA building where Merv Griffin served as master of ceremonies. Joan Crawford, Helen Hayes, Mary Martin, and Ed Sullivan were honorary chairpersons for the event, the proceeds from which would be donated to provide program services at the USO's 165 global centers, including those in Vietnam.

As much as she enjoyed all the accolades, Maggie already had plans for her return to Vietnam, where she hoped to take an abridged version of *Hello, Dolly!* In early June, it was announced that Betty Grable would replace Maggie in the Broadway *Hello, Dolly!* "Miss Raye," the show's spokesman said, "is tired and in need of a rest."

A three-month rest could have been just what the doctor ordered for the entertainer. Certainly there would be no rest for her when she took her *Dolly* troupe to South Vietnam. In the meantime, Maggie did some guest shots, appearing on *The Jerry Lewis Show* and then, along with dancer Juliet Prowse, on *The Carol Burnett Show* in September. "Three Stars Demonstrate That Their Legs Are Something to Sing About," *TV Guide* boasted of the trio's appearance, with a photo of the three, each wearing black fishnet stockings and displaying the neat turn of their ankles while giving "thanks to their shanks."

After her abbreviated *Hello, Dolly!* production was approved by President Johnson, General Westmoreland, and David Merrick in September 1967, Maggie and her cast left for Vietnam. In early

October, two hundred American soldiers, sitting outdoors at Camp Davis near Saigon, watched the first performance. The weather was hot and humid, the sun merciless as Maggie launched into one of her strenuous dance numbers. When she collapsed onstage, a medic rushed to her side. Maggie managed a weak smile. "Don't worry, honey," she mumbled. "I've had worse hangovers." It was typical Maggie bravado. She was taken to Saigon Hospital and treated for heat exhaustion.

Two days later, Maggie was back with her troupe, ready to continue the tour. By the end of November, the troupe had traveled to various camps and bases, giving its ninety-minute performance. But Maggie still was committed to visiting remote outposts where most celebrities never went. It was not surprising, then, that as she returned from an area north of Saigon, she decided to make an unscheduled stop at a mountain outpost at the peak of what was dubbed, by American forces, the Mountain of the Black Widow not far from the Cambodian border.

If the name of the jagged mountain, looming more than three thousand feet, was forbidding, so, too, was the fact that the lower areas of the Black Widow were controlled by the Vietcong. Dwight Whitney of the *New York Times* reported that a most unusual arrangement existed with the Vietcong, who allowed South Vietnamese porters, after payment of protection money, to haul water containers from the mountain base up the dangerous slopes to the American Special Forces and radio-relay operators stationed at the mountain peak. Since Maggie and two other members of her troupe could gain access to the American outpost only by helicopter, they clambered aboard an available aircraft and were soon lifted to heights that they had never before experienced in a chopper.

Maggie was already at work, entertaining the Americans, when Vietcong mortar shells began exploding in and around the mountaintop campsite. The *Dolly* audience ran for their guns while radio operators relayed an emergency call for help in rescuing "some VIPs."

First Lieutenant Gerhard Weis and Warrant Officer Richard Bashline responded to the call as they were returning in their large helicopter from flying troops into combat. The only way they could have known that the American entertainer was stranded at the camp would have been if they had recognized the call-name "Mike Romeo," used by radio operators to identify Martha Raye.

No casualties were reported among the Americans who manned the outpost, but Maggie later claimed that she had a piece of shrapnel in her foot when she and two other performers boarded the troopship helicopter and flew five miles to another Special Forces camp, Tayninh East. Maggie also said that at Tayninh East a medic removed the shrapnel from her foot. She herself set the bone, she added. "Set it wrong," she told a reporter. "But I can't tell the boys. They'll never trust me again."

On her return from the tour, she was invited to Valley Forge, Pennsylvania, to receive the National Service Medal given by the Freedom Foundation "for her light-hearted entertainment, giving cheer to lonely patriots far from home." The only previous recipient of this award had been Bob Hope. Maggie and Bob were still crossing paths, both in Vietnam and in the States.

There were other awards, too, before she went back to Vietnam in October 1968. The first was the USO Board of Governors' Special Award for Gallantry, presented for her repeated tours of Vietnam under the USO banner "in the face of gunfire and personal danger in 'the show must go on' tradition." The second was P. T. Barnum's "The Circus Honored Saints and Sinners Award" accompanied by the presentation of $3,000 to the USO in Maggie's name.

Only two weeks before the entertainer had gone back to Vietnam in October, Maggie's daughter, recently divorced, had arrived at the Bel Air home with her son. Mother and daughter agreed that Melodye would stay at her mother's home, along with Nick, who had been living there for the past three years, while Maggie was touring Vietnam. This could have been a convenient arrangement for all of them. For the couple of weeks that Maggie remained at home, she seemed to enjoy the opportunity to get reacquainted with her grandson. Then, adding to the sense of "togetherness," Maggie invited her daughter to appear with her on Joey Bishop's show, where Melodye sang "Feelin' Groovy."

Not too long after Maggie's departure for Vietnam, her daughter began to shop for cases of chocolate-covered cherries, dried apricots, and cans of tuna and Dinty Moore beef stew to send overseas in time for the Christmas holidays. Maggie had been spending each Christmas in Vietnam with servicemen, and she liked to have goodies to distribute during the holiday season. But her daughter already had made up her mind that, on her mother's return, she would leave the Bel Air home. It was the only way, she suspected, that she and her mother would be able to get along; she knew that too much togetherness had always been, and still would be, fatal to their relationship.

14

Colonel Maggie

Returning home in February 1969, Maggie was surprised when her daughter left the house quickly, taking her son with her and saying only that they were going to San Francisco. Her daughter, she knew, was getting very little, if any, financial support from her ex-husband. But Maggie had many other things with which to occupy herself, including a quick invitation from Bob Hope to appear on his television show with Bing Crosby, George Burns, and Diana Ross and the Supremes. Then there was her work as national vice president for the POW-MIA organization awaiting her attention on the home front.

Soon afterwards, the evening of April 15, 1969, turned out to be a thrilling occasion for Maggie when she took her place among her peers—Frank Sinatra, Burt Lancaster, Ingrid Bergman (long since forgiven for adulterous behavior), Natalie Wood, Diahann Carroll, Sidney Poitier, Rosalind Russell, Don Rickles, Tony Curtis, Walter Matthau—at the glittering forty-first awards presentation by the Academy of Motion Picture Arts and Sciences. Jane Fonda, certainly no favorite of Maggie's, happened to be among the celebrities presenting awards. Although Maggie rarely spoke ill of other entertainers in public, she had never hesitated to speak out when reporters asked for her opinion of Fonda. "I feel very sorry for this person," Maggie told one reporter that evening, "because she was born American. She's not any more uninformed than she wants to be . . . yet she's very intelligent and a good actress. But she's a lousy American."

Just as frequently, Maggie was asked about her many divorces and ex-husbands. Her reply to writer Dora Albert was typical of the tolerant responses she had schooled herself to give on this subject. "It takes two to tangle. It can't be just one person's fault." This self-deprecatory tone helped to disarm the questioners.

Tonight, though, as a crowd of people estimated at three thousand gathered in front of the Dorothy Chandler Pavilion of Los Angeles County Music Center, and with a television audience estimated at 60 million, Maggie watched as Katherine Hepburn and Barbra Streisand (the latter wearing a daring black see-through pantsuit) received two gold-plated Oscars for the first dual award ever given in the Best Actress category.

Maggie's own moment in the spotlight came when Bob Hope presented her with the Jean Hersholt Humanitarian Award for her "devoted and often dangerous work in entertaining troops in combat areas almost continuously since World War II."

In June, Maggie appeared on the television show *Here Come the Stars*, as the guest of honor to be "roasted" in the testimonial production hosted by George Jessel. But for most of the summer, she played at summer theaters in the musical *Hello, Sucker*, the story of Texas Guinan's life in the 1920s.

Maggie took a brief break from the touring circuit on July 18, when she was invited to attend special ceremonies aboard the USS *Massachusetts*, the state's official war memorial. There, "Admiral Martha Raye" was presented with an honorary commission in the Massachusetts Navy for her service to American troops in World War II, in Korea, and in Vietnam. Then, when she wanted to return to Vietnam in the fall of 1969, she simply canceled a well-paying engagement in Las Vegas and boarded a plane headed for Saigon.

Nick complained, "If the war keeps up much longer, we'll both be broke." His deeper concerns, his worries about Maggie's safety, remained unspoken—at least to reporters. But he could not have helped wondering why Maggie was not content to stick with a group of USO entertainers in relative safety when she was in Vietnam. Instead, she remained in the war-torn country for months after a USO group would have departed, making her usual treks to outpost Special Forces camps where there was imminent danger of attack by the Vietcong. She had only recently been presented with General Westmoreland's Special Award for Nursing, which Maggie, who often had boasted of being a registered nurse, had proudly accepted. Actually, she was neither a registered nor a practical nurse, although this lack of certification hardly diminished the devoted service she had given to the wounded of both World War II and the Vietnam conflict.

Even Nick, who knew her best, could not fully explain the depth of devotion that Maggie felt and displayed for the troops in Vietnam. He knew, though, that she was not doing it for acclaim. She loved these soldiers with the purest kind of love, a blend of admiration with the sacrificial maternal love of a kind she had never before experienced, except for her love for the men in World War II. But her strong attachment to the boys in Vietnam had still another facet to it, a protective loyalty rising from her resentment of the treatment thrust upon veterans returning to their own country and being reviled and spat upon by protesters. For the rest, most Americans seemed apathetic toward the war. Maggie resented the apathy almost as much as she hated the protesters.

There was no selfishness involved on Maggie's part, no sense of furthering her own career through the publicity engendered by her role in Vietnam. For Maggie, it was not a role at all but a thorough immersion of self on behalf of a greater cause, totally apart from any role she had ever played—actress, singer, wife, or mother.

Had she not done enough now? Nick asked. For Maggie, it was not enough. In her devotion to the brave men in the outpost camps, she had taken extreme measures by undergoing paratrooper training and making five qualified parachute jumps in her determination to be a very real part of the Green Berets. But she was careful, she told Nick, careful to wear her St. Christopher medal day and night. After all, she knew that no part of South Vietnam was safe from the treachery of Vietcong sympathizers. Poisoned bamboo traps were set up by Vietnamese boys, the same smiling children who may have thanked American soldiers for chocolate bars the previous day.

Always, she carried a supply of St. Christopher medals and

mezuzahs and distributed them in the Special Forces camps. Many of the men wore the medals constantly, along with their dogtags. And if an encampment of Green Berets happened to get word ahead of time that Maggie was on her way to their outpost, the men made a special effort to have a supply of 100-proof vodka, their visitor's preferred drink, on hand.

The nine Green Berets who occupied Special Forces Camp A-322 at Katum near the Cambodian border had managed to get hold of a fifth of 100-proof vodka just before she arrived there during the monsoon season of 1969. Years later, First Lieutenant Mike Zielinski would recall that Camp A-322 was "the pits, even for Vietnam." Mortar attacks were so numerous in the area that "the complex was built two-thirds underground," and the rooms, or "hootches," had little ventilation and were stifling. Roaches "the size of a pack of chewing gum" and poisonous millipedes inhabited the hootches, along with giant rats. Nonetheless, Maggie arrived in a two-seater plane, to the accompaniment of an enemy mortar barrage, "holding two cartons of Newports in one hand and her own bottle of 100-proof vodka in the other."

There was little or no sleep for anyone at Camp A-322 that night, which was just as well, since the visiting "lieutenant colonel" had no overnight bag. In fact, she brought nothing but the vodka and cigarettes with her, Zielinski now remembers. She must have had a lipstick tucked away in her pocket, though, since Zielinski says that "her famous mouth was heavily lipsticked, which had started to smear in the tropical heat and humidity."

He also recalls that she looked old for her age. She was fifty-three, and what woman wouldn't look beat with no makeup kit and under such conditions? If she had been in her own milieu—onstage or in the television studio—and wearing her black fishnet stockings, the Green Beret and his pals might have thought she looked young for her age. But now the jungles of Vietnam were her milieu, by her own choice, and the guys at Camp A-322 clustered around as if she were Marilyn Monroe while she entertained them with jokes and songs and told them the latest Hollywood gossip. At the same time, she chain-smoked, swigged down vodka, and used the same cusswords the men used. Most of all, though, they talked about 'Nam and "the whole stinking mess"—all of them impassioned and none more so than Maggie as, in turn, she listened carefully to their opinions. She also listened to their expressions of disillusionment at America's loss of interest in, if not actual opposition to, the soldiers who had carried the burden of duty to their country into the dangerous jungles and rice paddies of South Vietnam.

And here was Honorary Lieutenant Colonel Maggie, showing them how much she cared by her lively presence and entertainment, by her daring and courage, by the hands-on nursing care they knew she had given to the wounded, and by her tears, falling on the faces of the dying.

The American troops loved her then, in South Vietnam. And those who survived would honor and revere her years later, in their own country, as their Florence Nightingale. Even their Joan of Arc.

On Maggie's return home, she brought letters with her, letters written by her "boys" in lonely jungle outposts which she had promised to hand-deliver to their families. Then came the opportunity for her to take part in two motion pictures. One was *Pufnstuf*, a fantasy in which she played a witch, with Billie Hayes and Jack Wild starring in the Universal picture. Then she worked with Joan Blondell and Michael Ansara in *The Phynx*, a Warner Brothers production.

Unfortunately, both pictures turned out to be shoddy affairs that did nothing to attract other offers from producers. Although Maggie insisted that a career was second in importance to Vietnam for her, she was disappointed to the point of melancholy when the movies failed.

Still, television producers Sid and Marty Kroft offered Maggie a boost to her career when Nick okayed a contract for her to have a role in *The Bugaloos*, a children's series that would be televised on Saturday mornings. Maggie would play Benita Bizarre, a witch who lived in a jukebox, wore a turkey feather boa, and constantly battled a British rock group. After Maggie finished taping the first *Bugaloos* episodes (which she termed "high camp"), she prepared to leave for her eighth tour in Vietnam.

First, though, Bob Hope gave her another opportunity to guest on his show, set up to poke fun at the women's lib movement. He had an all-star cast of comediennes including Ruth Buzzi, Imogene Coca, Phyllis Diller, Edie Adams, and Zsa Zsa Gabor. The show was so successful that Hope would arrange for a follow-up program in September 1971, with most of the same cast and the addition of Dr. Joyce Brothers. In the follow-up, Hope would play the role of an astronaut zooming onto a planet occupied by man-hating females.

Maggie admired Bob Hope, not only for the frequent opportunities he gave her to guest on his long-running television show but also for the time and energy he had spent bringing entertainment to American troops in South Vietnam. She was aware, too, that because she was a woman and because of the nursing chores she performed, it was easier for her to get close to the Americans fighting in Vietnam. But for a man whose legend was as massive as was Hope's and who traveled with an extensive entourage, there was an invisible barrier, as much as he was admired by the troops, that was difficult for him to vault, in Maggie's opinion. "It's breaking his heart," she confided to reporters.

In between the two shows with Hope, Maggie prepared to leave for Vietnam. "I'm planning to stay for five months," she told reporters. And in response to their questions about injuries she had received, she told them she had suffered five broken ribs when her Jeep had been overturned by terrorists. "But I've had worse hangovers," she said, cracking the same joke she had used many times. It was still good for a laugh. And what about the two Purple Hearts she had received? "One was for the rib injury; the other for being wounded by shrapnel," she replied jauntily. Purple Hearts? Neither Nick nor his daughter knew anything about the Purple Hearts.

Melodye had held a variety of jobs in the nearly two years that she had spent in San Francisco, working at more than one job at a time to support herself and her son. Since getting into the entertainment business was what the young woman really yearned to do, she began singing and entertaining at night, moving from one club to another until she was finally hired by Cal Tjader to sing with his Quintet at El Matador. She sang with the Quintet for nearly two years and enrolled her son in an Arizona boarding school. True, it was a replay of her own childhood separation from her mother, but it was necessary. When her two-year stint with the Quintet ended, she decided to move back to North Hollywood and live with a former girlfriend who was willing to share her apartment.

As soon as possible, she drove to Arizona and picked up her son, then temporarily settled into Maggie's Bel Air home (as a cost-saving measure) when her mother returned to Vietnam.

In Vietnam, Maggie posted her home address and telephone number at each camp (just as she had in previous tours) to encourage veterans to get in touch with her when they returned to California. But on her return to the States this time, Maggie had problems of her own that needed immediate attention.

Her badly neglected teeth had given her pain that vodka and pills could scarcely numb. "The condition of your teeth is very poor," the dentist said. "They'll have to be pulled." Anything, she decided. Anything to be relieved of the pain. The teeth were removed, and Maggie was fitted with dentures just in time to begin filming more television programs for *The Bugaloos* as the series became a success.

She did not make her usual October flight to Vietnam in 1972. Instead, she began rehearsing the fast tap dance she would be doing in *No, No, Nanette* when, in November, she would take over Patsy Kelly's part as the doleful maid. Ruby Keeler was also leaving *Nanette.* So Maggie's part was expanded to include Ruby's tap routine and a new song, "Don't Turn Your Back on a Bluebird."

Even while Maggie prepared for *No, No, Nanette,* she agreed to do a week's gig near Baltimore at the Painters Mill Music Fair, performing in *Minsky's Burlesque, '72.* In some ways, the gig seemed to Maggie to be a throwback to her early days in vaudeville as, girdled into a green and gold brocaded gown and with a green boa around her shoulders, she followed a topless dance act. Once onstage, though, Maggie quickly took control of the audience as she belted out the song that had made her famous, "Mr. Paganini," then went into her slapstick comedy act. But it was the finale that brought noisy cheers from the audience as Maggie slid into her combat boots to make an impassioned plea for support for the boys still in Vietnam.

"They ask so little and give so much," she told the audience. "The least we can do back home here is to give them the love, the respect, and the dignity that they, our flag, and our country deserve."

Although Nick had shared Maggie's home for the past several years, she continued to shrug off questions about their relationship. While the two were in Maryland, reporters repeatedly asked if they were going to remarry. Maggie shook her head. They were friends, she said. Very good friends who trusted each other and enjoyed each other's companionship.

Maggie even agreed to make personal appearances in stores where she signed autographs for customers as she plugged Painters Mill Music Fair. A vigilant Nick stood by, still agile but aged slightly by a few extra pounds and the silvering of his dark hair. Maggie had put on more weight than Nick, though, since her rigorous years in Vietnam. Still, she looked trim enough in her carefully fitted red tunic and white pants to attract complimentary remarks from most visitors to the store. But Nick sometimes heard remarks that were less than complimentary, remarks regarding how long she had been in show business and whether she had undergone a face-lift.

There had been no face lifts for Maggie, who had suffered the ministrations of doctors, as well as dentists, only when she was too weak or in too much pain to fight back. She smiled her wide smile at the toughest of questions, flashing her white dentures, and continued to make her closing speech of support for American troops in Vietnam.

Nick was pleased when the audience clapped loudly at her final words; he knew how important audience response was to Maggie. Vietnam remained an inflammatory issue, and Maggie was quickly incensed when anyone accused her of being "hawkish" in her attitude.

"I'm neither a hawk nor a dove," she frequently retorted. "Those are two idiot names. I'm not promoting the war. I'm promoting empathy for our fighting men." Her responses were sharper when, invariably, she was asked about Jane Fonda's antiwar activities. "I question her patriotism," Maggie would say, adding that she also questioned the patriotism of the press for publicizing harsh measures taken by U.S. forces against the enemy, while ignoring the atrocities performed by the Vietcong.

Maggie lived her patriotism. Visitors to her Bel Air home were startled when they saw, outside the house, a crudely lettered sign bearing the name "Maggie's Team House." To the uninformed, Maggie explained that "team" referred to Green Beret teams. Inside the home, the walls of her enlarged den were a background for plaques, citations, insignia, and artillery taken from captured Vietcong. The den was also home to a three-and-a-half-foot stuffed monkey named No-Nuts, which in life had been trained to warn a team of Green Berets whenever it sighted the enemy.

Maggie's conversation, no matter with whom she talked, was peppered with army terms. "Chow" for food. "Bunk" for bed. Even "latrine" for powder room. If her friends found it wearying, Maggie was too caught up in her love affair with the military to notice or to care. Even when she was invited out to dinner, she was likely to show up in the Special Forces fatigues and the jaunty beret that she proudly had worn ever since President Johnson named her an honorary lieutenant colonel in the Green Berets. LBJ called her "the first person outside the elite corps [Berets] who may wear their proud symbol." She was probably also the first woman to be given so many other honorary military titles: honorary colonel in the Marine Corps, gunner's mate first class in the 101st Airborne, master sergeant of the infantry, and an honorary U.S. army nurse.

As free and easy as Maggie, wearing her boots and fatigues, appeared to others, however, she remained a woman plagued with insecurities. The insecurities popped up each time she committed herself to some new "show-biz" project, when she was invariably besieged by first-night jitters. Still, once she agreed to take part in a show, it never occurred to her to back out, despite her nerves and fidgets (except for the one time she had cancelled a Las Vegas show to leave for Vietnam). Real troupers simply went ahead with the next job, whether it was good or not. The important thing was to keep working. To keep performing. Not to do so would be a kind of death for an entertainer like Maggie, who had never known or wanted any other kind of life.

Maggie was happy after *No, No, Nanette* opened in New York, but still she plainly showed her bitterness toward Hollywood when she was interviewed by a *New York Times* reporter. She complained that most of the movies she had made had been of the "mindless" type, adding that *Rhythm on the Range* and Chaplin's *Monsieur Verdoux* had been the exceptions. She had treasured the *New York Times* clipping in which critic Bosley Crowther had praised her performance as Annabella Bonheur in Chaplin's movie, terming it "brilliant." But for the rest, she said, she felt she had been "badly used" in motion pictures.

As the holiday season passed, Maggie knew that she would not be returning to Vietnam. A cease-fire, aimed at ending the war, was signed in January 1973. Some prisoners of war returned to the States in early February, and by the end of March, all U.S. ground combat troops were withdrawn from South Vietnam.

In Bob Hope's book *Don't Shoot, It's Only Me*, written with Melville Shavelson, the comedian's feelings about Vietnam, certainly echoed by Honorary Lieutenant Colonel Raye, were poignantly expressed. "Most of the country [the United States] was happy to forget Vietnam," Hope said. "But I'll always remember."

Maggie, too, would always remember. Her gung-ho personal life seemed strangely empty without the expectation of going back to the Special Forces' camps in South Vietnam. She realized now, though, that the honors and awards she already had received for her work in Vietnam had kept her name alive in newspapers and magazines despite her lengthy absences from the States. Although she never had gone to Vietnam with the expectation of furthering her career, she hoped now that her professional life might begin to benefit from the sacrifices she had made.

In February 1973, Maggie took part in a CBS special, *Ed Sullivan Presents the Comedy Years*. When no other television offers followed, she chafed at idleness and put on some more weight. That summer, though, she kept busy playing theaters in Ohio. In September, Nick arranged for an appearance on an upcoming *Merv Griffin Show.* Condos was asked if his daughter also would appear on the show.

"How about it?" Nick asked Melodye. "Would you like to do the *Merv Griffin Show* with your mom?"

Of course she would. There was no doubt about that. It might be just the boost she needed to get some good offers of gigs right here in Los Angeles. But nothing more was said about the show to Melodye after Maggie returned from Ohio. In early October, Maggie appeared on the *Merv Griffin Show,* alone.

Griffin introduced her to the audience as "that great lady of theater, radio, television, and movies," an "electrifying" personality with "a heart as big as her mouth." Wearing a softly flowing caftan, Maggie came on stage and scurried, in typical Raye style, to the guest chair next to Griffin. With her gray hair gently waved and her lips curved into a smile that softened the lines in her face, she made a demure appearance as she discussed some of the highlights of her career.

Admitting to being "a little nervous" when she was asked to sing, she walked to center stage, smiled widely, and belted out a rhythm song with no trace of nervousness. As she finished singing, she tossed the hand microphone into the air and caught it with a confident gesture, knowing that she had done a good job. To Griffin's comment that the lyrics sounded Portuguese, Maggie grinned and admitted she was singing "double-talk." And she had been improvising vocally as only talented singers like Ella Fitzgerald could do.

When Marty Allen, also a guest on the Griffin show, recalled Maggie mixing a cake on top of his head for a previous television act, Maggie laughed so hard that her eyes watered as she confessed that slapstick was her first love. But her favorite movie, she told Griffin, was the classic she had made with Charlie Chaplin years ago, *Monsieur Verdoux.* The film was slated for a reshowing on November 20 at Royce Hall, she told the television audience.

November turned out to be a good month for Maggie. In Hollywood she received an award from Dennis Weaver, president of the Screen Actors Guild, in honor of her thirty years of performing for American troops. Later in the month, Maggie played the role of a jealous plumber's wife on the comedy series *Love, American Style*. Novelist Jacqueline Susann was the object of Maggie's jealousy in the skit.

But guest appearances on television were not occurring as often as the comedienne-actress wished, and she found herself with more free time than she would have liked. She used the time to visit veterans' hospitals, where she began working with amputees. She had become accustomed to doing the grubbiest of nursing chores in Vietnam, and now, with equal fervor, she tried to ease the sufferings of veterans bound to Stryker frames or wheelchairs. "Nursing the military is first with me," she repeated frequently and gamely. But to Nick and her closest friends, she continued to complain of how deeply hurt she was that Hollywood people, especially television producers, seemed to have forgotten all about her. Or, worse yet, they were deliberately ignoring her.

Active in both the POW-MIA movement and in VIVA, the organization formed to assist families of men missing in action, Maggie seized every opportunity to express her opinions about the lack of government effort to obtain more information about American servicemen listed as missing in Vietnam. It was, she claimed, a national disgrace that Vietnam veterans had very little support during the war and little honor following the war. She further stated that she would like to talk to Henry Kissinger about 318 Americans still listed as missing from the Korean War.

If such an unlikely meeting could have taken place, some people were of the opinion that Maggie would have been out of her depth, since she knew almost nothing of history or politics. It's likely, too, that Maggie had never heard of Sojourner Truth, the eloquent speaker for the rights of blacks to vote, but it was Sojourner Truth who said simply, "I can't read, but I can read people." Maggie, too, had an uncanny knack of "reading" people and may have been able to talk more successfully with Kissinger, given the opportunity, than might have been expected.

In the privacy of Maggie's home, Nick heard the same fervent sentiments expressed often. He knew that it would be much wiser for Maggie to confine such opinions to her family and close friends if she wanted opportunities to work in or near the Los Angeles area. But Maggie was Maggie—outspoken, and never more outspoken than when supporting those who had served in Vietnam.

When Maggie got the opportunity to play in *No, No, Nanette* for the San Bernardino Civic Light Opera Company, she was happy to work near her home and pleased by a review that lauded her for doing "what Raye can do splendidly: squeeze a dozen zany gags and grimaces into every available opening."

Because movie roles and television appearances were not forthcoming, Maggie was away from her comfortable home much of the time, usually a good deal farther away than San Bernardino. There was no other choice, she reminded Nick as she left Los Angeles to tour the country in the stage play *Everybody Loves Opal*, performing the starring role of an old junk woman.

It would have been rare for anyone to accuse Maggie of being a temperamental star. But since she was an avid animal lover, she made one demand of the *Opal* director. Maggie wanted someone to go to the local animal shelter each time the show moved on to another town. The selected person was supposed to choose a homeless cat, an animal scheduled to be put to death, to take part in the play. When the show was ready to move on again, the celebrity cat would be in demand for adoption.

Continuing to tour in *Everybody Loves Opal*, Maggie made a special effort to be amiable to reporters. She gamely answered questions that might have upset her in earlier years. Questions about her suicide attempts were the toughest. "That happened a long time ago," she would reply. "It was rather infantile on my part," she would add, saying that she was "very content" with her life now.

The many telephone calls she made to influential former friends and acquaintances in Hollywood, as she desperately searched for work in television, belied her claims of contentment. Only Nick knew the depths of her disappointment as her phone calls and letters to producers went unanswered. "My phone just stopped ringing," Maggie deplored.

Part of the problem, she realized, was the "warmonger" image that ultra-liberal Hollywood had of her. Still, when reporters continued to ask for her opinion of "Hanoi Jane" (as Jane Fonda had been dubbed for her outspoken support of the North Vietnamese), Maggie did not mince words. She thought of herself as being unfairly ostracized—both for her patriotism and for her love of the men who had fought for survival in the jungles of South Vietnam—in much the same way that Charlie Chaplin had been ostracized in an earlier era and then pressured to leave the United States because of his outspoken political views. United Press International reporter Vernon Scott referred to Maggie as "the only Vietnam war casualty in Hollywood, surreptitiously blacklisted as a warmonger for devoting 10 years, off-and-on, to working with medics under fire in the field."

Maggie would not back down when she was asked about Vietnam; she was thoroughly aligned with the veterans who had returned home not to parades but to near-ostracism in some places. But she was less than honest at times in declaring to reporters that she was happy with her work as she toured (usually for six months of the year) with *Everybody Loves Opal*.

There were good reasons, of course, why she had to work, she explained to those who asked. All of her ex-husbands, except for Nick Condos and Neal Lang, "had collected small fortunes" as the divorces took place. "And I'm not getting residuals from my old movies," she told a reporter, not mentioning the money that had been lost to gambling and through lack of personal supervision of her funds. At age fifty-six, she said candidly, she was lucky to be working because in show business there was always someone just as good, or better, who was ready to replace an aging actress.

The thought of retirement was anathema to Maggie. Something better would come along soon so that she would not have to continue on the tiring treadmill of touring the country. She was sure of that.

15

The Big Mouth

While Maggie was having her own problems in acquiring television bookings, she heard that her daughter was entertaining at various clubs in the Los Angeles area—the Rose Tattoo, Papa Choux, the Biltmore Hotel, and then at a Beverly Hills club called Hogan's, while beginning to work for a Beverly Hills literary agency. At the same time, like her mother, Melodye was sending out résumés to television producers. When she had no positive results, she began to suspect, on the basis of rumors and peculiar responses she had received from producers, that her mother was sabotaging her efforts.

Maggie was uptight about her own rejection by producers. When her daughter came to the Bel Air house and began demanding answers to her suspicions, Maggie, whose self-respect already was being shredded by her own rebuffs from producers, reacted to what she saw as a threat and ordered Melodye to leave the house. "I don't have a daughter anymore!" Maggie shouted.

Maggie's prospects changed, though, when a breakthrough occurred through the efforts of Leonard Stern, head writer on the old *Steve Allen Show.* "Hey, Len, I'm still looking for television work," Maggie invariably reminded Stern when the two met at parties or other Hollywood events.

At this time, Stern was executive producer of the popular television show *McMillan & Wife* starring Rock Hudson and Susan St. James. Stern knew that comedienne Nancy Walker was planning to leave *McMillan & Wife* to take the part of Valerie Harper's mother on *Rhoda*. How about writing in a comedy role for Martha Raye in the two-hour *McMillan & Wife NBC Mystery Movie* that was to be filmed? he asked his staff. If Stern's intention was to make Maggie a permanent part of the television show, he did not mention it. He was well aware that others were voicing doubts about Maggie's ability to remember her lines after so many years away from Hollywood. Maggie was not so young anymore, they reasoned. Would she be physically and mentally able to handle the part?

When she finally received Stern's offer, she was elated. Happily, she pointed out to Nick that there could possibly be a continuing role for her in the series if she did well as the comical housekeeper Agatha Thornton in the movie. With great patience, Nick read and reread the script to her at home until Maggie had her lines memorized so well that she felt confident as she made her first appearance on the set, where she exerted every effort to make friends with the other cast members.

The movie, *Greed*, aired in February 1976. Maggie's performance was so good that she became one of several nominees for best supporting actress for a single performance in a drama or comedy series at the Emmy Awards ceremony. There was tough competition from Helen Hayes, Sheree North, Pamela Payton-Wright, and Kathryn Walker, the latter walking off with the award.

Although finishing again as an "also ran," Maggie was thrilled by the expectation that *McMillan & Wife* producers surely would offer her a contract for the upcoming season. As she waited for her telephone to ring, bringing good news, her spirits sagged. Soon her secretary began sending out letters, citing Maggie's recent nomination for television's best supporting actress award and her availability for work.

Once again, Maggie was convinced that Hollywood's most powerful moguls were exercising pressure to make sure that she would never again have steady work in television or motion pictures. She was sure that the blacklisting continued because of only one thing—her outspoken support for Vietnam veterans and veterans' organizations. Just when Nick began to despair of bringing

Maggie out of the cycle of moodiness and depression that possessed her, things began to change once more.

Steve Allen, slated to begin a new weekly television series called *Steve Allen's Laugh-Back* in June 1976, invited Maggie to guest on his opening show along with his wife, Jayne Meadows. Maggie was thrilled to join regulars Don Knotts and Louis Nye on that first show, which was to resurrect excerpts from Allen's old shows of the 1950s and 1960s.

Before long, Maggie received another call from Len Stern. She was invited back for more appearances on *McMillan & Wife,* now known simply as *McMillan* with the departure of Susan St. James. Universal Pictures had given Rock Hudson a $1.6 million contract for the first six episodes of the new show, and had agreed to give him the right to approve casting. Hudson made it clear that he wanted only congenial people in the cast. Remembering how congenially she had worked with Hudson in the movie, Maggie was certain that Stern's invitation to join the cast was largely because of Hudson.

As Nick Condos went into negotiations on Maggie's contract, she received another invitation from Steve Allen to appear on *Laugh-Back* in December. This time, her daughter was included in the invitation.

The sixty-year-old Maggie wore a flowing flowered dress with bat-wing sleeves to the television studio. Allen introduced the unusually quiet, silvery-haired Maggie as an "original comedienne— one of a very few such in the business." When she began to sing "Pennies from Heaven," it was obvious that her voice had not changed and that her sense of rhythm was as strong as ever. Then her face lighted up and she looked years younger as she ripped through "That Old Black Magic" with a fast, strong beat. Nostalgia was "in," and Maggie still could handle the old favorite rhythm numbers.

Next, the cameras followed Melodye to the piano. Although she did not read music well, she had mastered enough chords to accompany herself at the piano while she sang. As she shifted into "I Miss You," a song she had composed in 1971 and that Don Ho subsequently had recorded in Hawaii, the cameras moved back to Maggie who, looking on proudly, wiped tears from her eyes. It was a touching moment, not only for Maggie and her daughter, but for those who realized that the two talented women, who looked so much alike, had experienced troubled times in their relationship. But mother-daughter ties were not easily broken beyond repair; their appearance together on the Steve Allen show had once more threaded together, if not entirely mended, the scarred relationship between them.

Maggie's first appearance on the regular *McMillan* set boosted her confidence when she discovered that Universal Pictures had supplied her with a limousine and a three-room dressing suite. First class all the way, she told Nick, with appreciation for the perks.

As usual, Maggie was ready to go to work. Cast member Shirley Jones, always a perfectionist, was ready to go as well. Rock Hudson appeared to be ready to start, but as they went into rehearsal for the first scene, Hudson began to laugh as Maggie duck-trotted across the room with a cup of coffee for him. His uncontrollable laughter messed up the scene. More rehearsal attempts followed, each broken off by Hudson's laughter at Maggie's every move. At her comical nearsighted stare. At her voice whenever she little-girled her famous "oh, boy" expression. Maggie laughed, too, but she feared that the very ladylike and controlled Shirley Jones, along with other cast members, did not appreciate the delays. Strangely, director Lou Antonio seemed to have a great deal of patience, even though they were on a tight schedule. But Maggie suspected that the director's patience would not last much longer and that it existed only because Rock Hudson was the star and the one who wanted her in the cast. Eventually the scene was filmed, however, and the first episode was approved. A jubilant Maggie would remain with the show for the rest of the 1976-77 season.

In March 1977, she joined Bette Midler, Pearl Bailey, Paul Anka, and Rosemary Clooney on stage at Ambassador College in Pasadena to tape a CBS special honoring Bing Crosby's fiftieth year in show business. Bob Hope took part, as did Debbie Reynolds, Donald O'Connor, and Crosby's wife and children. But as he finished one of his songs, Crosby tripped and fell into the orchestra pit.

Assuming her favorite Florence Nightingale role, Maggie rushed to his side. Then she rode with the seventy-two-year-old entertainer to the hospital. He was treated for cuts and bruises while, apparently unruffled, he hummed some of his favorite songs in the emergency room and made jokes about his fall. Doctors, not quite so cavalier about the accident, decided that Crosby should stay in the hospital for a couple of days.

For Maggie, who claimed she had been at home for the Christmas holidays only twice in twelve years, it seemed to be an enjoyable experience to put up Christmas decorations that year and to wrap gifts and pile them beneath the tree for twelve-year-old Nicholas. It was great fun, too, for Maggie to arrive home from the studio with people she had invited to "come and party," and to kick off her shoes and enjoy a few drinks while surrounded by the conversation and laughter of friends, plus the yapping noises of five little dogs running around underfoot while someone picked out a tune on the grand piano.

Jack Oakie, whom she had known since the 1941 filming of *Navy Blues,* was frequently invited to her home, as were Rock Hudson and his companion, Tom Clarke. Nick was usually on hand, as was Maggie's secretary. Melodye was invited only occasionally. Mother and daughter were again facing the fact that they got along best when they saw each other the least—a strange paradox for Maggie who loved company and movement and anything but being alone with herself. Because being alone meant there was no one on hand to bolster her opinions and give her the complimentary feedback she needed, solitude was frightening to her. At that point, when she could find no one else to come to her home for a visit, she would phone her daughter.

Frequently, Maggie would invite her grandson to go to dinner at one of her favorite restaurants, usually Matteo's, or sometimes they would dine at her home. Melodye would drive her son to the restaurant specified by Maggie or to Maggie's home, and would pick him up later when he telephoned for a ride. Melodye took no offense at this arrangement; she was pleased that Maggie and Nicholas were buddies.

Vietnam veterans still appeared on Maggie's doorstep from time to time, and she was delighted to see them, feed them, spend the evening sharing their experiences in Vietnam, and provide them with beds for the night if they chose to stay. And during the summers, when she went back to touring summer theaters in *Everybody Loves Opal*, Vietnam veterans often showed up in the audience. Afterwards they would come up to shake hands with the woman they respected for her work with medics in Vietnam under fire.

After *McMillan* expired, Maggie had the opportunity to appear in a *Love Boat* episode in 1978, playing opposite Ray Bolger. She wore her silvery hair short and curly now, and her expressive eyebrows looked like horizontal question marks each time she grimaced on the show, which was frequent. She spoke in short, terse snatches of sentences in the Bugs Bunny tone of voice that viewers found amusing.

Maggie enjoyed doing guest shots, but when Universal Pictures offered her the opportunity to play a character role in *The Concorde: Airport '79* (the fourth in a series of *Airport* movies), she was overjoyed to sign up for her first Hollywood movie in ten years. Robert Wagner and Susan Blakely had the lead roles. Maggie played the part of a woman who went back and forth to the ladies' room for most of the flight. "It's almost the story of my life," she told reporters, adding that she empathized with the character "because I have only one kidney myself."

As far as can be determined, Maggie had never lost a kidney. This, too, appeared to be some of the fast-talking entertainer's hype.

In a cryptic *Times* review, Vincent Canby admitted that a great many people, including the reviewer himself, found the airport movies irresistible in a kind of dreadful fascination. The movie is "devoted to the Concorde, the supersonic jetliner developed jointly at great expense by British and French aviation interests while American airline people scoffed," he wrote. "For people who treasure expensive, supremely tacky Hollywood claptrap," he added, the movie "is SHEER JOY! THE FUNNIEST FILM OF THE DECADE." Of course, he pointed out, none of the airplanes in this series of movies could be mortally damaged by anything, however terrifying. "Martha Raye," he wrote, "who plays the movie's comic-old-lady character, gets roughed up when she's caught in the toilet as the Concorde executes a few barrel-rolls and loop-the-loops to avoid the guided missile." He concluded, "The worst is best." But Maggie was hopeful that the popular near-disaster movie would be a stepping stone for her into other movie roles. Until that happened, however, she intended to continue touring in *Everybody Loves Opal* as a bread-and-butter role. And just one week before Christmas, she took part in an NBC two-hour musical-comedy special: a country-western version of Dickens's *Christmas Carol*, with Barbara Mandrell. Maggie took the role of the Ghost of Christmas Past and Hoyt Axton performed as Skinflint.

In 1980, Maggie stopped worrying about "bread-and-butter" roles when Polident offered her a three-year advertising contract at $250,000 a year. Real money, once again, Nick told her. No more financial worries. And all for joining the club of aging celebrities advertising on TV. June Allyson promoting adult diapers. Elizabeth Taylor touting her Passion and, later, White Diamonds perfumes. And soon, George Hamilton hawking the merits of Diamond Mortgage and James Whitmore advertising Miracle-Gro.

Maggie quickly signed the contract. Wearing pearls looped three times around her neck and knotted in the front, she was filmed dropping dentures into a glass containing Polident denture cleanser. Smiling widely to display her own "pearly whites" as a recommendation for the use of Polident, she confided, "I've worn dentures for years. Take it from Martha Raye, the big mouth." When Polident sales zoomed, Maggie knew she was "in" as the company's spokesperson.

There was also a Universal Television movie for Maggie in early 1980 as she played the part of Georgia O'Hanlon in *The Gossip Columnist*. The movie was a star-studded affair with Steve Allen, Jayne Meadows, Jim Backus, Jack Carter, Allen Ludden, and Betty White. Afterwards, Maggie did a *Love Boat* episode with Milton Berle and a guest spot on *Circus of the Stars*.

Nick's brother Steve Condos, who took medication for cardiac problems, stepped proudly back into the limelight when the movie *Tap*—

celebrating the history of tap dancing—was produced in 1981. When Nick visited his brother on the *Tap* set, he was able to renew his forty-year friendships with Gregory Hines, Sammy Davis Jr., Sandman Sims, and Harold Nicholas, who were among the many fast-stepping black hoofers who had great respect for the talents of the Condos Brothers.

Nick, of course, had long ago given up dancing to devote himself to the advancement of Maggie's career. Because of the closeness between Nick and Maggie over the years, rumors still persisted that the two had remarried. Nick was not free to marry anyone, however, until Barbara finally decided to officially divorce him in 1982 because she wanted to marry someone else.

At this time, Nick was involved in working out a contract for Maggie to begin touring the country with *The New 4 Girls*, replacing Rose Marie (of the old *Dick Van Dyke Show*) in a singing group that included Rosemary Clooney, Helen O'Connell, and Kaye Starr.

One night, after a performance, Maggie and Rosemary were drinking in the limousine that was returning them to their hotel when Maggie ordered the driver to pull over to the curb and stop. She then opened the door, pulled up her dress, stuck one leg out of the back seat, and urinated into the street—at least, partly into the street. Years later, Rosemary's nephew, George Clooney, would relate the incident on David Letterman's show.

One of the highlights of *The New 4 Girls* performances was appearing at the JFK Special Warfare Museum/Cumberland County Auditorium at Fort Bragg, North Carolina. Clooney proved to be a real trouper that night as she went onstage to perform while sweating out a 102-degree fever. Since Fort Bragg was home to Special Forces, Green Berets Airborne, the singers' reception there was especially warm because of the presence of "Lieutenant Colonel Maggie."

Maggie was honored in Hollywood that month, too, along with Carol Burnett, who had got her start in the industry many years previously on *The Garry Moore Show* when Maggie—who was slated to guest on the show—was too ill to appear. Burnett had been the replacement. Some years after that, the two had recorded an album:

Martha Raye–Carol Burnett Together for the First Time. Now Raye, Burnett, and Elizabeth Taylor prepared to appear in *Soaps—An American Celebration,* a four-day observance of the fiftieth anniversary of soap operas on radio and television.

Maggie was a fervent fan of daytime dramas when she was at home. And she was pleased to keep her name "out front" by taking part in the anniversary observance because she knew that major advertisers such as Polident liked their celebrity figures to retain their status in the eyes of the American public.

With Nick handling details of still another contract, Maggie began appearing in the popular and long-running television series *Alice,* starring Linda Lavin as a waitress at Mel's Diner. From 1982 to 1984, Maggie appeared several times as Mel's wacky mother, Carrie Sharples.

In early December 1982, Maggie appeared with Debbie Reynolds and Mickey Rooney, as ringmasters, on the CBS two-hour presentation of *Circus of the Stars.* No longer did the entertainer have time to fret about being forgotten or neglected. But she did fret about an interview her daughter gave to a writer, Raymond Strait, in 1983. It was quite possible that the writer checked back with Maggie in regard to the material her daughter had provided. If not, she heard about the interview in some other way, although Strait's manuscript was never published.

"It's ridiculous," Maggie said to reporters, denying that she ever had punished her daughter by cutting off her ponytail or had picked up the Christmas gifts she had given her daughter and taken them back to the store. "Don't bother me with that. That's a lot of junk," Maggie protested. "Never heard anything like that. She's not my daughter. She's the devil's daughter."

Invited to take part in the televised Bob Hope special, *Bob Hope's Road to Hollywood,* Maggie could look back forty-five years to her first association with Hope in *The Big Broadcast of 1938.* Dorothy Lamour and Jane Russell also were among the guest on the television show, which used film clips to salute Hope's long career.

Soon after her sixty-ninth birthday, Maggie agreed to entertain for one month at the Ballroom, a New York cabaret. Fortified with a few drinks, she began her act with a comedy number in which she pretended to play a zither. When she caught her heel in a rung of the stool on which she was perched, she fell awkwardly to the floor but pretended it was just part of the comedy routine. She then repeated this fall nightly. After the comedy bit, she sang ballads in pure, nostalgic Raye style: "Little Girl Blue," "My Funny Valentine," and "I'll Remember April." The cabaret patrons loved it, and a *New York Times* reviewer complimented Raye's "big, vital voice."

She had done this type of singing a long time ago, Maggie reminded reporters. When she had been married to David Rose in the late 1930s, Rose had arranged for her to record popular ballads, including "Body and Soul." And this had earned her some "58 cents in royalties," Maggie pointed out, laughing. But now singing ballads turned out to be a profitable venture.

If taking a stand on controversial issues was risky, careerwise, Maggie appeared to be unconcerned about it when she accepted an invitation to serve as grand marshal of a lesbian parade that wound its way through Hollywood and into West Hollywood. To many people, leading such a parade marked Maggie as a lesbian. Lesbians and gay men were "coming out of the closet" by this time, demanding recognition and their "rights," and because she had so many friends in the gay community, Maggie was sympathetic to their goals.

It seemed paradoxical that Maggie should be so closely aligned with both the military and gays—groups quickly categorized by many to be at opposite ends of the spectrum. But Maggie was concerned only with what she saw as loyalty to people she cared about. It turned out that there was less flack than Nick had expected from her appearance at the head of the gay parade.

Maggie continued making her Polident commercials and was pleased when Nick arranged for her to play the part of the Duchess in the television movie *Alice in Wonderland*. The movie, shown in two-hour segments on CBS in December 1985, was a fun deal and an ego booster for Maggie, who enjoyed being part of a star-studded cast of comedians that included Sid Caesar, Carol Channing,

Imogene Coca, Sammy Davis Jr., Harvey Korman, Steve Allen and Jayne Meadows, and Jonathan Winters.

She then played the part of Miss Hannigan in a revival of the Broadway success *Annie*. Opening in Atlanta in July 1986, the musical began a cross-country tour. When *Annie* played in Los Angeles, the audio was bad in at least one of the performances and Maggie was the only cast member people could hear clearly.

Maggie always had managed to make herself heard. Now, when her tour with *Annie* ended and regardless of her recent complaints about the rigors of being "on the road," she returned to *Everybody Loves Opal* and continued to tour in that oldie with a gusto that defied her age—seventy years.

When she learned that her old friend Rock Hudson was dying of AIDS, she was very depressed. Soon after his death, she appeared with Cleo Laine, Don Scardino, John Herrera, and other celebrities at Manhattan Community College in an evening of music, *Close upon the House*, to benefit the "American Run for the End of AIDS." Then it was back to *Everybody Loves Opal* for Maggie, who clung to the familiar rites of performing onstage, as she grew older, as a panacea for her doubts and fears—all of which lay in the darkness just beyond the footlights. Since the age of three, she had lived with the sounds of applause and curtain calls; in her seventies, she was fearful of releasing her clutch on the erratic pulse of the theater.

She had other anxieties as well, including a great fear of losing Nick. His fast and reckless lifestyle finally had caught up with "the iron man." He could walk only a short distance before becoming short of breath. He suffered from angina. He stopped smoking cigars and drinking Dewar's White Label. And still his condition deteriorated until he required quadruple bypass surgery in 1986.

His daughter spent a great deal of time at the hospital until Nick was sent home to recuperate. Then she watched over him as he spent hours each day, lying on a chaise lounge in direct sunlight as had long been his habit. In previous years, he would lie in the sunlight with his head back and a phone in his hand to carry on his business. Now, as he toasted himself to what he called a "healthy tan," he ignored warnings that too much sun could be damaging. The sun felt wonderful, he insisted.

On March 5, 1987, the host of *Late Night with David Letterman* suddenly joked that he "saw the most terrifying commercial on television last night featuring Martha Raye, actress, condom user."

Neither Maggie nor Nick watched Letterman's show. There were a number of popular comedians whom Maggie disliked, including Lenny Bruce and Steve Martin in addition to Letterman. But Maggie, the perennial "good sport," soon heard about the recent Letterman show and was not amused. She was further incensed when Nick read a report of Letterman's comment from a newspaper. Nick tried to soothe her by suggesting that possibly he could arrange for her to get a television appearance out of the incident, at least. But Maggie was not interested in that. She quickly filed a $10 million slander suit against Letterman and the producers of his show.

The suit charged that Letterman's remarks implied that Raye was "sexually promiscuous," that she had "frequent intercourse or relations with persons infected with or exposed to AIDS," and that she used condoms "in some form of deviant, aberrant or socially unacceptable . . . behavior."

"Ms. Raye, in fact, is not a condom user," the suit stated. But the suit was soon dismissed as a "frivolous action." Entertainers, it seemed, were fair game for kidding, no matter how tasteless, by other entertainers.

By this time, Maggie had more important things to concern her. Nick's failing health was now attributed to cancer of the throat. He gave up his last indulgence, sunbathing, and soon followed his doctor's advice to go into the hospital for an operation. He underwent a full laryngectomy in 1987 and had to learn to speak with the use of two electronic vibrating instruments.

Now working for Viking Entertainment Company, Nick's daughter gave up her job to be with him. It was a difficult time for both her and her mother to see the formerly garrulous, expansive, and cocky Nick Condos looking to his ex-wife and daughter for reassurance as he physically shrank and mentally faded right before their eyes.

Maggie wanted to help with his care, but she was so shaken that it could have been dangerous for her to attempt to put a cleaning tool down his trachea. So Nick's care became largely his daughter's responsibility because Maggie simply could not deal with it, despite the nursing chores she had done in Vietnam and the pain she had suffered to see limbs amputated from those vulnerable young men and to hold them as they died. Nick was just too close to her; she was completely unnerved by the thought of losing him.

In the early summer of 1988, Nick's condition worsened. He became so ill that he had to be taken back to the UCLA Medical Center. He slipped into a coma on June 8 and was still in a coma in early July when Maggie left town to attend a Special Forces convention in Fort Bragg, North Carolina. Nick died on July 8.

Melodye telephoned Maggie at Fort Bragg to break the news, then took care of the immediate details. Maggie arrived home the day before the memorial service, planned by her daughter, took place. Reports circulated that mother and daughter were estranged immediately because Maggie was enraged by Melodye's plans to have her father's body cremated.

In reality, both women had known for quite some time, as had Nick's brother Steve, that Nick wanted to be cremated. But it was typical of Maggie to ignore unpleasant realities. It was also typical for her to feel "second-best" when her daughter, who had taken over Nick's care at Maggie's home, had now planned the memorial service and cremation. Maggie was, in fact, in denial of her own inability to function in the planning and programming area, to ad lib her way in territories completely foreign to her.

Also, Maggie was emotionally distraught over Nick's death and in pain from a fall she had taken in her bathroom at Fort Bragg. She had not gone to a doctor but was sure she had fractured a couple of ribs. And so she had taped them up. There was nothing else that could be done for fractured ribs, she stubbornly insisted.

Maggie's attorney, Shirley Woolf, escorted her to the memorial service and assisted her as she hobbled into a pew apart from the one occupied by Nick's family—his daughter and grandson and brother Steve and his wife. Maggie refused to move when Melodye approached and asked her to join the rest of the family.

Maggie was truly devastated by the death of the man who for many years had been her protector. Her shield. Her rock. But she was not too devastated, it seemed, to have her lawyer draw up a new will immediately following Nick's death—a will which cut off her daughter and her grandson from sharing in her estate and named Woolf as executor, and as recipient of Maggie's Mercedes Benz automobile.

In an earlier will of 1963, Maggie had left her entire estate to Nick until his death when everything remaining would go to her daughter. Twenty-one years later, she drew up another will specifying that 75 percent of her estate should go to her daughter and 25 percent to her grandson. But now neither daughter nor grandson would get anything.

Before Woolf returned to Florida, she hired a woman to take care of Maggie and to make sure that all important mail was sent directly to the lawyer's Florida address. When Melodye called and asked to speak with her mother, she was refused.

When the 1,300-member Friars Club in Manhattan, presided over by Frank Sinatra, had complied with a court edict to admit female members in 1988, Liza Minnelli, Sinatra's pal and costar in stage shows, became the first woman admitted to full membership. Soon after Nick's death, Maggie learned that she and Barbara Sinatra, Lucille Ball, Carol Burnett, Eydie Gorme, Barbra Streisand, Elizabeth Taylor, Dinah Shore, and Phyllis Diller were elected to honorary membership in the prestigious eighty-four-year-old club. But Maggie was listless now over an honor that would have thrilled her only weeks earlier.

She sat for hours, window drapes drawn, watching soap operas and daytime talk shows, a drink often at her side as she sank deeper into depression. She frequently saw her own Polident commercials, still running on television. She was paid very generously for the ads; the checks were sent on to her lawyer by the William Morris Agency.

Realizing now that her entertainment days were nearing an end, or possibly had already ended, Maggie was losing interest in everything except her two little dogs and the dramas that continued to play endlessly on the television screen. But that would change—and soon.

16

Newlyweds

Nick Condos had wanted his assets to go to his daughter at his death. Before he slipped into a coma, he had given her a letter, authorizing her to take possession of the cash that he had placed in the safety deposit box at the bank—a box with three names registered: those of Nick, Maggie, and Melodye. He also told her that, in his bedroom at home, there was a packet of cashier's checks for various amounts, some of which were made out to her, some to both father and daughter and others to both mother and daughter. When Melodye and her son went to the house, shortly before Maggie's return from Fort Bragg, she had opened her father's desk and picked up the packet of cashier's checks.

When she had gone to the bank, on the day after the memorial service, to look inside the safety deposit box, bank employees informed her that her mother and her attorney already had emptied the box and were not renewing the rental.

A trip to the bank that had issued the cashier's checks was equally frustrating. The checks could not be cashed, she was told, but little explanation was offered in answer to her questions. She did learn, though, that bank officials already had spoken with her mother and her "accountant, Miss Woolf."

Because Nick Condos had filed no formal will, the court appointed his daughter as executor while his assets were probated. As executor, it was her obligation, as she saw it, to pursue any possible leads to collect known assets. In her opinion, such assets included commissions from the Polident payments—commissions which she was convinced that her father, as Maggie's personal manager, had not received from his wife's earnings for four years prior to his death.

She hired an attorney to sue the William Morris Agency, to which the Polident checks had been sent and which, in turn, had quite properly taken out its 10 percent fee before sending the remainder of the money on to the Florida attorney. But Melodye claimed to be dismayed to find that the first petition her own lawyer filed in the suit for the Polident commissions also named Maggie as a respondent.

Maggie was furious when she learned, from Woolf, that her daughter was suing her, and the daughter promptly had her mother's name removed from all further papers. Soon, dissatisfied with her own attorney's work, she hired another lawyer to take over the case regarding the Polident commissions and also to file suit against the bank for its refusal to honor the cashier's checks. In the meantime, she made regular phone calls to her mother in attempts to repair their troubled relationship. Even on the telephone, it was clear that Maggie was deeply depressed. When Melodye went to the Bel Air home to check on her condition, Maggie refused to respond to any attempts to rouse her from her apathy.

To make conversation, her daughter had to compete with the constant drone of the television and the blankness of her mother's hazy blue eyes as Maggie stared at the television screen. She muttered protests when her daughter opened windows and found dog poop behind the drapes and in corners. When Melodye spoke louder to get Maggie's attention, she pressed the volume button on the remote control to drown out her daughter's words. At the same time, she gathered her pampered Yorkie, Rocky, and her little Lhasa apso, Weenie Bean, into her lap and murmured babytalk to them, still complaining about the glare of sunlight on the television screen.

"Mom, you can't just sit there and sip vodka all day long," her daughter protested. Not only was the drinking bad for Maggie, but she was neglecting personal hygiene and her diet was poor. She refused to eat what she called "greens" but munched on sweets and fatty foods. Each time Melodye left the house, she was frustrated and her mother was plainly irritated. If the daughter had been a coaxer, instead of an order-giver, she might have accomplished more. But she was not the kind of person to fawn over anyone. She could, and claimed she did, tell her mother that she loved her, but she could not force herself to keep reassuring Maggie that she had been the greatest entertainer of the century.

Some of Maggie's acquaintances flattered her constantly when they visited, reminding her of past triumphs to make her happy. Perhaps that was one reason the former entertainer found herself very lonely these days; people were tired of handing out compliments. On occasion, Maggie resorted to giving money to some acquaintances who consented to visit and talk with her. She even phoned one of her daughter's friends and coaxed her to visit, then insisted on giving her money before she left. When she was alone, Maggie would worry about her current Polident contract expiring in another year or so. Perhaps it would not be renewed. That could end everything.

Maggie found little relief from her loneliness and anxieties. When she staggered and fell in her home, she was in such pain from reinjuring her previously fractured ribs that she had to be taken to the UCLA Medical Center. By the following day, she was in such a state of confusion that her daughter was called to the hospital. As Melodye listened, Dr. Saxena asked Maggie simple questions. "Who's the president?" he asked. "Truman," she replied. It was obvious to the doctors that the patient's eyes were not focusing properly, that she had no concept of time, and that alcoholism was a problem in her life.

Regardless of the confusion that sometimes clouded Maggie's mind, she would be roused to fury each time she was informed by Woolf of the progression of her daughter's legal suit. The eighty-three-year-old judge, Thomas Murphy, had taken it upon himself to blend the two issues (the Polident commission issue and the charge against the bank for failing to honor the cashier's checks) into a single case.

By this time, Maggie was refusing to take any more phone calls, much less visits, from her daughter. When the legal decision finally went against the younger woman, Maggie was further incensed after Melodye filed an appeal in the appellate court.

On January 5, 1990, less than five months after observing her seventy-third birthday and one and a half years after Nick's death, Maggie suffered a stroke and was rushed back to UCLA Medical Center in serious condition. Her daughter hurried to her bedside, bringing a fresh bouquet of flowers from her garden and hoping she would not be rejected. Maggie admired the flowers as Melodye expressed her concern for her ailing mother. There was some relief on both sides when the rift in their rocky relationship was, in part, repaired once more.

Maggie had been taken to UCLA because it was close to her home. But once her condition was stabilized, she was moved to Cedars-Sinai Hospital, where her physician was a resident.

News of the former entertainer's stroke, which left her paralyzed on the left side and caused her mouth to droop, roused an appeal from several veterans' groups asking Congress to help obtain the Medal of Freedom for the ailing Maggie. Bob Hope had received this prestigious medal from President Lyndon Johnson, and it had rankled Maggie's supporters that despite her long service to her country, she had not yet received the coveted trophy.

Two women—Mildred "Noonie" Fortin, an army reserve sergeant from Texas, and Belle Pellegrino, a retired marine from Albany, New York—had been in the forefront of the movement since 1986 with their "Medals for Maggie" campaign. The two were selling Colonel Maggie T-shirts, mailing newsletters to veterans, contacting politicians, and trying to get media coverage for their crusade.

Cardinal John O'Connor, writing in the weekly magazine for the New York archdiocese, joined veterans' groups in petitioning Congress to award the medal to Raye for her outstanding dedication to servicemen during World War II and the Korean and Vietnam Wars. "Raye didn't need the big showcases, the extravaganzas that played at big bases for thousands of troops," the cardinal wrote. "She went into the jungle, into little caves and lean-tos, into the holes dug out of the sides of mountains."

After several weeks, Maggie was released from the hospital when she promised to report for therapy sessions three times weekly and have home nursing care around the clock. But soon therapists' reports indicated that the patient was actively resisting therapy. At other times, Maggie would telephone to give what the therapists called "questionable" excuses for not keeping appointments. The practical nurses who cared for her at home, when questioned by hospital personnel, admitted that the patient often was uncooperative. Sometimes she refused to eat; at other times she would not allow nurses to bathe her.

By the middle of February, Maggie had sunk into a deep depression, developing what one psychiatrist called "significant suicidal ideation." In a session with the psychiatrist, Maggie denied that she had any such "suicidal ideations" in the past. She did admit, however, that she drank about three glasses of vodka a day. Her physical therapist reported that the "three glasses" could be understated and that the patient also was using sedatives.

The doctors agreed that twenty milligrams of Prozac each morning could be helpful, but one of the other two antianxiety medications the patient was taking was discontinued after Maggie experienced an episode of confusion and disorientation. When her medication was adjusted, Raye became more cooperative and less depressed.

Over the Labor Day weekend, Belle and Noonie arrived in Marina, California, for "Colonel Maggie's All Services Airborne Drop-In." There they met the entertainer they so much admired, sitting in a wheelchair attended by two nurses. Afterwards, they went to her Bel Air home where they spent five days reading her the letters they had received from servicemen who described their memories of Colonel Maggie during wartime. "All the way back to World War II," Noonie said later. Maggie laughed and cried at the veterans' stories, astonished at the incidents they remembered.

To date, the women told Maggie, they had forwarded petitions with more than fifteen thousand signatures of servicemen and women to President Bush. And they would send thousands more.

Soon after the departure of her visitors, Maggie received news of the death of Nick's brother Steve. At age seventy-one, Steve had died immediately following his performance as a "tap-dance virtuoso" at the Lyons International Dance Biennial in France. He had received a standing ovation, then walked down the steps and collapsed. "He died with a smile on his face," said his wife, Lorraine, who had accompanied him on the trip. It was reported that the festive spirit of the celebration of American dance, with appearances by seventeen U.S. dance companies, was broken by Steve's death.

His death was a poignant reminder to Maggie of her own mortality. Like Steve Condos, she would have chosen to perform onstage to the end and to "go out" with the sound of applause ringing in her ears. But her hopes for improvement, and for a chance to return to the stage, diminished as less severe strokes took their toll.

In June 1991, she fractured her right shoulder in a fall in her home. Taken to UCLA Hospital, she underwent surgery. She suffered a second stroke while still in the hospital, then was thoroughly examined by a UCLA psychiatrist, Dr. Bruce H. Dobkin, and by Dr. Saxena. The diagnosis was that the patient suffered from dementia possibly caused by alcohol abuse or earlier subcortical strokes. A brain scan indicated that earlier strokes could have caused infarct dementia. They also felt that Maggie had suffered the onset of Alzheimer's at least a year earlier.

Dr. Dobkin, a geriatric neurology expert, noted that Raye, whom he advised to stop drinking alcohol, was unable to recall recent events, generate a list of words, or follow three-part instructions. He offered his opinion that the patient was unable to handle her personal affairs.

The appeal of the daughter's court case was still pending in the appellate court when Bette Midler's film, *For the Boys*, debuted in 1991. Movie critic Michael McWilliams, an open admirer of Midler as an actress and singer of "expansive gifts," predicted that the movie would be hugely successful. In fact, he said, it would be hailed as a masterpiece. The hype accompanying the Twentieth Century Fox movie's debut upset Maggie because she suspected that the movie was based on her own life.

Nearly ten years earlier, Nick had asked one of his buddies to put together a ten-page treatment, centering around Raye's wartime experiences, which they titled "Maggie." Nick had envisioned Midler starring in the movie that he hoped would evolve from the outline, and he invited Midler to the Bel Air home. Then, at Melodye's suggestion, Nick's buddy had taken his "treatment" to the Los Angeles Writers' Guild to have it registered.

For Maggie's seventy-fifth birthday in August 1991, President George Bush and his wife, Barbara, sent her an autographed photo of themselves. That same year, in the wake of the war with Iraq, President Bush presented Medals of Freedom to General Norman Schwartzkopf, General Colin Powell, Secretary of Defense Dick Cheney, Secretary of State James Baker, and National Security Adviser Brent Scowcroft. Maggie, it appeared to her supporters, would not receive the medal she so urgently desired.

When Maggie's old friend, comedian Bernie Allen, phoned from Las Vegas in the middle of September 1991, Melodye was astonished. The astonishment was not because Allen called; he had been a close friend for years. But his message was a surprising one.

He had some reservations about Maggie's relationship with a much younger man and he thought Melodye should know about it, he said. He also wanted to apologize for having introduced Maggie to the forty-two-year-old Mark Harris. He had never suspected that anything other than a casual meeting would come of the introduction, but now he feared that some kind of attachment had already developed.

Melodye asked when the two had been introduced. When Bernie replied that the introduction had occurred only about a week earlier, some of her fears were eased. Still, Bernie's remarks circled in her mind for the next two or three days. *Says he's a producer. But told me he's mostly an admirer of Martha Raye, ever since he was a kid.*

Harris had asked Bernie to arrange a meeting with Martha Raye. Just to meet the famous entertainer would mean so much to him.

Bernie Allen was the kind of loyal pal who often visited Maggie, now that she had become a shut-in. So he tried to cheer Maggie by telling her about the young man who was eager to meet her.

A short while later, Harris telephoned and Maggie agreed to talk with the caller. It did not take long for Harris to persuade her to give him permission to visit.

When Harris arrived at the house, Bernie was still there. A nurse escorted Harris into the bedroom, where Maggie was propped up with pillows.

Maggie was quickly charmed as the dark-haired, blue-eyed guest kissed her on both cheeks. ("Violet eyes, like Liz Taylor's," Mark Harris often described his own orbs.)

Bernie watched and listened patiently as the attentive Harris, a glib talker, told Maggie of the various things he had done, in and out of show business. He had been a singer, worked as a designer in New York's garment industry, hosted a TV pilot, and been both an agent and a producer in Las Vegas, he said. Oh, yes, and he was a licensed cosmetologist. He would absolutely love to wash, trim, and style Maggie's hair.

But, first, there was dinner to be prepared. Harris, it seemed, was also a great cook. Bernie quickly was pressed into service to go to the grocery store with a list prepared by Harris.

On Bernie's return, Harris took over the kitchen and fixed an appetizing meal. After dinner, Bernie went home. But the nurse was still there to watch over her patient as Harris entertained Maggie with his admiring chatter. And Maggie was so enchanted that she was reluctant to have him leave. One week later, the two agreed to marry. At that point, Harris went back east and then quickly returned after arranging to have his grand piano shipped to his new Bel Air address.

In the meantime, he had performed the promised hairdressing chore. ("Her hair hadn't been washed with water and shampoo in a year and a half," Harris later would tell Howard Stern on Stern's controversial radio program. "It's difficult for a stroke victim to put her head back for a regular shampoo.") Maggie was tired but pleased with the results.

There were varying answers from people to the question of how long Harris and Raye had known each other before the young man transported Maggie, along with her wheelchair, to Las Vegas on September 25, 1991, to be secretly married. "Three weeks," some people said later. "Two weeks," said others. But her daughter insisted it was more like nine days.

On their arrival at Vegas, Harris promptly filled out a marriage application at the Clark County courthouse. Accompanied by a courthouse clerk, he returned to a limousine in which Maggie waited to sign her name to the document as Harris guided her trembling hand. Her hair, highlighted with a silver rinse, was cut short with bangs, and Mark had carefully applied her makeup. Her appearance was vastly improved, no doubt about that.

A short time later, the couple moved into the bridal suite at the Golden Nugget. Attended by one of the groom's male Vegas pals, and with Maggie propped up like a rag doll on a stool in front of the suite's small bar, they were married by a rabbi engaged by Harris. It was Maggie's seventh wedding, which placed her in the Zsa Zsa Gabor category for multiple marriages.

As listed on the marriage license, Harris (who was born with the surname Bleefield) had been married once previously and was, he claimed, the father of three grown daughters. (There were rumors, however, that he adopted his wife's three children.) And according to information Harris later gave to radio host Howard Stern, he also had an illegitimate daughter born to the woman with whom he lived after the divorce from his first wife.

Eased back into her wheelchair after the ordeal of sitting up on the bar stool, Maggie shared wedding cake and champagne with her husband. Since she was not good at cards or gambling, reports that the bride and groom spent the evening playing blackjack may not have been accurate. But after retiring to their bridal suite, the bride suffered such severe abdominal pains during the night that she had to be whisked away by ambulance to nearby Desert Springs Hospital.

By the time Maggie returned home the next day, news of the wedding had reached Los Angeles. Maggie's old friends were shocked, but none of them could have been as shocked as was her daughter. Harris took his wife directly to St. John's Hospital in Santa Monica when, in great pain, Maggie began passing blood.

Ruth Webb (who had served, on occasion, as Maggie's agent

for special arrangements) was unaware that her client was hospital-ized when she phoned the Bel Air home. Harris did not tell her that Maggie was hospitalized, and for a few moments, the two argued. The argument ended abruptly when Harris informed the agent that he was now his wife's manager; Webb's services would be entirely unnecessary in the future.

Mark immediately took action to prevent any more unwanted telephone calls to his wife. He had Maggie's unlisted number of the past thirty years changed to a new, unlisted number.

Ruth Webb announced to the *Globe* that she was ordering her attorney to file an emergency lawsuit to try to prevent Harris from removing, spending, or transferring any of Martha Raye's assets until Raye's competency to manage her own affairs was decided. Holly-wood buzzed with gossip about the newlyweds, and the tabloids were having a field day when reporters discovered that Harris was quite willing to talk with them.

Frantic with worry, Maggie's daughter asked a lawyer if the marriage could be annulled. She explained to the lawyer that her mother was ill and dependent on a wheelchair and nursing care and that she certainly was not competent to make a decision about getting married. In fact, she insisted, her mother was suffering from Alzheimer's dementia.

News soon leaked out that Raye was recuperating in Santa Monica from an intestinal inflammation that Harris said was diver-ticulitis. Hemorrhaging was an infrequent complication of the con-dition. Later, though, the episode was reported (from information supplied by Harris to journalists) to have been diagnosed as inter-nal bleeding caused by blood thinners that the patient had been given for clotting problems.

After the possibility of having the marriage annulled was the sub-ject of several tabloid articles, the question arose regarding whether the marriage had ever been consummated. "I'm having sex for the first time in years," Maggie was quoted in the *National Enquirer* as having told anonymous "friends."

One year later, newspaper writer Jane Wollman Rusoff stated

unequivocally in a magazine article that "Harris and Raye do not have sex." The contradiction could have arisen from the hype that had always colored Maggie's responses—flip answers that, even now, emerged from the debilitated former entertainer like flashes of light in a shadowed room. Mark injected still another colorful segment into the kaleidoscopic views of the Harris-Raye marriage by openly acknowledging that he was bisexual.

Rumors circulated that Maggie had changed her will as soon as she married Harris, that Harris had drawn up the "will of Margie O'Reed" only four days after the marriage, leaving the daughter one dollar and everything else to her husband.

Rumors did not seem to bother Harris. He developed various plans to keep his name in print. "He takes care of me," Maggie said, pointing out that her husband did everything from making cocoa for her to making her look good when he took her out to parties—lots of parties.

Still, the nurses, always under strict orders from Harris, were on hand to assist Maggie while Mark was busily trying to advance his career, arranging for interviews with Howard Stern on radio as well as with Phil Donahue, Montel Williams, Sally Jessy Raphael, and other TV talk show hosts. He also was involved in redecorating the Bel Air home, getting rid of Maggie's colonial furnishings and replacing them with "my antique collection," as Mark phrased it. "I have a lot of furniture from Europe," he said in a Stern radio interview.

He replaced window drapes, tore out carpeting, rewired the house, and installed a new Jacuzzi, because the Jacuzzi that was already in the house (a gift from Raye's veteran friends) was the wrong color. The house "was very colonial before," Harris pointed out, "and now it's eclectic."

He admitted to hosting many parties, claiming that he knew a lot of celebrities and invited them to visit Raye's home. "I do my best to keep Maggie's spirits up," he said. He also did his best to foster the notion that his wife was not helpless. He and the nurse would get her out of the wheelchair and she would "take a few steps, as long as we hold her."

In casual conversations, Harris spoke of trying to sell one of his sitcoms to Norman Lear or trying to make a deal on Maggie's life story. Although Maggie did not like it when Mark went out of town, he felt he had to keep trying to advance his own career, and he loved to talk of marvelous "possibilities." On returning to Los Angeles, he would do whatever he had to do to coax Maggie back into a good mood by cooking the special foods she liked and recalling her past triumphs.

One of Mark's recollections, which he said Maggie particularly enjoyed, was of his youth, when he and his parents would watch *The Martha Raye Show* in their Brooklyn home. Mark would tell Maggie about special incidents he remembered from the show, especially his father's reaction when Maggie, wearing a brief costume and black fishnet stockings, would appear on the screen. "Aah, the legs. The legs," his father would say admiringly.

In the evenings, Mark often dressed his wife in one of her after-five gowns, used skin tape to lift her eyes, combed her bangs over the tape, applied makeup and a touch of her favorite perfume, attached her jewelry, and took her to parties where, very often, she fell asleep in her wheelchair. There were those who criticized, saying the former entertainer was too sick for late-night parties, that she should be at home in bed. Others defended Harris, saying that Maggie enjoyed being "prettied up" and relished the attention she was receiving. It had given her a new lease on life, they added.

On November 24, after two months of marriage, Mark wheeled his wife into the popular Matteo's in Westwood, lit a cigarette, and placed it between her lips. Then they ordered dinner. Before they had finished eating, Maggie's head drooped. She was not dozing this time; she was having some kind of attack and had to be taken to the UCLA Medical Center. "A mild stroke," was the attending doctor's diagnosis. She was kept in the hospital overnight, then released to return home. A little more than twenty-four hours later, Mark took her to the drag queen club, La Cage aux Folles, in Los Angeles. And two evenings later, they showed up at a private party hosted by Roger Dauers. One of Dauers's guests told a *Star* reporter that Maggie would be talking to someone and would fall asleep in midsentence. "She told people she was tired, but felt that Mark wanted to attend this gathering, so she came along."

One week before Christmas, Melodye filed a suit in Los Angeles Superior Court to have her mother declared incompetent as the result of a series of strokes. She asked to have conservators appointed to manage her mother's assets and her "person."

In response, a temporary conservator was appointed to handle Raye's estate. But for now, the court awaited the receipt of medical reports before appointing a conservator to make decisions about Raye's personal care.

The lawyer representing Maggie admitted that her client had suffered several strokes. But regardless of previous findings by physicians, the lawyer stated, the strokes had had "no impact on her ability to function mentally." Mark Harris was not reluctant to speak out on the matter, claiming that Maggie's daughter was financially motivated in filing suit. The suit would surely fail, he predicted. But Melodye's attorney pointed out that she was acting solely out of concern for her mother's well-being and was not seeking personal control of her mother's assets.

Within a day or two after the conservatorship lawsuit was filed, an agreement, dated December 23, 1991, was signed by Mark and by Maggie, in a shaky signature. The agreement stated that in the event of Maggie's death, she "hereby confirmed, assigned, and transferred" to her husband all monies due her, plus all claims and causes of action against Twentieth Century Fox, Bette Midler, Midler's partner Bonnie Bruckheimer, and Mark Rydell, producer of *For the Boys.* The agreement concurred with a filing of a $5 million suit by Mark Harris, on behalf of his wife, Martha Raye, naming Midler, Twentieth Century Fox, Bruckheimer, and Rydell as defendants. (The Harris-Raye signed agreement would be brought to the attention of the court later and its validity would be questioned after Raye had declared by way of a deposition that she had not given anyone any right to anything.)

Reporters quickly got in touch with Midler to ask for her comments. The actress admitted having gone to Raye's home years previously and seeing some sort of outline of Raye's life. But Midler protested that she hadn't known the occasion was a business meeting; instead, she had thought it was entirely a social affair.

Then, as if to reinforce his marriage in the eyes of Hollywood and the entire country, Harris planned a ceremony in which he and Maggie would renew their wedding vows. If it did not satisfy Harris's earlier declared fantasy of having celebrities taking part en masse in the affair, the ceremony was in keeping with Maggie's commitment to the military. Held in the rented Friars Club dining room in Los Angeles, the ritual took place beneath a chuppa made of camouflage netting with twenty-five army reserve members in attendance.

One hundred guests attended, most of their names taken by Harris from an address book that Maggie had kept years previously—a book in which she had listed a great many people she had met only casually. While Nick was alive, he had kept the book up to date by crossing out names and addresses of people who died, but Maggie never bothered with such details. Mickey Rooney, Margaret O'Brien, Barbara Rush, and fashion dictator Mr. Blackwell were among those who watched as the broad-shouldered Harris and the silvery-haired Maggie, sitting in her wheelchair, repeated their vows. But Maggie's longtime friend Bernie Allen, the man who had introduced the wedding couple and the man whom Maggie had frequently referred to as being like *"mishpocheh"* (Yiddish for family), was not invited. Nor, of course, were her daughter and grandson.

Maggie's pal Cesar Romero and Anne Jeffreys ("a good friend of mine," Mark boasted) served as best man and matron of honor. When Harris bent down to kiss his wife, cameras clicked. Maggie licked her lips afterwards in comic reaction.

Apparently unperturbed by the controversy over whether he was or was not a fortune hunter, Harris went on with the fun things that seemed to give him great pleasure. Parties, mostly. Planning parties and giving parties. (Martha got so much enjoyment from them, he pointed out.)

He splurged with one of his larger parties near the middle of January 1992 (two weeks after the renewal of the couple's wedding vows) when a teary-eyed Maggie greeted guests from her wheelchair. The high point of the evening, and a complete surprise to Maggie, occurred when her husband, reveling as master of ceremonies, focused everyone's attention on a flamboyant figure who promptly burst into song.

Maggie's mouth dropped open in astonishment. Party guests looked at one another in surprise. How dared Bette Midler show up when Raye had a court suit pending against her? But, of course, it was not Midler. No, the singer was not even a woman, but a clever female impersonator with a powerful voice.

As soon as the Midler impersonator finished singing, Mark Harris launched into a humorous song with words written for the occasion. Guests laughed, though a bit uncomfortably, because the lyrics contained the names of all seven of Maggie's husbands. Obviously pleased with the response to what he had planned as the pièce de résistance of the evening, Mark bowed and looked at Maggie, the perennial good sport, who nodded and flashed at least part of her famous grin. Facial muscles, on the left side of her face, had been partly numbed, impairing her ability to smile.

17

On the Edge

Ruth Webb, who had represented Maggie for certain gigs, had a number of clients who were making headlines, including the notorious Joey Buttafuoco and John Bobbitt (the latter of the reattached penis fame). But the agent had not pursued the lawsuit she had told the *Globe* that she filed to determine Maggie's competency. Mark Harris had talked to Webb again and at length, turning on the considerable charm of which he was capable, until Webb had done a turnabout. She was now supportive of Mark and what she saw as his efforts to bring some happiness into the life of his ailing wife, who, he now claimed, had proposed to him in the first place through her nurse, pointing out that marriage would be a protection against her only child—"the dreadful daughter" (so named by Harris) who, Maggie had been convinced, was determined to put her in a nursing home.

The marriage had existed for four months when a January court hearing was held, at which time a declaration by Maggie was presented, objecting to the appointment of conservatorships. Harris then petitioned to be appointed as his wife's conservator, both of estate and person. This was denied by the judge. Melodye also presented a request at the hearing, asking the court to authorize a psychiatric evaluation of her mother, referred to as the "conservatee."

Maggie's attorneys quickly objected to the latter request. The proposed "conservatee" (named on many of the official documents as Margaret Yvonne Theresa Reed, a.k.a. Martha Raye) did not need the services of a psychiatrist, they stated.

While these matters were under consideration by the court, Harris flew to New York for the first of what would become a series of radio interviews on the controversial *Howard Stern Show.* Stern gave Harris an opportunity to recite a litany of his many accomplishments. One of them was his claim that he "spoke both French and German."

"You're horny in three languages," the sex-oriented host commented.

Harris ignored the gibe and said that now, serving as Raye's manager, he was trying to sell the story of Maggie's life. And he might do a live act at the Sands Hotel in a few months, he concluded.

At that point, the disruptive Stern switched the conversation to the Raye suit against Bette Midler. Was Stern aware, Mark asked in an attempt to turn the questioning in a different direction, that he, Harris, had sung with Bette Midler some twenty years previously?

Stern did not take kindly to clever maneuvers by guests to avoid the host's frequent sex-oriented questions. He pressed Mark for more definite answers now. Everybody was faxing him, Stern said, wanting to know if Harris and Raye were really man and wife.

"Could this marriage be annulled?" Stern's sidekick, Robin, asked.

"No, it cannot be annulled," Mark replied, but would go no further, saying it was "disrespectful to Martha."

The interview then shifted focus, but only slightly. When Stern asked if Harris was gay, Mark replied that he was heterosexual, although he had been tagged at various times as either gay or bisexual. "I've worn more labels than Calvin Klein," he quipped, using a one-liner, Maggie-style, on which he would rely in similar situations. It was only the beginning of frankness for Harris, who soon was admitting in other interviews that he was bisexual. Indeed, he had told Raye of his bisexuality just before they married. Although it was likely that he had not known previously of Maggie's affinity for gays and bisexuals, he realized it by the time of the marriage with her response that gay and bisexual lifestyles were not unusual for artists.

Shortly after Harris's radio interview with Stern, Raye was referred by Dr. Alan Frankel (brought into the case by the conservator of the person) to psychiatrist Bruce Dobkin, who had examined Maggie nine months earlier when she was an inpatient at UCLA Hospital.

Dr. Dobkin soon discovered that the recently hired nurse's aide who accompanied the patient to his office, and Mark Harris, the husband of less than six months, could supply few details on the patient's past progress or regression. Maggie complained of left scapular pain that was not totally relieved by Darvocet, muscle relaxants, and other medicines. Soma had been prescribed for her back pain, and her current medications included Warfarin, Synthroid, Xanax, and a variety of other drugs. Her difficulties with perception possibly fluctuated in relation to the use of various medications, the doctor concluded.

The patient and aide agreed that Maggie needed help bathing and dressing. She had become incontinent about a month before her marriage. She could stand only "with maximal assistance," the doctor noted. Maggie admitted that she watched television most of the day, did not keep up with current events, and had never been a reader. "I've always been a dumb-dumb," she told the doctor. She admitted, too, that she was not responsible for any of her financial affairs, but just signed credit card slips.

Maggie had been honest in her admissions. She never had kept up with current events. "I only voted twice in presidential elections," she had often told friends. "For Franklin Roosevelt and for Kennedy." But this claim was not true. Maggie had never registered to vote.

The psychiatrist's cognition testing revealed that the patient did not know the number of pennies, nickels, or dimes in a dollar and could not draw the correct numbers on a clock face. The doctor again made mention of "her good social skills" and her ability to converse well about her past. But he remarked that she had difficulty with recent memory and simple calculations. He observed that "her left hemiplegia is such that she has virtually no level of recovery of the motor deficit and this has made her wheelchair bound."

He also believed that "the patient does need supervision and clearly needs assistance in any matter that requires planning and sound judgment."

Plans were made to hospitalize Maggie at UCLA Medical Center for a few days, beginning on March 30. Dr. Frankel felt that the patient needed to have her medical condition and her medications evaluated.

On March 30, however, the UCLA Medical Center learned that the patient had not been brought in for the scheduled evaluation. Instead, she had been taken to a psychiatrist at another hospital who had prescribed Thorazine for her without having learned much about her medical history. So now she was taking a powerful antipsychotic drug, in addition to Prozac, Seldane, Naroxin, and other strong drugs. And then the Harrises left for Las Vegas where, it was reported, Maggie wanted to see Debbie Reynolds's stage performance.

It was doubtful that Maggie ever saw the Debbie Reynolds show. Instead, there was partying at both the Mirage Hotel and the Sands Hotel. On the morning of April 2, Maggie suffered a stroke in her Las Vegas hotel suite. Paramedics transported her to Desert Springs Medical Center to stabilize her condition.

USA Today reported that Martha Raye had become irrational while she was hospitalized in Las Vegas. At that point Raye was transferred back to Los Angeles, where she was returned to UCLA's Neuropsychiatric Institute for treatment.

By the time the court called an emergency hearing in May, Maggie had recovered sufficiently from her stroke in Las Vegas to be wheeled into court by her husband, accompanied by their attorneys. But Maggie was not as perky as she had been when she appeared in court the previous December with the original filing of her daughter's petition for the establishment of conservatorships. At that earlier date, Maggie had boasted to writer Cindy Adams, "I dressed up and I looked great. Even put in my falsies—the teeth, not the tits," she had quipped.

The "looking great," however, had not been achieved without a lot of help from her husband and nurse. And now, at the May emergency hearing in Superior Court, Los Angeles County, even the hairset and makeup (much less the falsies) did not restore Maggie's former flippancy.

According to the court's findings, the allegations of the petition filed by Maggie's daughter were "true and sufficient." Maggie was found to be unable to provide for her own personal needs and "unable to manage properly her financial resources or to resist fraud or undue influence." A permanent conservator of the person was appointed, and the previously appointed CPA would continue to oversee Maggie's financial affairs as she received a monthly allowance of $5,500. A careful review was to be done of the drugs used to medicate Raye. She continued to chain-smoke Benson & Hedges ("I don't inhale," she insisted), although she stopped drinking.

"I think it stinks," Maggie complained to reporters who interviewed her after the latest court ruling. "My daughter and I have never been friends. I don't like being told how to live in my own home or how to spend my money," she insisted. "My daughter said I'm crazy. She wants to take my house and money."

Although described in various newspapers as "paralyzed and ill with Alzheimer's disease," Maggie was quick to vent her criticisms of her daughter to visitors. "She's the devil's daughter," she said repeatedly. "I wish she was dead."

On the first of June, Maggie suffered another stroke. Her husband characterized the stroke as not as severe as those she had in the past. "The problem is her mind is slipping more than her physical abilities," he explained. But Maggie was kept at the hospital for a full week because she had some trouble swallowing.

He was preparing a book, Harris told reporters at this time, entitled "Maggie and Me." It would be a book "about caring and genuine love, and that I wasn't a con artist."

Honoring his wife's seventy-sixth birthday in August 1992, Harris again rented a section of the Friars Club. Like a queen in her sequined dress, Maggie was wheeled into the club after everyone else was seated and was taken to the dais where Cesar Romero, Anne Jeffreys, Ruby Keeler, Red Buttons, Dorothy Lamour, Bob and Dolores Hope, and Jimmy and Gloria Stewart awaited her arrival.

There was wild applause from the guests when a telegram from President Bill Clinton was read. Everyone knew that a pro-Raye petition, bearing 32,000 signatures, had been sent to the president to request the Medal of Freedom for Raye because of her meritorious service to troops in three wars. "If all goes well, I'd love to be able to present it [the medal] to you," the president had written.

The rest of the entertainment was typical Harris style. After Bob Hope did a repeat of presenting Raye with the special Oscar she had received many years earlier, La Cage aux Folles staged a drag show. One of the Folles male performers, dressed as Martha Raye in the 1940s, sang "Mr. Paganini" as Maggie wept. Dorothy Lamour commented that Maggie was "very much in love with Mark, and he with her."

Jimmy Durante's widow, Marge, always had good things to say about the couple. The marriage had changed Maggie's life for the better, she said.

For her part, Maggie summarily refuted any reports that claimed Harris was taking advantage of her. "He knows how to talk about business to people," she told one reporter. "So I'm very lucky. "I know from *gournish* [nothing] about money and business." Her use of Yiddish expressions had become even more frequent since her marriage to the Jewish Harris.

Milton Berle also supported the Hollywood view that the Raye-Harris marriage had been beneficial to Maggie. "She should enjoy the rest of her life," he said. "If they have comfortability and companionship and love, it's their business."

Maggie's lawyer gave her supportive opinion to writer Jane Wollman Rusoff, insisting that Harris had helped Maggie find a new life. "She looks wonderful," Shirley Woolf said. "From laying in bed and just vegetating, she has become again 'Martha Raye.'" Harris had other things to tell reporters. His wife suffered from memory losses now and was becoming very frustrated. He also told them that he was not dependent on his wife's money; he made his own money, some of which came from appearing on talk shows. But in legal papers he previously had filed with the court in regard to the establishment of conservatorships, he stated that he had no income and had not filed taxes for three years.

Maggie did not like Mark to go out of town, and although there always was a nurse on duty in the Raye home, Harris knew that his wife was very dependent on his presence. But publicity and the money he received for appearing on talk shows were important to him. So he left for Chicago to appear on Jenny Jones's talk show in September 1992 and discuss his year of marriage to Martha. He and his wife would celebrate their first anniversary that month, he reminded viewers.

When he returned home, Harris expressed disappointment with *Jenny Jones*, claiming that he had not expected the topic of the show to be "male gold diggers who are not ashamed to admit they are." Still, he agreed to appear on *The Jane Whitney Show* in October to discuss the subject of marrying well.

Before he left in October, Mark threw an anniversary party. It was an at-home affair with an early-evening, elaborate buffet set up for the guests, only a few of whom—like eighty-six-year-old vaudevillian Eddie Rio—were longtime friends or acquaintances of Maggie's. Looking very fragile in her white suit, Maggie cracked a few tired jokes from her wheelchair as she greeted their guests. Shortly before nine o'clock, a nurse quietly wheeled her out of the room and into her bedroom while the party went on. Mark continued to play the genial host to the largely senior group, but his ailing wife did not rejoin the guests.

By October 1992, when plans for management of the Raye estate were presented to the court, Maggie was complaining that she felt she was under intense pressure to agree to turn over all her affairs to the conservator for the estate (as long as the conservator was not her daughter, she specified). According to the newly established plan, the conservator would handle Maggie's routine bills and provide her with $3,000 in personal allowance (reduced from the previous $5,500) each month.

Maggie remained bitter about the arrangement; bitter, too, about her daughter who had appealed to the court for a reduction in her monthly allowance. "I bought her a house," Maggie said in an interview. "But she wants everything."

The statement was not true, her daughter retaliated. She had bought her own modest home and had the papers to prove it. And she was making her own mortgage payments.

The misunderstanding about who had bought the house had

begun years earlier, Melodye pointed out, when Nick Condos had told Maggie that he had bought the house for his daughter. She could not explain why her father had lied about it when actually he had given her only one-third of the down payment. Had he lied because he had come up short when accounting to Maggie for some other expenditure? Had he gambled money away? To defend herself, Melodye claimed to have delivered copies of the house contract and mortgage papers to her mother several years ago, so that Maggie could have someone explain to her that Nick had not bought the house. Nonetheless, Maggie clung stubbornly to her claim that she had given the house to her daughter.

Harris, who had recently announced that he was about to make a deal for a Broadway musical based on his wife's life, was now answering questions from reporters about his wife's will. Maggie had signed a will shortly after their marriage, he said, in which she left the bulk of her fortune to him. But recently, he added, she had signed a new will leaving him the Bel Air house, with much of the remainder of her estate going to charity. The "dreadful daughter," he said, would get one dollar.

Harris's personal plans were as diversified as ever. He told friends he wanted to find a play in which he and Maggie could star together. But when he seized upon the play *When Night Falls*, starring a female character in a wheelchair, Maggie reacted negatively after she learned that the wheelchair-bound actress was going to be decapitated and have her head displayed in a box. Besides, there was Maggie's problem of dozing while in her wheelchair; she had done some of that during a Fourth of July parade as her husband wheeled her down the street to the cheers of spectators.

The most exciting escapade of which Maggie seemed capable these days was to allow herself to be lifted from her wheelchair into the 1976 Rolls-Royce that Harris had received from an unidentified donor. Then he would drive his wife, propped up on the seat with pillows, to the ice cream store for a strawberry shake, even though ice cream was on the doctors' not-recommended food list, along with the cheese and potatoes she loved. The short trip invariably was tiring enough to Maggie that, despite the frequent dozing she had done during the day, she would be ready to go to bed for the night on her return home.

The wait for an appellate court decision in regard to the assets of Nick Condos had dragged on much too long, his daughter decided as she obtained an order from the court for "a mandatory settlement conference." Since she could no longer afford to run up bills for lawyers, she was ready to settle for what she could get. She soon learned that the bank, where she had tried to cash the cashier's checks immediately following her father's death, had reissued the checks after they were reported "lost" by her mother's attorney. They were not lost, the daughter told the court. She still had the original checks, as entered into the court record, in her possession.

The court fined the bank for reissuing the checks without authorization. According to the settlement, Melodye would get the face value (no interest) of the cashier's checks that were made out only in her name. Maggie would get the face value of the checks made out to her and Nick and those made out to both daughter and mother. Melodye collected on three of the checks, but had only a small portion left after paying her legal fees. She was disappointed, too, when the appellate court refused to change the negative ruling of the lower court on her suit to try to collect the Polident commissions she thought should have been paid to her father.

On January 27, 1993, the House of Representatives formulated Resolution 30, expressing, with the concurrence of the Senate, that "Whereas Martha Raye is truly both an unsung hero and a national treasure . . . the President should award the Presidential Medal of Freedom to Martha Raye in honor of her meritorious service to the United States." A copy of the resolution was sent to Maggie.

In the year and a half since her marriage, Maggie's condition had continued to deteriorate. On a typical day, she remained in bed until early afternoon when she was wheeled into the den and settled into her orthopedic chair, surrounded by the military citations, medals, photos, and plaques that decorated the walls. One particularly interesting plaque, which Maggie proudly pointed out to visitors, had been made by a young man in the service of his country, who had worked for weeks to polish the hardwood, to arrange the inlaid lettering, and to print his heartfelt tribute.

Lt. Col. Maggie Raye
In Recognition of
Outstanding Service:
More sacred than Joan of Arc,
More Beautiful than Helen of Troy,
More like Maggie
The world should enjoy.

Mostly, though, Maggie fastened her gaze on the television screen until, at frequent intervals, her eyes closed while she dozed. Beside her, a portable commode stood ready for duty.

Whenever she had a visitor, Maggie would brighten considerably. Without her dentures, and because her left lip was partly paralyzed, her speech was slurred. Still, there were flashes of the old Maggie now and then. She continued to smoke. Mark, she boasted, made everything as convenient as possible for her. He took very good care of her, she added as Mark, hovering nearby, came in to check on the invalid. Visitors rarely stayed long. It was evident that Maggie's thin, little voice became tired very quickly.

Harris was in the news again in April 1993, when he complained publicly that President Bill Clinton had reneged on a promise to present seventy-six-year-old Maggie with the Medal of Freedom. Boasting of taking out $7,000 worth of ads pushing for the medal in the current *Variety* and *Hollywood Reporter*, Harris was not reluctant to call the president a liar. "Which should get a medal pinned to Raye's chest by about the year 2525," one newspaper joked.

18

Martha Raye, Civilian

There was some movement in the Martha Raye–Bette Midler law-suit in March 1993 when a Los Angeles Superior Court judge dismissed as "frivolous" all but one of the complaints filed. Breach of contract was the only complaint left intact.

Bette Midler, who wanted to be rid of what she considered a nuisance suit, twice offered a small compromise payment to Mark Harris if he would drop the remaining complaint. But Harris wanted $5 million, and he refused to compromise.

There still had been no official pronouncement concerning the award from President Clinton by the second week in October 1993, when Maggie's nurse observed that a toe on her patient's left foot was turning black. Taken to Cedars-Sinai, the hospital famous for its clientele of Hollywood stars, Maggie underwent surgery on October 12.

Five hours of circulatory surgery had taken place, Mark Harris told *Variety* columnist Army Archerd, and doctors had amputated one of Maggie's toes. Since his wife's life expectancy might not be more than a few months, he said, he was following her wishes and making arrangements for an Irish wake and for burial services at Fort Bragg, North Carolina.

Harris had slightly different news for other reporters. His wife was very ill from a failing liver, and her doctor had given her less than three months to live, he told them. "She probably is suffering from years of alcohol abuse," he added.

Because everything was in place for around-the-clock nursing care at Raye's Bel Air home, she was permitted to return home the following week. But soon an ambulance took her back to Cedars-Sinai. "Gangrene has set into one leg," Harris told reporters. "Doctors expect that leg will have to be amputated."

On Friday morning, October 29, Raye was taken back into surgery and her left leg was amputated just below the knee. Later that day, she was listed in critical condition.

Maggie still was fighting her battle for survival in the hospital when it was announced that President Clinton finally had awarded her the Medal of Freedom, the nation's highest civilian honor. His citation recognized her "great courage, kindness, and patriotism."

How sad, friends said, that the prestigious award that Maggie had longed to receive had come when she was so debilitated that she scarcely was aware of what was going on around her.

Within a short while, though, it seemed that Maggie's fighting spirit was overcoming great obstacles; her doctors permitted her to go home in time to personally receive the Medal of Freedom with appropriate ceremony. Seated in the orthopedic chair in her den, she wept with gratitude as Medal of Honor winner Master Sergeant Roy Benevidas pinned the prized medal to her chest, saying, "She's the Mother Teresa of the armed forces." Lieutenant Colonel R. S. Teilmann, rows of ribbons decorating his uniform, presented her with the official document bearing President Clinton's signature.

The conservator for Raye's estate was once again trying to reduce to $1,000 the monthly allowance the court had established for Maggie's "personal use" after her daughter had filed a request for a reduction to $500. The daughter had pointed out in the request that her mother's personal wants were few and that all bills were paid by the estate.

Frumeh Labow, conservator of the person, objected to the reduction. She filed a declaration with the court, stating that she had talked with Raye at the time of the presentation of the Medal of Freedom and that Raye had expressed her affection for Harris. Raye also had said that she did not like Mark to be away on business. She wanted him to stay at home.

Labow claimed that Mark Harris had "created a special environment" for Raye, "designed to boost her self-esteem." Labow said she was aware that funds were being diverted to Harris on a monthly basis. "But if it is necessary for him to be out of the house to earn a living, it will make Maggie very unhappy."

Harris filed his own objections to any further reduction. At Raye's insistence, and because of his caring for her needs, he claimed that he was no longer able to engage in employment. He went on to declare that he had devoted a great deal of time and energy to the care and comfort of his wife, and had been "pushed to my physical and emotional limits" by her latest illness. "Most recently," he stated, he was "instrumental in arranging for her to receive the Medal of Freedom at a ceremony in her home."

One of the tabloids also claimed some credit by stating that Raye received her medal after that paper "told how the plucky USO performer was wounded twice while entertaining troops in three wars," prompting an "avalanche of letters" from its readers.

The twice-wounded claim matched the nonexistent Purple Hearts, Raye's daughter claimed. She wanted it known that many veterans' organizations, politicians, newspapers, and others had played an active part in trying to get the prized medal for the former entertainer. But most of all, Melodye was convinced that the continuing efforts of "Noonie" and Belle had led to the award, and she wanted the two women to get the credit they deserved.

Before the arrival of the new year, Maggie suffered two more strokes. Once again, doctors permitted her to go home where she faced what she now realized was inevitable. The death of her longtime friend, eighty-six-year-old Cesar Romero, from pneumonia on New Year's Day, 1994, seemed to add to her resignation. One of her happiest memories was of Romero appearing with her on the first episode of her television show. But all that was left now were her memories—the most cherished of which seemed to be of the young servicemen whom she had entertained and nursed in World War II. In Korea, the "forgotten" war. And in Vietnam, that inglorious conflict which still was largely ignored by Americans whose lives had not been personally scarred during those long years of jungle warfare.

It was a comfort to Maggie to recall that many of the Green Berets had assured her, years previously, that they would do everything possible to make sure she was buried at Fort Bragg.

On January 17, 1994, a severe earthquake rocked the Los Angeles area, killing fifty-eight people, collapsing freeway overpasses, and leveling bridges. Mark Harris was out of town when the earthquake struck. When he returned a few days later, it was clear to him that his wife's house would require extensive repairs since the northern section of the home was badly damaged structurally. Harris and the conservator realized that some important decisions would have to be made about Raye, who was very upset. One suggestion was that she could be moved into the old actors' home, where she would be with her peers. On being informed of this suggestion, Raye's daughter visited the actors' home but decided that it would not be suitable for her mother. The case worker, assigned to Raye by the court, talked with Melodye before a final decision was made, at which time it was decided that a hotel might be a more appropriate setting for the ailing woman. They finally decided on the Radisson Hotel, which was comfortable and located next to UCLA Medical Center. As quickly as possible, Maggie and a few personal accessories were moved into the hotel along with her nurses and medications. She was settled into the hotel for only a short time when, before the end of January and through early February, a rash of sensational statements, reported to have been made by Harris, appeared in several tabloids and journals including the *Las Vegas Review Journal*. Each article stated that Harris was peddling a sizzling biography of Martha Raye, including her so-called lesbian affair with Joan Crawford. The book would also describe her many sexual liaisons with actors as well as with hundreds of GIs during wartime. Maggie, of course, knew nothing of this book.

By this time, Melodye had another request pending with the court. She wanted to see her mother. Mark Harris, she charged, had prevented her from visiting her mother by issuing restrictive instructions to hospitals and nurses.

In February, Maggie had to be treated for pneumonia, although she was not immediately moved back into the hospital. But as she weakened, she was taken to Cedars-Sinai only one day before Bette Midler took the witness stand in court to deny that *For the Boys* was in any way based on the life story of Martha Raye. Midler recalled seeing a treatment of Raye's life at Raye's home, and discussing the treatment, entitled "Maggie." But, Midler said, "It was pretty choppy and pretty episodic. It was unfilmable, I felt."

The lawyer representing Raye stated that his client's inability to testify because of illness "significantly impaired" his case. But that did not seem to make much sense; he had known for some time that his client would not be able to testify to anything. For one thing, she never saw the Midler film, which depicted the story of a married couple in their sixties, a former song and dance duo, who reminisce about their life together and the experiences they had when they entertained troops in World War II, Korea, and Vietnam.

Defendants admitted that Martha Raye had "inspired" the movie, but Midler insisted that Raye was just one entertainer whose wartime experiences in entertaining had been researched for materials for the book. She had also researched the experiences of Pearl Bailey, Gypsy Rose Lee, Ann-Margret, and "all the Miss Americas."

Midler, who had admitted to friends that the box-office failure of *For the Boys* "nearly killed me," was relieved to put the whole affair behind her when the judge dismissed the case without a complete trial. The judge pointed out that there was no proof that the movie was based largely on Raye's life. It was, he declared, a "non-suit."

In Maggie's weakened condition, she was unlikely to survive the pneumonia. Still, her will to live prevailed, despite the sense of resignation that had motivated her to talk about her funeral. She was allowed to return to her hotel room even though she was having serious circulatory problems in the right leg.

Before the end of February, Mark Harris filed a declaration in response to the request to the court by Maggie's daughter to allow visitation rights. Harris stated that he never had prevented Melodye from visiting her mother; in fact, he declared, he had encouraged Martha to speak to her daughter and had always given the telephone to Martha when Melodye called. He went on to accuse Melodye of having hired someone to threaten his life "or even to kill" him. And he asked the court to order a psychiatric examination for his wife's daughter.

In conclusion, he pointed out that Martha was now hospitalized again "awaiting surgery for amputation of her right leg above the knee." It was not the proper time for Melodye to see her mother, he claimed, when Martha had always indicated she did not want her daughter to visit.

Harris also filed a request to have his wife's estate pay the attorney's fees for Raye's dismissed case against Midler. Midler also sued the estate for her legal expenses. Eventually, the Raye estate would have to pay more than $46,000 in costs for the failed Midler suit.

Part of Raye's right leg was amputated at Cedars-Sinai at the end of February. While she remained in critical condition, her daughter appeared in court on March 1. Because her attorney was ill, she was representing herself in regard to her earlier proposed reduction in monthly personal allowance paid to Maggie, "but used largely for Harris," the daughter had claimed. Despite the presence of three attorneys representing Raye's interests, the court found that the "allegations contained in the 'Amended Petition' are true and correct," and the personal allowance was reduced to $500, as requested.

Until now, except for rare emergency visitations, Melodye always had to rely on the conservator to inform her about her mother's condition. But soon she obtained court permission to visit her mother twice a week in the presence of the conservator. There were difficulties in this process, however, because it entailed setting a specific time that was convenient for the conservator. Sometimes the conservator would cancel without notification. At other times, Melodye would arrive but the conservator might be late without having called the facility.

Nonetheless, Maggie's daughter was relieved to be able to work around the difficulties and to see her mother at the hotel. Harris was still out of town much of the time, often being interviewed on Howard Stern's show.

While Melodye visited with her mother, she asked if Maggie would like to see Nicky, her grandson. He was now working as a security guard, and he played electric bass in a band as a hobby.

Maggie shook her head sadly. She did not want Nicholas to see her in her present condition. "I want Nicky to remember me the way I was," she said.

The quality of life for Maggie was very low at this time. Occasionally there was a rerun of one of her old movies on television and, at this, Maggie expressed some interest. But her eyesight was poor. Still, she watched the flickering television images of a young and vital Martha Raye, the shadowy forms sharpened into focus by sounds and vivid, wistful memories of her glory days in Hollywood. And she continued to survive, day after day, week after week.

During the summer, Harris claimed to have shared his wife's hotel room for a few days while he recovered from plastic surgery on his neck and to remove his double chin. He would say then, and after Maggie's death, that his wife never knew that she had lost both legs. Indeed, she never knew that she had lost even one leg. "We never told her, and the nurses were warned not to tell." He would point out, too, that his wife's neck had stiffened so that she could not look down.

Harris's so-called warnings had never reached Maggie's daughter. And if they had, they would not have mattered to her. Shortly after the first amputation and before the daughter obtained regular visitation rights from the court, she had obtained permission from the conservator for an emergency visitation when her mother was still in serious condition and while Harris was out of town.

When Maggie had begged plaintively to know, "What's happened? What's the matter with me?" her daughter hesitated only momentarily. She remembered, very clearly, how her mother never had liked the matter-of-fact, truthful answers that her daughter had given to her in the past. Yet now the daughter realized that she was the only source of reality for her mother in the confined world of this hospital room where everyone was feeding her soothing little lies. And despite the Alzheimer's that ravaged her mother's mind, there were many moments of lucidity when she was deeply disturbed by realizing there was something terribly wrong. But what? Her daughter decided that it was Maggie's right to be told.

In February 1994, after the second leg amputation at Cedars-Sinai, Maggie's daughter had seen her again through the power of the conservator while Harris was out of town. She went through the same explanations when her mother questioned her.

As Maggie began to recover, she was allowed to return to the hotel room—her "home." And her daughter was now able to make regular use of her court-ordered visitation rights.

On Monday, October 17, Maggie suffered from diarrhea and vomiting and was in need of transfusions. She was taken once more to Cedars-Sinai Hospital from the Radisson Hotel. Harris left strict orders that Melodye Condos should not be permitted to enter Maggie's room. Then he left for New York. But as soon as Maggie's daughter was notified by the conservator of her mother's condition on October 19, she visited the hospital. She asked to see Martha Raye.

There was no Martha Raye registered as a patient, she was told. She tried to explain the circumstances, pointing out that her mother could not have been discharged because she was seriously ill. She learned, then, that Harris had left instructions barring her from her mother's room. The court-appointed conservator had the authority to make such decisions, Melodye informed the hospital employee. But they were unable to reach the conservator at this point.

Disappointed and confused, Melodye returned to work to ponder her next step. She was sitting at her desk with a small radio beside her when a news report snagged her attention. Martha Raye had just died, at age seventy-eight.

Shocked and angry, Maggie's daughter hurried back to the hospital to demand answers. Ms. Raye had died of pneumonia at 1:35 P.M. The body had been picked up by mortuary employees at 2 P.M. Her mind seemed to click off at the mention of 1:35 P.M. *She had been right here at the hospital thirty minutes earlier, and she had been denied the right to be at her mother's side when she died.*

Except for the presence of a private nurse, her mother—who loved company and conversation and fawning attention—had died alone at Cedars-Sinai. This was difficult for Melodye to accept. When *National Enquirer* reporters called, she told them that although she and her mother had reconciled recently, Harris had left orders at the hospital barring her and her son from visiting the dying patient. Harris was interested only in her mother's fortune, she added. "I'll see he never gets away with it," the tabloid quoted her.

Harris issued denials to the same reporters. There had been no reconciliation between mother and daughter, he insisted. And it was Maggie's own choice not to see Melodye.

"Not so," the daughter retaliated. "The visitation papers stated that Mom had said she wanted to see me, which was a condition of the agreement."

Following Maggie's death, outrageous articles appeared in tabloids such as the *Examiner,* which claimed that "loved ones" were accusing Bette Midler of hastening Raye's death. When the $5 million suit against Midler had been thrown out of court, the article stated with sickening sentimentality, it plunged Raye "into a despair that robbed her of her will to live."

The article also quoted her "shattered" husband, Harris, as saying that his wife was never the same after the court suit was dismissed. And it quoted agent Ruth Webb as declaring that the suit had killed Raye and that Midler was "a miserable human being."

Maggie would have been pleased with her obituaries, though. In *Variety,* columnist Army Archerd described her as a "true soldier in grease-paint who deserved more medals than she ever received." Longer obituaries featured the accomplishments that had been most important to Maggie. The song that brought her success and recognition as a singer, "Mr. Paganini," and twenty-six Hollywood films. The description of her "most notable role" as an actress—that of Charlie Chaplin's wife in *Monsieur Verdoux.* Her many tours to entertain American troops. And the prestigious award of the Medal of Freedom by President Clinton.

Even before the obituaries appeared in newspapers, Harris had planned a service that would be held in a Santa Monica chapel. Many people who were strangers to Raye were invited, but her daughter only found out when a reporter phoned her three hours before the service began on October 20.

A couple of men from the district attorney's office were kind enough to drive Melodye to the Santa Monica chapel where she was very much aware of heads turning at her entrance. She sat on the right side near the front section of pews only to be told, "You can't sit there. This is Colonel Tyler's place." She moved back one pew and sat alone at the far end near the wall, looking around to see Mark Harris and his male companion, wearing matching black velvet jackets, sit at the front. She spotted only a few other people she recognized. Actress Rose Marie. Ruth Webb, the flamboyant agent who now was Harris's friend. A. C. Lyles, who had been a Paramount producer. Gloria Allred, who would be Harris's attorney for only a short time and who later would represent a member of the Brown family in the O. J. Simpson murder trial. Allred, in fact, slid into the same pew in which Maggie's daughter sat and, as the service began, whispered words of sympathy to her.

The priest, who had never met Raye, gave his memorial talk, and then Lyles began to speak in a conversational tone, as if he were talking to Nick Condos. "Isn't that right, Nick?" Lyles asked, looking into the pews as if the deceased Condos were sitting there.

Rose Marie commented on the good relationship between Mark and Maggie. When it was Mark Harris's turn to speak, he began by saying how much Maggie had loved him—enough to request a Jewish wedding ceremony. She had told him she wanted a plain pine box at her funeral, he said, inclining his head toward the coffin. She did not want any fanfare at all, he added.

When Harris concluded his talk, Maggie's daughter quickly rose to make her own unrequested comments. She began with an apology to the many people who were not among those attending the service; to her own friends, to the military, civilians, and her mother's fans who did not know about the service. "Who were not notified, just as I wasn't," she added.

When she sat down, Harris stood up and hurried to the podium. He spoke quickly and loudly, elaborating on his theme that Maggie wanted a Jewish funeral even though she was Irish Catholic.

Melodye suspected that the pine box had not contained her mother's body. When a reporter phoned her the next morning, she learned that the body had previously been shipped on to Fort Bragg in preparation for burial on Saturday in the military cemetery where no civilian ever before had been buried. And this was Friday morning. She immediately began making phone calls. First she called a press officer at Fort Bragg, who seemed astonished that she hadn't known about the funeral arrangements. He had been informed that she knew all about it and that one of the tabloids was paying her plane fare to the funeral.

As Melodye was arranging for her flight, Barbara Caplin phoned. Barbara had just had a call from Steve Condos's widow, Lorraine, and Lorraine was already at Fort Bragg. Melodye wondered if everyone in the world had known about her mother's funeral arrangements before she learned of them. (She was unaware, she said, that television, radio, and newspaper reports had described the arrangements.)

Melodye had to spend considerably more than $1,000 for her flight to North Carolina, but her son stayed at home because of the expense. In a flurry of activity, she packed her bags, took a shuttle plane from Burbank to the Los Angeles airport, boarded a large airplane, and would have to switch to another full-sized plane and a final shuttle before arriving at the North Carolina airport where five Green Berets from Fort Bragg were waiting. They drove to visiting officers' quarters where she was settled into a comfortable room. She discovered that Lorraine Condos occupied the room across from hers.

Later, when her escorts returned, they asked what she would like to do. They took her to the Green Beret Club where servicemen—all of whom, it seemed, had known "Colonel Maggie"—treated her royally. Veterans from World War II brought her yellowed newspaper clippings, faded photos, and, best of all, their stories of Maggie doubling as a nurse, even as a surgical nurse, and helping to cleanse and bandage their wounds. They told of Maggie's seemingly inexhaustible exuberance.

One Vietnam veteran, William Holloway, remembered Maggie coming into Long Bien Hospital, bringing beer to her wounded "boys." "We weren't supposed to have it," he recalled. "But nobody could tell

Maggie she couldn't do something when she wanted to do it." He smiled, recalling that Maggie was "a real good woman. We've lost a good friend." Retired Army Sergeant Major Al Warok added, "There were a lot of tears among the old-timers." He recalled the time he had put Raye up for two weeks while she was visiting Bangkok, where so many serviceman in South Vietnam went for R&R.

"When Maggie showed up, she brought life," retired Army Command Sergeant Major Willie C. Lewis told Melodye. "She didn't hold back. She loved all people. Made everybody feel special, that's what she did." He pulled a photograph from his pocket and pointed to a youthful sergeant first class with Raye, dressed in fatigues and grinning widely. "That's me, back in the fifties," he said. "I just had time to give Maggie a big hug and then it was back to the field for me."

Veterans had poured into Fort Bragg by plane, bus, or car. Mark Harris drove up in an extra-stretch limousine to attend the service, accompanied by A. C. Lyles and one of the daughters from Harris's first marriage.

Wearing a black dress, dark glasses, and a black lace mantilla wrapped about her head and shoulders, Melodye arrived for the ceremony, accompanied by her aunt. They were approached by an intermediary for the Harris "entourage" with the information that Mark did not want Maggie's daughter to sit with the rest of the family at the foot of the grave. "I *am* the family," Melodye replied.

But the two groups were not seated together. Melodye and Lorraine were seated, by their Green Beret escort, beside Raye's grave, with Secret Service men standing behind them. It was quite possible that, in this comparatively quiet moment of waiting, thoughts of the possible battle, or battles, soon to come might have entered the minds of both Maggie's husband and her daughter, even though they avoided looking directly at each other. Maggie's daughter had the advantage here, though, because of the black veil covering her face.

Melodye would soon discover, as Harris already knew, that her mother's will would leave her $50,000 on the condition that the comparatively small inheritance would be lost if the daughter challenged the will's provisions. Harris would get the bulk of the $2.4 million estate including the Bel Air home. The grandson would be left nothing at all. The military would get Raye's collection of memorabilia, and People for the Ethical Treatment of Animals (PETA) would get $100,000, it would be reported in various newspapers. Actually, it would turn out that Raye's contribution to PETA would come to only $7,000. And the very mention of PETA would be anathema to Harris, who would soon be planning to market a line of fur coats. If animal rightists didn't like this idea, "Let them eat steak," Harris would quip. "The fur is flying over Martha Raye's estate," one newspaper would comment.

Maggie's daughter already had been billed for large amounts of money for the court suits she had filed and lost. She had not worked, until very recently, since giving up her job to take care of her dad in 1988. She drove a 1974 Volkswagen, and it was difficult for her to keep up with her mortgage payments. She had learned the hard way the expense of court suits and now would be fearful of engaging in another suit and possibly losing her inheritance. She would try to break the will, though, by filing suit in her son's name to claim a portion of his grandmother's estate on the basis of Raye's "incompetency," but the attempt quickly would fail because witnesses to the making of the will and codicils were ready to testify that Raye knew what she was signing.

But all this was not yet public knowledge. And the many veterans who had come were at attention when a Special Forces honor guard solemnly bore Maggie's coffin to its resting place. The press stood near a fence, kept back by the veterans who attended. Civilian spectators, who had been shuttled to the cemetery from a parking lot, also were kept at a short distance.

A Special Forces chaplain presided over the forty-five-minute ceremony, with many tributes to the woman who was the only entertainer to visit consistently the lonely outposts in Vietnam where "hang-tough" Special Forces men lived under primitive and threatening conditions that Maggie often shared. Because Maggie was an honorary lieutenant colonel and not an official Special Forces member, it was not possible to give her a full military burial with the traditional booming of a twenty-one-gun salute and then "Taps." The ceremony was impressive, nonetheless, as Special Forces veterans fanned out around the canopy above the pine coffin and the grave. The band played "Mr. Paganini," and uniformed veterans stood at attention as the clear and stirring notes of "The Ballad of the Green Berets" triumphantly rang out over the cemetery.

Mark Harris was presented with the folded U.S. flag (contributed by the Special Forces Association) that had covered Maggie's coffin. He was asked by reporters for his comments as he left the grave site. "This, to Martha," Harris said, nodding at the folded flag in his hands, "is worth more than Hollywood."

That was hardly news to the veterans attending the service; they were quite aware of the career sacrifices Maggie had made to spend month after month, year after year, in the jungles of Vietnam; aware, too, of how costly her outspoken support of her "boys" and her scathing criticism of Vietnam dissenters had been to her career. Now her prized green beret was on display in the John F. Kennedy Special Warfare Museum at Fort Bragg.

"Being accepted by the Green Berets was the proudest moment of my mom's life," Melodye Condos told veterans. When she left Fort Bragg on Sunday, she had not slept for three days. Yet she was hardly aware of her exhaustion in the fresh and proud realization of how much these GIs had loved her mother. Retired Sergeant Major Fred Davis had pointed out how dedicated Colonel Maggie had been to visiting Special Forces units. "She always hung with the tough ones, the guys who had the most casualties," he said admiringly of "one hell of a gal."

Melodye knew that, with "her boys," Maggie had always been a giving, joyous, and understanding woman. But her own relationship with her mother had been very different. Even though they had reconciled, the daughter's mourning was now for what she considered to be her lost childhood, she would admit.

Maggie's grave was, as yet, unmarked by a tombstone. But soon an unpretentious marker, inscribed "Martha Raye, Civilian," would be in place—a marker similar to those at other graves, all of them undistinguished by any indication of rank in the unity and dedication of proud Green Berets, from various wars, to their unit and their country.

An early morning visitor, standing alone, looking about the quiet cemetery and listening intently, might catch—or might imagine catching—the sound of faint strains gradually rising out of the prevailing silence; a muted echo, spiraling from the morning mist, of bagpipes playing "The Ballad of the Green Berets" to the silent but steady ghostly accompaniment of marching feet of proud battalions of Green Berets and the clunky combat boots of an equally proud "Colonel Maggie."

Filmography

Rhythm on the Range	1936	Paramount
The Big Broadcast of 1937	1936	Paramount
College Holiday	1936	Paramount
Hideaway Girl	1937	Paramount
Waikiki Wedding	1937	Paramount
Mountain Music	1937	Paramount
Artists and Models	1937	Paramount
Double or Nothing	1937	Paramount
The Big Broadcast of 1938	1938	Paramount
College Swing	1938	Paramount
Tropic Holiday	1938	Paramount
Give Me a Sailor	1938	Paramount
Never Say Die	1939	Paramount
$1,000 a Touchdown	1939	Paramount
The Farmer's Daughter	1940	Paramount
The Boys from Syracuse	1940	Universal
Navy Blues	1941	Universal
Keep 'Em Flying	1941	Universal
Hellzapoppin	1941	Universal
Four Jills in a Jeep	1944	20th Century Fox
Pin-Up Girl	1944	20th Century Fox
Monsieur Verdoux	1947	United Artists
Jumbo	1962	20th Century Fox
Pufnstuf	1970	Universal
The Phynx	1971	Warner Brothers
The Concorde: Airport '79	1979	Universal

Sources

Bibliography

Allen, Steve. *More Funny People.* Briarcliff Manor, N.Y.: Stein and Day, 1982.

Bacon, James. *How Sweet It Is.* New York: St. Martin's Press, 1985.

Berle, Milton, with Haskel Frankel. *Milton Berle: An Autobiography.* New York: Delacorte Press, 1974.

Caplin, Barbara. *Hard Candy.* New York: Morrow, 1988.

Chaplin, Charles Jr. *My Father, Charlie Chaplin.* New York: Random House, 1960.

Henry, William A. III. *The Great One: The Life and Legend of Jackie Gleason.* Garden City, N.J.: Doubleday, 1992

Hope, Bob. *Five Women I Love.* Garden City, N.J.: Doubleday, 1966

Hope, Bob, with Melville Shavelson. *Don't Shoot, It's Only Me.* New York: G. P. Putnam, 1990.

Johnson, Catherine E., ed. *Twenty-Five-Year Index to TV Guide.* Radnor, Pennsylvania: Triangle Publications Inc., 1981.

Milton, Joyce. *Tramp: The Life of Charlie Chaplin.* New York: HarperCollins, 1996.

O'Day, Anita. *High Times and Hard Times.* New York: Putnam, 1981.

O'Donnell, Monica M., ed. *Contemporary Theatre, Film, and Television.* Vol. 4. Detroit: Gale Research, 1987.

Parish, James Robert. *The Slapstick Queens.* San Diego: A. S. Barnes, 1973

Shipman, David. *Judy Garland: The Life of an American Legend.* New York: Hyperion, 1993.

Smith, Bill, *The Vaudevillians.* New York: Macmillan, 1976.

Steinberg, Cobbett. *Film Facts.* New York: Facts on File, 1980.

Terrace, Vincent. *Encyclopedia of Television Series, Pilots, and Specials.* Vols. 1 and 2, 1937-1973. New York: Zoetrope, 1986.

Sources

Thomas, Bob. *Joan Crawford.* New York: Simon and Schuster, 1978.

Archives and Library Resources

Detroit Public Library, Performing Arts Archives
Chicago Public Library, city directories and vertical files
Library of Academy of Motion Picture Arts and Sciences, Beverly Hills
New York Times Indexes, 1935-1994

Interviews

Steve Allen
Melodye Condos
Doris Granata
Harry Neigher
Mike Zielinski

Newspapers

Bridgeport Sunday Post, April 29, 1956
Detroit News, February 17, 1938, and others
Detroit Free Press, August 12, 1937, and others
Examiner, November 8, 1994
Fayetteville (N.C.) Observer-Times, October 23, 1994
Globe, November 12, 1991, and others
Hollywood Reporter, October 9, 1992
Las Vegas Review Journal, June 6, 1994
National Enquirer, November 8, 1994, and others
New York Post, December 23, 1991, and others
New York Times, August 1, 1936, and others
Sacramento Bee, December 24, 1991
Sarasota Herald Tribune, January 7, 1995
Star, April 21, 1992
USA Today, June 8, 1992, and others
Washington Post, December 28, 1991, and others
Westport Herald, May 13, 1954, and others
Westport Town Crier, May 3, 1956, and others

Sources

Periodicals

American Weekly, April 26, 1937, and others
Colliers, May 1, 1937
Etude, June 1941
Good Housekeeping, November 1975
Life, May 3, 1954
Look, February 9, 1954
Los Angeles Magazine, November, 1992
New Yorker, July 9, 1973
Parade, April 18, 1954
People, August 28, 1992
Photoplay, March 1974
Playgoer, July 7, 1940
Radio TV Mirror, April 1954 and others
Saturday Evening Post, May 7, 1955
Scholastic, March 29, 1943
Time, March 1, 1954
TV Guide, November 20, 1954, and others
Billboard, February 19, 1944
Variety, December 23, 1942, and others

Miscellaneous Publications

Medals for Maggie Committee publications ("Maggiegrams"), March 12, 1991, and others

Court Documents

Superior Court of the State of California for the County of Los Angeles, March 1, 1994

Public Records, Vital Statistics

Jacksonville, Florida
Lansing, Michigan
Helena, Montana

Index

Index

Index